Published by
Mike Grenville,
Forest Row, RH18 5DX, England

www.renebesnard-ww1diary.org

© 2014 Mike Grenville

All rights reserved

ISBN-13: 978-1497438255

ISBN-10: 149743825X

Dedication

To my mother Lilian Monique Armfield, her brother Robert and my father Stephen Comyns Grenville, who lived during the the Second World War.

To all my grandparents who lived through the First World War.

For everyone working to create world peace in our hearts.

Profits from the sale of this book will be donated to 'Médecins Sans Frontières' (Doctors without Borders): www.msf.org

CONTENTS

Préface	vii
Origins of our death phobia	ix
Foreword	1
1915	5
1916	99
1917	183
1918	265
1919	343
Photos	353

Préface

René Besnard was born 20 April 1878 and died 17 December 1948 at home in Nogent-sur-Marne, near Paris, aged 71 years. He is buried at the Père Lachaise cemetery in the family tomb.

At the start of the Great War, believing like many others, that it would only last a few months, René responded to the call up to the French army. For most of the war he was stationed around north eastern France. He spent the first part of the war as a stretcher bearer and later as a driver. In September 1917 he was awarded the Croix de Guerre for his bravery.

By the end of 1914 when it became clear that the war was going to go on for a while, René decided to keep a daily personal diary for his own memories afterwards. He then wrote it out into a bound book of 738 pages.

René's sister-in-law, Yvonne, whom he also calls Vonvon in this diary, was my grandmother, who died in 1945 before I was born. The original hand written diary was passed on to me by my mother and with the centenary of the war, I felt a responsibility to share it.

This diary is published in both in English and the original French titled VÉCU ET SURVÉCU. I am grateful to Nichola Lewis for her work in typing it up from the original, additional research and translation into English.

The photos included in this diary were in the original.

It has been said that war is 90% being bored stiff, 9% frozen stiff and 1% scared stiff, which is certainly reflected in this diary!

Mike Grenville

Origins of our death phobia

In preparing this diary for publication, I began to wonder whether there was a connection between our phobia around death and the impact of the experiences of this war. Although death is featured on the front pages of daily newspapers, Western society today has become death phobic. Talking about death is so taboo that we actively avoid people who have been recently bereaved. A century ago, life was more precarious and we all came across death many times in our lifetime. In 1910 most people died in their own bed at home while a hundred years later in 2010, 58% of all deaths in England took place in hospital and only 19% in their own home. While just under half a million people die every year in England, which is about one every minute, many adults may have never experienced someone close to them dying, and few have ever seen a dead body. Children are frequently kept away from funerals even when it is someone close to them and when they specifically request to be there.

While all life naturally seeks to avoid death, this is not the same as fearing it. If a branch falls from a tree, we step away to avoid it. But we have an additional fear of what will happen to us after we die. Since fear of death is not the experience for every culture, it must be something that is somehow taught. In part this could be explained by a our cultural story of there being a judgmental God. But why over the last century have we become so phobic about death? The conclusion I have come to are that the seeds of our death phobia were sown during the Great War, later named World War one, compounded by other factors in later years.

Firstly the trauma of the war itself. The total number of military and civilian casualties in World War I was over 37 million. There were over 16 million deaths (which includes about 10 million military personnel and about 7 million civilians) and 20 million wounded ranking it among the deadliest conflicts in human history. About two-thirds of military deaths in World War I were in battle, unlike the conflicts that took place in the 19th century when the majority of deaths were due to disease. Nevertheless, disease, including the Spanish flu and deaths while held as prisoners of war, still caused about one third of total military deaths for all belligerents in WW1.

The horror of the war for those who survived was so great that afterwards they did not want to talk about it, and those back home did not want to hear it either. The curse of the famous British 'stiff upper lip', or sangfroid. At the time, most shell shock victims were treated harshly and with little sympathy as their symptoms were not understood and they were seen as a sign of weakness. So instead of receiving proper care, many victims endured more trauma with treatments such as solitary confinement or electric shock therapy.

Although men were not compelled to fight until Conscription was instated in 1916, there was enormous social pressure on men to volunteer. For example, at the start of the war in August 1914, Admiral Charles Fitzgerald founded the Order of the White Feather. The organization aimed to shame men into enlisting in the British Army by persuading women to present them with a white feather if they were not wearing a uniform. By the end of the war, the slaughter of millions of idealistic young men appeared catastrophic and senseless. This created some sense of guilt in many who had been so enthusiastic supporters of the war at its outset and so had their own reasons to participate in the conspiracy of silence.

The trauma of these deaths was compounded by the fact that no bodies were brought home for a funeral or to bury. In the early days of the war a handful of officers bodies were repatriated to the UK with the cost paid by relatives. However repatriation from a war zone was banned from mid-1915 mainly because of the logistical, health and morale problems the return of thousands of bodies would create. So all a family received was a telegram that began "Deeply regret to inform you...".

At the end of World War One, the 1918 flu pandemic (that lasted from January 1918 through to December 1920), infected 500 million people across the world, including remote Pacific islands and the Arctic. It killed 40 to 100 million of people—three to five percent of the world's population. To maintain morale, wartime censors minimized early reports of illness and mortality in Germany, Britain, France, and the United States; but the newspapers were free to report the epidemic's effects in neutral Spain, creating a false impression of Spain as especially hard hit—thus the pandemic's nickname 'Spanish flu'. The virus predominantly killed previously healthy young adults and brought large scale death right into the heart of communities.

One more significant event in the 20th century has compounded this disconnection from death in society has been the National Health Service in 1945. This has taken both birth and death out of the community and into institutions and the hands of professionals. This is compounded by the pervading view that considers death in hospital to somehow be a failure.

The collective agreement of how to deal with large scale trauma and death at the end of the Great War, was to not talk about it. Tragically, far from being "the war to end of all wars", WW1 scarred western society whose sons were sent to die in another war within a generation. This became parental patterning that taught the generation that lived through WW2 to not talk about it. From my own experience I know almost nothing of how my mother lived under occupation in France and only a handful of wartime snippets from my father he only told me in his dying months. Of my grandparents I know almost nothing, a gap in our family story that I hear echoed from so many people when I ask what they know about how their grandparents lived through WW1. For a family and a whole culture to not know the story of our ancestors is to be cast adrift without a map.

So it seems that WW1 marks the point where we stopped telling the next generation about where they had come from. Losing respect for themselves, the next generation had no elders to look up to and learn from. Today we have replaced elders with celebrities chosen from amongst our peers without substance. This brings with it the fear of growing old and the loss of respect. We have become a 'competence addicted society' so we fear this loss of abilities since it is only in our being able to do things that we derive our worth.

There is another important reason why we need to face our WW1 stories. Studies with mice have found that the genetic imprint from traumatic experiences carries through at least two generations. This means that the trauma of past wars is passed down through the generations, not just in the stories but in our DNA. So my conclusion is that this collective and individual unhealed trauma is a significant part of why we are unable to deal with death as a part of life in modern society. All these factors taken together have contributed to society focusing as little as possible on death as an integral part of life.

The Preamble to the Constitution of UNESCO declares that "since wars begin in the minds of men, it is in the minds of men that the defenses of peace must be constructed". The 1914-1918 centenary presents us with an opportunity to critically reflect on both the legacy of World War I and the continuation of war in our world. By doing this, together with connecting with our own family stories, we can begin to heal the pain passed on to us from our ancestors and contribute to a world without war, bringing about the more beautiful world our hearts know is possible.

Mike Grenville

Original handpainted cover

FOREWORD

Why have I written these lines – or rather, these daily notes, which have now accumulated into a veritable tome? To be honest I have no idea. I think it came about one day when I was bored and a perhaps a little depressed and I felt it would be better to record events rather than to rely solely on my memory, which I had already done. Then it became a sort of obsession to record the details of a more or less full day. I remember too, one of my comrades telling me how he had quite a good way of doing it. Every time his wife wrote to him, she would leave a blank page in her letter so that he in turn could recount his doings since his last missive. I did not think that such a bad idea and thought that, at a later date, he would be very pleased to be able to re-read the letters with his family; but many of his letters have been lost, which is why I prefer to keep the notes I make in my possession.

So now, why did I only start the diary on December 29, 1914, and not on August 3 of the same year, the day I left home? I think the reasons are quite straightforward I did what everyone else did and became my own backroom strategist. I told myself that, given our equipment and weapons, the war however horrible, could not last very long. It was a matter of three months at the most. We would defeat the Boches in short order, and in less than six months it would be over. Oh! How ill judged, when I think that this hell lasted for fifty-four interminable months! It must be that man went mad. Anyway, it is over and done with.

I did not write my diary for anyone other than myself, but I enjoy re-reading it, which I do quite often because to be honest, if at times I wept, I also laughed a lot.

To give some logic to the beginning of this book, here are a few sketchy notes of my activities at the beginning of the war.

On August 3, 1914, in the company of a few neighbours, I left home heavy-hearted, as you may imagine, for embarkation at the Pont de Charenton. Here I met up with some comrades from the regular army, who like me were heading for the depot at Auxerre. It was a relatively quick journey. We arrived at Auxerre station at four in the morning just as the fourth infantry line and our 37th territorial regiment were embarking. We went to the barracks. No one had time to look after us and we were told to report again the following morning. We went to a hotel in town and we spent the rest our day in discussion and speculation. It seemed logical, we thought, that as territorials we would be guardians of territories taken from the Boches. In which case we would here for a while until someone needed us. Alas! We were soon disillusioned.

The following morning we arrived at the Vauban barracks at the same time as the 204th Reserve Regiment were setting off for the front. We were kitted out fairly well and we were each issued with a rifle, because we learnt that at dawn the following morning, we would be leaving for an unknown destination. What fun.

Back at the hotel we made parcels of our civilian effects and left them with the hotel owner who would keep them until our return – if we did return.

Next morning, in tight formation, we left the barracks for embarkation at the station. We travelled all day in cattle cars, of course. At four o'clock, we stopped at the Malesherbes station. Where the devil could we be going? The journey dragged on very slowly all day and then night fell once more, then daybreak. At six o'clock we disembarked at Épinal. We were exhausted from the journey, but we still had to march on foot to Uxegney one of Épinal's fortifications, where we stayed for a month for training and use of arms. One fine day we were taken to the village of Golbey, where we learnt how to construct trenches. Then we went progressively to tiny country places such as Chavelot and Le Prey. Apparently, we were posted to defend the Grand Couronné de Nancy.

How ridiculous! When one thinks that they made us stand at the ready in open fields in all weathers and only if we heard the cannons. In November, there was serious talk about sending us to the front to reinforce the troops serving in the Lorraine. At that time, they were forming a unit of regimental stretcher-bearers – allocated four to a company. I was taken on because I had been a bandsman when on active service. At first, I thought it was a sinecure because I was no longer required to mount guard, and our work consisted of hospital rounds, visiting the sick with the medical officer and then dressing wounds.

It was indeed a sinecure for a time, but later, I was frequently proved wrong. However, I was lucky in that I was good at dressing wounds, which amongst my fellow-brancardiers, earned me the title of Group Leader – honorary only, as I did the same work as all the others. We trailed from village to village, and then on December 29, I started my diary.

In these notes, I have sketched accounts of my daily, sometimes hourly, activities. When, on occasion, I have made disagreeable remarks about certain commanding officers, it is because it galled me that some of them sported stripes of undeserved and ill-used rank. In any case, I have been discreet, but that does not mean that what I have not wished to write, is not engraved forever on my memory.

René Besnard

MY NOTES FROM 1914 to 1919

29 December 1914

A quiet day. In the morning – drill. In the evening, showered at Rambervillers. I still can't move because of my sprain. We have learnt that we leave the day after tomorrow for La Chapelle St-Michel-sur-Meurthe.

30 December 1914

Rest all day in preparation for our departure tomorrow, which is now official. My sprain is a bit better.

31 December 1914

Seven o'clock. I get into the medical supplies wagon. There is ice. It is extremely cold. I cover myself as best I can with my rug. We go across Saint-Benoît into the Sainte-Barbe forest. We are heading for La Chapelle Saint-Michel-sur-Meurthe.

The road running through the forest is wonderful: superb slopes and ravines. There are fragments of German and French clothing everywhere. My friend Lièvre leaves the cannons and returns with us. I'm pleased. At the end of an increasingly attractive drive, we go beyond the woods and come to Thiaville where we leave the fifth and sixth Companies. Twelve hundred metres further on we arrive at La Chapelle-St-Michel-sur-Meurthe. These last two small villages are intact.

We are billeted in a paper factory. The Boche occupied this for three weeks, but nothing was destroyed because apparently, it is a German factory – but nobody really knows. As a billet it's not very good and is quite distant from the villages. It seems we will be here for ten days. The cannons are thundering quite a bit, and it seems to me that they're not far away.

1 January 1915

Last night we opened fire and filled the night with dense smoke. During the night we heard the cannons and then, not very far away, a fusillade. We don't know the outcome. Because of my sprain, I stay put. The comrades have gone off to the trenches. Somebody brings us cigars and chocolate and promises us a New Year's Day breakfast. A poor show this New Year's day – the first time in thirty-six years that I have spent it away from my family. At ten o'clock, as well as the usual fare, we have: dried ham, two apples, and a mandarin, a piece of chocolate, tobacco, a cigar, half a litre of wine, and a quarter litre of champagne. This little feast seemed to me rather funereal. I can't understand why on the one hand and in the present circumstances, they should give us any kind of libation, and on the other, this forced revelry makes me think of our family get-togethers every year where everyone's good wishes are expressed in the same way. Today, it just seems so sad to me. The captain sent a message of good wishes. Very nice of him, but he could have done it in person. In the afternoon, my comrades return to the trenches. I would like this day to be over. I have tears in my eyes. Eight o'clock at night – the day has passed without incident.

2 January 1915

The day after the party (Oh irony!). An uneventful day. I am still nursing my sprain, which is getting better. The others have gone to the trenches. At one o'clock, there's an announcement that a billet inspection will be made by General Franckfort. At two o'clock, he has still not arrived. The others go looking for straw to make their bedding more comfortable; it is certainly needed. I have tried wearing my shoes – it doesn't feel too bad, but it's still not quite right. I know I need more rest, which I take. The sun is shining. It does one good. They have given us clean straw, which is only slightly cleaner.

3 January 1915

At eight o'clock last night, the cook came back drunk. What a performance. Then a few of the men started to snore so loudly that no one else could sleep. What a racket they made; it went on for half an hour. There were no letters yesterday either, because the post had a day off on the first. So I sincerely hope, there will be something tonight. Another quiet day. My sprain is improving. This morning the men had practice drill. This afternoon they will work on the trenches, and this evening at seven o'clock, they will occupy them. Yesterday, I trimmed my beard and cut my hair – one way of passing the time. The commanding officer has left to inspect the barracks. He grabbed every man who was off sick. Thanks to my armband, he excused me as my duty is to stay here. Which is all for the best. This evening the rain fell so hard that the occupation of the trenches has been cancelled. Our letters have arrived. I have received five.

4 January 1915

Resting today. At nine o'clock, as I am leaving the infirmary after having my foot bandaged, I learn that there will be an inspection by the Colonel of the 141st Infantry Regiment. We waited for him and saw him at a distance but he didn't come over to us. This afternoon more rest. A lot of the men play cards to pass the time, but most them just sit around in contemplation, and are bored.

5 January 1915

A very quiet day. Trenches. My sprain is much better. I could get my shoe on for a bit. The question has been raised as to what a stretcher-bearer's work should entail. One of the comrades has just come back from seeing the authorities. No one was able to give him a definite answer. We are also hoping for the solution we want. Let's hope the reply will be favourable.

6 January 1915

The decision is in the report. The stretcher-bearers will act as orderlies, two a day, and mount guard at the police post. They will participate in the same work and exercises as the Company. Thanks very much. It is a long way from what we expected. In the meantime, I am still nursing my sprain. It has not stopped raining since this morning. A gloomy time. Boredom has taken firm hold

7 January 1915

It is still raining incessantly. Rest this morning as the comrades are relieving the guard. This afternoon, they have gone to work on the trenches with the rain beating down on them. The stretcher-bearers go too, but as medics. They are there in case any of the men hurt themselves. I still have my sprain, and I make the most of a little peace and quiet. That is all I have to do.

8 January 1915

It hasn't stopped raining. I am still nursing my sprain. Nevertheless, it is much better. The men are lining the trenches with pine. Other than that an uneventful day.

9 January 1915

Still raining this morning. A little sun this afternoon. But will it last? It is a little colder. My sprain is really much better today. Tomorrow I am on guard duty as stretcher-bearer at the police post. The men are still lining the trenches with pine. Boredom still reigns. We have had no orders to leave tomorrow, as we had thought. There is talk that we have another six days here.

10 January 1915

I have been on guard duty the whole day as stretcher-bearer-orderly. I took a telegraph operator to the infirmary to apply a tincture of iodine. It has been cold today. I kept my shoes on all day today and tonight my foot was swollen. I can't bear wearing the bandage at night. I slept little because of the constant coming and going of the guard as well as a tempestuous wind and rain.

11 January 1915

This morning at six o'clock, I leave my orderly duty and with the rain beating down, I go back to the factory to sleep. At nine o'clock an arms review. While that is going on I go to the infirmary to get a massage. But the review is late and I get back just in time to be inspected. The lieutenant asks after my sprain. I tell him I still need quite a few days of rest. He says nothing. I am tired from guard duty and a sleepless night. I am going to make the most of this rest, because soon everybody will be off resting.

12 January 1915

A quiet day, but how sad – grey and rainy. The men are going to the trenches in spite of the bad weather. I am still nursing my sprain, but God, I'm so bored. Rather like everyone else, I have caught a sort of cold, due to the excessive humidity, which reigns in our factory. When will this end?

13 January 1915

Everyone was coughing so much last night, we couldn't sleep before ten o'clock. Our billet is inordinately damp, and so more and more people are falling sick every day. The weather today is grey and snow is expected – a cheerful outlook. I am still nursing my sprain. But still, it is getting better.

14 January 1915

A noteworthy incident marked the day. At two o'clock, four labourers who were on duty repairing a footbridge at Pont de la Meurthe – the enemy had blown up the main bridge – fell into the water. We immediately raced to find a doctor and stretcher-bearers (including me) but it was too late. One of the men was rescued by a fisherman who stretched his rod out to him. Another managed to save himself, but we couldn't rescue the two others who were carried away by the current, and no doubt perished. With the doctor, we searched the banks but to no avail. It caused a big stir and was the talking point of the whole evening.

15 January 1915

Uneventful day. This morning rest for the section who were on guard duty yesterday. This afternoon, the men went to the trenches, but had to return at two thirty because of the rain which is still falling. Rumour has it that we leave next Tuesday. Some say we are going forward; others, that we are returning to the Épinal sector. But in fact, nobody really knows anything.

16 January 1915

In the morning all work is impossible because of the rain. In the afternoon the men go to the trenches but return early under an avalanche of hail and rain. In the evening, since there was nothing much on offer in the mess, a couple of mates and I went to the village to eat fried potatoes.

17 January 1915

It is Sunday, and we are at rest. In the morning there is a tool review but nothing serious. It has snowed incessantly since two o'clock this morning. The countryside is marvellous. The pines which surround us have taken on a grandiose appearance. But God in heaven, it is not warm. In the afternoon we stay in the factory and try to keep ourselves warm the best we can.

18 January 1915

This morning it is snowing so much, it is impossible to take the men to the trenches. In the distance we heard the cannons and fusillades, which lasted for quite a while. This morning in view of the projected move to Épinal, I went to see the field-doctor to exempt me from carrying field kit when we return to Épinal.

And talking of Épinal, I have it officially that we leave Wednesday morning at six-thirty for Raon-l'Étape, Neufmaisons, et Pexonne, which is to say about 15 kilometres forward – a dramatic development which we were far from expecting.

This afternoon, brilliant sunshine and the men are in the trenches. The locals say it is going to freeze. On top of the snow, that will be good.

19 January 1915

A very quiet day. Rest in preparation for departure. They want me to leave at four forty-five, with the forward party, but I don't want to leave before six – that is, with the medical supplies wagon.

20 January 1915

Departure at six. It is white with snow everywhere, but it is still very dark. It is so slippery, the road is almost untenable. With my sprain, I have to be very careful. We cross Thiaville and come to Neuville-les-Raon, and then we cross Raon-l'Étape. It is now daylight. The centre of Neuville-les-Raon has been badly damaged, and many houses destroyed.

After Raon we go through the Petit and Grand Reclos forest. An idyllic and marvellous sight; and the pine trees lining the road have at least 20 centimetres of snow on their branches. With ever-changing scenery, the road winds upwards for four kilometres, then down again and two kilometres on, we leave the woods for the plain. We can now hear the cannons.

We arrive at Neufmaisons, where we take leave of a company. Then finally, we get to Pexonne at ten thirty. The town was occupied for six weeks, but hasn't suffered much damage except for the station. On arrival, I take an orderly stretcher-bearer to the police post and then replace a comrade (Gérard) who is unwell.

What snow – I have never seen so much except in Switzerland. I have a shift of two hours during the day from one to three o'clock and then two hours and a quarter at night from three to five o'clock. At four o'clock the wind gets up and it is not warm. I am completely stiff as I have hardly slept.

21 January 1915

Guard review at 7 o'clock. We are informed that we leave tomorrow to take up an outpost east of Badonviller. We drink tea to celebrate our departure. A good night spent in the hay of a barn. It has thawed a bit. It is very dirty.

22 January 1915

Up at seven thirty. I feel a bit better and I am less stiff. We leave at ten. For a while, I shall be leaving my job as stretcher-bearer to take up active service at the outpost. My knapsack on my back, I march with my comrades through Fenneviller, which has suffered little damage, and then through Badonviller which is devastated. There is nothing left of the village centre. We go into the Bousson forest. Lots of snow. The road is a sheet of ice and we have tremendous difficulty walking; staying upright is almost impossible. We get to our post – a black lair – nothing more than a hole made of packed earth. A quartermaster's sentry-box. The Boches are about 1200 metres away, but in one place, only 200 metres away.

We are with the 309th Infantry Regiment and the 70th Alpine Chasseur Battalion. It is extremely cold. We are actually at La Chapelotte, so called because of the little chapel in wood. La Chapelotte belongs to the woods owned by Monsieur Cartier-Bresson, who is mayor of the region at the far end of the Côteaux where he has his thread factories.

I take up guard at eight forty-five to ten o'clock. At nine o'clock, a man walks openly towards me. I cry, 'Stop! Who goes there?' The ground is so icy, the man slips and sits hard on the ground. I repeat my question and he replies, 'France'. It is my lieutenant, who has come to inspect the post and he recognizes me. We talk for quite a while. At six, I return and I shall try to sleep. The room is full of smoke from the fire which has been built at the back. The boards are really hard. Exhausted, I sleep, but not for long. All about us, the gunfire is almost constant.

23 January 1915

We left the service redoubt one month today. I get up at seven, frozen. I go off to shave at a stream little further away. Our guns at our shoulders, a comrade and I wander around the area. But we have to be extremely cautious. At nine thirty, we eat and then at ten o'clock we change guard.

So here we are, high in the mountains, with a wonderful view over the entire valley, which is covered in snow. Our shelter is a hole in the ground covered with pine branches which let in air and let out the smoke from the fire we have made. On sentry duty we wear a sheepskin for warmth. We are armed with rifles. The battle rages all around us; apparently it is the Alpine Light Infantry on reconnaissance. The enemy is, in fact, very close. I am on sentry duty at about nine fifteen. A sharp fusillade about 1200 metres away. Again, it is the Alpines in a trench who are giving their all. Impossible to sleep tonight as we are sitting on a plank making do as a bench and in spite of the fire, it is extremely cold.

24 January 1915

Daybreak. At seven, they bring us coffee, but it is cold because the kitchens are about 1800 metres away. At about eight, there is another fusillade, and the shots are no further than 500 or 600 metres away. We are very careful and are at the ready. A quarter of an hour later, it stops. At one forty-five, surrounded by the 309th regiment, we leave; and take a steep path, with a gradient of at least 30°, through snow and mud ruts. The countryside is idyllically beautiful, but we are sweating water and blood. Our knapsacks are more than heavy. By the first halt we are already at the end of our tether. Forest and more forest with rutted and treacherous paths. There is over ten centimetres of snow. At last we emerge from the woods and immediately find ourselves in Fennevillers. And then without a halt we push on to Pexonne a kilometre away. When we arrive, I wash myself thoroughly and I feel better. Then we eat. We drink tea and at seven thirty. I turn in.

25 January 1915

I get up at seven fifteen. I have slept like a log but I am still very stiff. I polish my shoes and clean my rifle, wash a couple of handkerchiefs and washed my face. Impossible to find tobacco. Eventually I find a low-grade packet for 0.63 – that's the way it goes. We have a lunch of cod and potatoes. I'm going to write a few letters at the house of a good woman.

This afternoon, we have to go to the trenches. I shall try to get dispensation. I don't know if I'll succeed. I did succeed, and I stayed behind. In the course of the evening we are informed that our 4th section, at the rallying point with the light infantry along with a section of the 309th, encountered the Boches. One man from the 309th has not returned. In fact, Section 4, only return at nine at night. We will hear more tomorrow.

26 January 1915

Up at seven o'clock. We leave again for La Chapelotte. At eleven thirty, we stop at the Light Infantry's rallying point, to pay our respects to the remains of our poor brother-in-arms from the 309th, who died in a hail of German bullets while he was on patrol with our own from the 37th and Section 4. The Commanding Officer of the 309th gives a moving speech on the sad fate of the deceased. Then prayers are said in open air by a stretcher-bearer priest. This gives rise to a comment by one of our comrades (Jubin) who said, "So Besnard the stretcher-bearer, if one us cops it will you be the one to do the honours?" Then we march past with fixed bayonets. We are going back to the highest post, where we were two days ago. It is not that cold tonight and we have a good fire going. But of course, it is impossible to sleep. An odd circumstance – not one single gunshot all day or night.

27 January 1915

So, a calm night. At eight o'clock we watch a patrol from the 5th Battalion of the Alpine Light Infantry depart. At nine o'clock an extremely heavy exchange of gunfire breaks out near us. An hour later I watch as the 5-Alpine Light Infantry patrol return at a run. I ask them what happened. They were attacked by about 40 Boches and had to take cover amongst the trees. Happily no one was hurt. They will get their orders from their sub-lieutenant.

There is now an uninterrupted roar of cannons – heavy artillery. At eleven o'clock we go back down to the main post to spend the night. Nothing much on during the day: fatigue duty fetching wood – dinner – and bed. Then at two to three in the morning, guard duty in dreadfully cold conditions.

28 January 1915

Up at eight. Unbelievably cold and snowy. We eat at nine o'clock; then armed with rifles a handful of comrades and I go on a mountain hike to the "Pierre à Cheval" from which point there is a superb view. We can see Allamont, where the Boches are, and we have to stay hidden so they don't spot us. Word is that we leave again for Épinal. If only that were true. At two o'clock we are off again, taking the high road to Pexonne. The road is a sheet of ice. It is impossible to stay upright, and progress is painfully slow. We arrive at ten to four. At eight o'clock we have tea and go to bed in the hay. A cold day – the temperature is 17° below freezing.

29 January 1915

A morning at rest. I get up at seven o'clock. I ask to speak to the captain about the question of the brancardiers which I'm still interested in following up. Impossible to see him. In the afternoon – the trenches. The sun is shining brightly and I go too. On the way, I talk to the captain and state that essentially, I would rather stick to my duties as a stretcher-bearer. He is most obliging and promises to talk to the Commanding Officer. In the evening we are on guard duty at the exits. I take the eleven to two o'clock shift. It is a mild, very clear night. Then I go back to bed.

30 January 1915

I get up at seven. Departure preparations. At ten o'clock we are en route for La Chapelotte. Fat flakes of snow are falling. The night before, we heard a sharp exchange of fire. It was the 309th and our men taken by surprise on a reconnaissance. Two men from the 309th fell, and another was wounded. The Commanding Officer, made a speech over one of the bodies which we buried in situ. The other was buried in the morning at Escombes where he fell. With fixed bayonets, and to the sound of the shells exploding near us, we file past the body under the snow, which is falling in large flakes. We move our position and go to the post, 'Vierge de Clarisse' where all we have to do is to mount guard and stand watch over the area. The sun has come out. It is fine but cold, and there is nothing but snow. The heavy artillery continues to roar. It seems now that we will be on duty here for at least ten days.

31 January 1915

A superb night – a marvellous moon and fairytale scenery. There are five of us going as reserves to the Light Infantry rallying point. There is nothing to do there. One hour's guard duty out of twenty-four. I have caught a cold. At three forty-five, two of our squadrons are sent on reconnaissance to protect those in the trenches. We shake hands and wish them luck – no one knows what might happen.

1 February 1915

At 11 o'clock, the patrol returns without seeing anything untoward. We are very glad. The men are exhausted and soaked to the skin, as it has been snowing incessantly since the night before last. We leave for Pexonne at midday. The path is hard in spite of the great flakes of snow falling. Nevertheless, it is warmer and there is a thaw. We arrive at two o'clock. In the evening we all chip in and make crêpes because it is Candlemas. We turn in at eight thirty.

2 February 1915

This morning I am up at seven, and have a nice cup of coffee and milk. I have a heavy cold. Fortunately we have a whole day's rest. The sun is shining brilliantly and is even warm. However, outside everything is so icy, you can't stay upright. In the afternoon we relax. we need it. We are not making preparations to leave tomorrow morning. In the evening, we make a hot toddy. We turn in at eight o'clock.

3 February 1915

I get up at seven o'clock. A nice coffee with milk. Hurray!! We have got what we wanted for the stretcher-bearers. The chief medical officer of the 309th has allowed us to lay down our rifles and bayonets and to put back our armbands. Knapsacks on our backs we leave at the rear of the company. This time, we are going to Allencombe – an extremely dangerous post close to the Boches and at the bottom of a valley. I am no longer on guard duty. We are lodged in a fairly big shelter. At nine thirty we are called by the sentry. Just two steps from us, there has been an uninterrupted and intense exchange of fire and heavy artillery all day.

4 February 1915

It wasn't a bad night, but I coughed a lot. I get up at seven o'clock then wander around a bit and then go to the mess to help me along. At one o'clock, my comrades go to their various posts. But another stretcher-bearer and I stay on duty at the Allencombe post. Everywhere around us the fusillades and cannonades continue without letting up.

5 February 1915

I cough for part of the night and I am feverish. At seven o'clock I get up and wander around for a bit. There is nothing else to do. Our comrades missed a good chance: twelve Boches passed close by them, but they fired too soon and the Germans got away. At two o'clock we go back to Pexonne in muddy and heavy conditions. On the way, we are told we have to go back to La Chapelotte at least once more, which doesn't delight us. We arrive and rest up. In the evening we have tea and turn in at eight o'clock.

6 February 1915

I get up at seven o'clock. I feel lousy with this cold. Fortunately, we are resting. I do a bit of washing and darn my socks – Ah! What a lovely job. After lunch I spend an enjoyable moment writing letters.

7 February 1915

Up at seven. At ten o'clock, departure for La Chapelotte. I am designated stretcher-bearer to the Light Infantry. We arrive. The cannons are thundering and the shells are whistling about our heads. Artillery is exploding all around us. We stand ready.

8 February 1915

We slept to the sounds of the cannons. A reconnaissance has gone out. In the afternoon, the tally is three dead and seven wounded from the 309th, and two men from the 5th and 37th companies have disappeared – a sergeant and a soldier. I am informed that in the morning we are returning towards Épinal. Wonderful.

9 February 1915

We learn that two German companies occupied Angomont yesterday afternoon, but they were driven out. A shell exploded 30 metres away from one of our small posts. Fortunately, no one was hurt. At two o'clock, en route for Pexonne. We arrive at four, and rest up in the evening.

10 February 1915

Up at seven o'clock. Preparations for a departure tomorrow morning. Rest all day. We are quite bored.

11 February 1915

Departure at eight o'clock. It is a wonderfully sunny day. At the first halt, I shove my kit bag into the wagon. It is much better like that. We get to Bertrichamps at 11 o'clock, where we billet. We had a difficult journey because of the mud. In the evening we treat ourselves to a party and live it up a little.

12 February 1915

Departure at six thirty. Twenty-six kilometres to do. Beautiful weather. There has been a bit of frost. We leave and again I bung my kit bag into the wagon. We pass through the infamous Col de la Chipotte. Nothing but graves all along the way, and a terrible stench. The dead are barely covered with earth. It is very cold under the trees and we keep climbing higher and higher. We arrive at Vannecourt where we are billeted. It is a big village where the 58th Battalion is already stationed. We are lodged in a stable along with the horses, cows and chickens. Along the way, we received a congratulatory message from General [Coffinant].

13 February 1915

Departure at six thirty. The weather is mild. There are still another 28 kilometres to cover. My kit bag is again in the wagon. The way is hard going. At about nine thirty, after Longchamps, we are caught in the rain and the wind gets up. The road becomes even more difficult. A kilometre from Golbey, we take a long halt in the pouring rain. There is muttering. At half past twelve we set off again and what with the wind and the rain beating down on us, it is difficult to stay upright. It is very heavy going.

At Golbey there is a review before General Franckfort. Finally we arrive at the service redoubt. We have marched 65 kilometres in three days and we are completely exhausted. We are given two days rest, which are certainly none too many.

14 February 1915

I had a fairly a good night. Excellent news. The stretcher-bearers are to give up their weapons. At nine o'clock, I go to the Colonel's office in Golbey and hand in my rifle. In exchange I'm given a Sabre – series Z. I am pleased. I have waited a long time for this moment. I expect my notes will be more spaced out as we have to stay here for 20 to 40 days. I'll come back to them when we leave again, as I imagine that life here will be much as it was before we left – that is, very quiet. The weather is beautiful – a little windy, but brilliant sunshine.

15 February 1915

I have been detailed as stretcher-bearer to the 3rd Section and to the 12th Squadron. It saddens me to leave all these good comrades who over the last six-and-a-half months I've become used to. I have caught a thundering cold.

16 February 1915

I am at Chavelot. A good bunch of men, thankfully.

17 February 1915

I am designated orderly stretcher-bearer. I have found a room with two beds for 5 sous. It's not expensive.

18 February 1915

A quiet life. I am left in peace and I have nothing to do. It is now a question of the next departure. We are told to make our preparations and to be ready.

No entries for 19 – 25 February 1915

26 February 1915

At eleven o'clock we receive orders to leave at two o'clock and to spend the night at Golbey. I have toothache which is bothering me a little. We have acquired portable tents. At Golbey I dine with my comrades. We sleep in a barn open to the four winds. It is freezing – minus ten.

27 February 1915

Departure at seven twenty. Knapsacks on our backs we leave for Vannecourt – 26 kilometres in muddy conditions. We arrive tired out, in the afternoon. In the evening, nine of us buy a rabbit and we have a little party. It cost us 12 sous each. I still have toothache.

28 February 1915

We leave at seven thirty. We are going to Moyen. Twenty-four kilometres to go in sleeting weather. I still have toothache. The road is hard going. When we arrive, my mate Schumff finds us beds at just five metres from the barracks. A wonderful room and a welcoming landlady. There is a hole made by a shell. We fill it with straw. We are dead tired and we turn in at seven o'clock. Apparently we will be here for 20 days.

1 March 1915

I get up at seven. I slept well but my toothache is getting worse. I hope to God it is nothing serious. My mate has made us a wonderful hot chocolate which we drink with relish. The weather is vile – wind, rain, snow, and of course, it is cold. Fortunately we are resting today. It has been a fairly good day.

2 March 1915

The stretcher-bearers have received orders. We have to attend the medical rounds every morning and do the dressings when needed. Good. That will help pass the time, for the rest of the day there is nothing to do. I still have toothache, which doesn't stop me from having another nice hot chocolate. For the others, some unimportant drill during the day.

3 March 1915

A good night and a good coffee with milk this morning. My teeth are a little better. Medical rounds, then off-duty for the rest of the day. In the evening, an incident. Apparently, at La Chapelle and at Badonviller, there has been a fierce engagement where our 1st company has surrounded a Boche company. So in the barracks we are on full alert. Our bags are packed and we are ready to leave. What a bore. We were nicely set up here. I shall certainly miss my bed.

4 March 1915

We did not leave last night. It seems that the incident at La Chapelotte went well for us. I get up and do the rounds. We still have to keep ourselves ready though. There is almost nothing to do this afternoon. It is a beautiful spring day and I relax in the sun.

5 March 1915

After a good night, I get up at six forty-five. I have a nice hot chocolate and then do the rounds. The doctors have recommended that all the men wear flannel cummerbunds, as there is an epidemic of kidney disease in the area. We have to advise too, that those who have not been treated must be extra careful because gonorrhoea is rife. I think the alert is over as confinement to barracks has been relaxed a bit. An abrupt change in temperature – the sky is grey and there is a very cold wind. I am off duty in the afternoon.

6 March 1915

Good night. Good coffee with milk. No letters and we don't know why not. Very quiet day. Rain in the afternoon. Everyone stays put. Tomorrow I'm on orderly duty.

7 March 1915

I'm on orderly duty. It has rained all day and I'm bored.

8 March 1915

I'm on sentry duty. The weather changed during the night. Everything is snow-covered and it is very cold.

9 March 1915

A terrible freeze – it is 9° below zero. I'm still on nursing service and am off duty in the afternoon.

10 March 1915

It is dreadfully cold and it's snowing. My comrades can't go to work. Still the same routine.

11 March 1915

Superb day – there is a thaw. It is almost warm. Same routine.

12 March 1915

A little rain, a gloomy day, and still nothing to do.

13 March 1915

An errand to run at Rambervillers for the doctor. I offer to go. Thirty-four kilometres by bike on a disgusting road (and what a bike). I am rather tired tonight.

14 March 1915

Incessant rain. After the infirmary, I have lunch and go to Mass. In the afternoon I stay in my room and read and write.

15 March 1915

No change. We are staying here.

16 March 1915

The same again.

17 March 1915

At one thirty, we receive an order to leave Moyen at six o'clock. At seven o'clock we leave for Chenevières and arrive at ten. We get ourselves organized. At four o'clock – alert! At five forty-five en route for Thiébauménil which we reach at eight o'clock and where we spend the night.

18 March 1915

At eleven o'clock departure for Bénaménil. One can sense the Boches. We arrive at midday. The troops are on the march all day – the 217th infantry regiment and the 6th Hussar artillery regiment.

19 March 1915

Troops and more troops. We are badly billeted. I go in search of the field doctor to the 6th Hussars, who receives me from his bed at seven thirty. He is a very nice fellow. Work on the trenches in the afternoon. I stay put.

20 March 1915

It is the same scenario as yesterday. The cannons are roaring. The 10th Hussars return from patrol with one man dead and a wounded lieutenant. Fatigue duty in the afternoon. I stay put.

21 March 1915

It is Sunday, but you would never think it. The men work to the sound of heavy artillery. They are working tonight, but only two stretcher-bearers go with them. I stay put. they return at half past midnight. Everything went well.

22 March 1915

I go with the guards' section to an old mill. It is a quiet here. Only the cannons are booming from both sides. Shells whistle about our heads. In the end we ignore them. We have had true spring weather for the last three days. What a joy. But it is wretched being here.

23 March 1915

A routine day – same as always. The cannons are roaring. At night four of us sleep on stretchers in the infirmary. It is cleaner and more peaceful here.

24 March 1915

A fairly calm day. But at eight o'clock at night, someone comes to tell us that at ten forty-five, we leave for Ogéviller, 24 kilometres away. We don't know what we will be doing there.

25 March 1915

We arrived at Ogéviller yesterday night at ten past midnight, and went to bed at one o'clock. At ten o'clock I go on duty as orderly stretcher-bearer. Not a lot to do and I am rather bored. It has rained all day.

26 March 1915

It's a fine day. At ten o'clock, I relieve the guard. Afterwards I go to the infirmary to rest. From eight to twelve at night, we are on fatigues. I don't know if I am to go or not.

27 March 1915

I didn't go on fatigue duty last night. Tonight the others are going to the outposts at Herbéviller. I stay on duty at the infirmary.

28 March 1915

We arrived at Herbéviller yesterday evening at eight thirty. Our sentry comrades were waiting for us to set up the first-aid station. It is a huge café with four bedrooms allocated. We slept on bedsteads and out of the cold. The men go to the trenches and to the outposts. I stay, here on call and at the doctor's disposal.

29 March 1915

A good night and today is quiet. We have a very young and very nice doctor from the Dragoons. Our men have been working solidly and are tired. Very close to us, the artillery roars uninterruptedly. It is very cold. Tonight we return to Ogéviller.

30 March 1915

Yesterday evening just as I was leaving, a young Dragoon was brought in; a bullet had gone through his calf. It was our sentry comrades who had taken care of him. We returned at ten o'clock at night in very cold conditions. On the rounds this morning. There are a lot of sick men as they have a whole day's heavy work ahead of them. I rest in the afternoon. We play cards. It is raining, which means milder weather.

31 March 1915

I get up at five forty-five for orderly duty. It is snowing heavily and it's cold. I am rather bored. At seven thirty we leave for Herbéviller

1 April 1915

Last night when we arrived, we had to make a first-aid post at the other end of the village as our men are to attack Domèvre. At one o'clock there are two wounded with bayonet injuries; then this morning, two dead from the 12th Dragoons. Let's hope that will be all for the day. The weather is superb. It is really miserable to be here still at this time of the year.

2 April 1915

Tonight we leave for Ogéviller. Last night at nine o'clock, by the light of a bright moon, we loaded the two fallen Dragoons into the wagon. It was not fun. For Good Friday, we fasted. Cod and potatoes morning and evening.

3 April 1915

Return to Ogéviller. Nothing new to report. Tomorrow it is Easter.

4 April 1915

Easter day. It is hard to believe. The rain and the cannons do not let up. Only sadness while thinking of the family festivities. The programme has changed. We will not be going to Herbéviller tonight. I have caught a bad cold thanks to my stint as orderly at the police station.

5 April 1915

Still the same story. Tomorrow evening we leave for Saint-Martin.

6 April 1915

No change. We will only leave on the eighth for Saint-Martin.

7 April 1915

Nothing new. Departure tomorrow for Saint-Martin – village of the big shells.

8 April 1915

Nothing new. We really are leaving at seven o'clock tonight

9 April 1915

Yesterday evening we left for Saint-Martin – four kilometres in a pitch dark night with the rain beating down and through mud and water higher than our shins. When we arrive, the men go straight to the trenches and we to the infirmary which is in the presbytery. We are very comfortable. There is a piano and we have bedsteads to lie on. After a good night we rise at seven. We have been told that there are to be two stretcher-bearers in the trenches every day. Two of our comrades go. It will be my turn next. What a godforsaken spot. Big shells are falling very near us, and in fact, we are extremely close to the Boches. It is awful to see the men return from the trenches. They are covered in mud, from top to bottom. Without any exaggeration, they are in water up to their knees. Active service here is no joke.

10 April 1915

Dawn is a busy time for the stretcher-bearers and it was my turn to go to the trenches last night. Oh, it is fun – a kilometre of wading through mud up to our ankles to get to the woods. Once there, I see my Captain in a filthy shack. I sleep on rotting straw in an even more putrid shack. Water pours in onto my stomach. Naturally, I am very cold, particularly my feet. At seven I am woken by a comrade. When I get back, I am so muddy, I have to wash my shoes and have a footbath. I rest in the afternoon. Tonight we are going to Fréménil.

11 April 1915

We left Saint-Martin at ten last night and got to Fréménil at half-past midnight – six kilometres. We were in bed by one thirty. The infirmary here belongs to the 217th. We have to sleep in the barn. Tiredness overcomes me and I sleep well. Up at seven thirty, I take part in the rounds with a tiresome doctor. The men are at rest. The weather is fairly good and I go off to the middle of a meadow to write and to enjoy the sun. The roar of cannons, mainly from our side, is intensifying.

12 April 1915

Rest. Fréménil is not an attractive spot and we are not comfortable here. At eight o'clock in the evening we pick up my comrade and colleague, Verport, an artilleryman who came off his horse. His leg is completely twisted.

13 April 1915

Still at rest and there is nothing to do. Our artillery is literally spraying the Boches with shells.

14 April 1915

I'm going to take the medical report to Ogéviller. I make the most of the trip and eat at a restaurant to boost my morale a bit. Tonight we go to Saint-Martin.

15 April 1915

Last night we arrived at Saint-Martin at eight o'clock. I slept at the infirmary and I am on medical duty from seven in the morning to seven at night. The woods have dried out a lot and we are not sinking into the mud quite so much. Quite a bit of heavy artillery around, but nothing explodes near us. I had a long conversation with my Captain. One of my comrades (Jarret) has killed a marten and its three kittens. He sold them to the Captain. I help the Captain skin them.

16 April 1915

Tonight we leave once more for Ogéviller. The cannons are very loud but nothing unusual.

17 April 1915

Return to Ogéviller. Late afternoon at five o'clock, there is a terrible attack on Saint-Martin. The cannonade is truly terrifying. One of our men is killed. Then five men from the 17th Light Infantry and from the 217th Infantry are wounded. There but for 24 hours – we had a narrow escape, for Saint-Martin has been shelled from top to bottom.

18 April 1915

Yesterday's attack was appalling. We killed 40 men and took seven prisoners, three of whom were wounded. One of our men was killed. This morning we took four of the prisoners to Ogéviller. They are Saxons. They are far from being under-nourished and are not hurt as the newspapers would say. We are not going to Saint Martin tomorrow.

19 April 1915

After the storm, a little calm. The battle continues but less fiercely. There are more wounded from the 17th Light Cavalry Regiment. But we have won this round and have pushed the Boches back.

20 April 1915

Tonight I'm going with about one hundred men to work on a ridge in the plain in front of Chazelles. It is risky. Today is my 37th birthday.

21 April 1915

Everything went well. In all, there were about 3000 labourers to dig the trenches, which they speedily accomplished. We were subjected to a fusillade to begin with, but nothing more. All the same, I am whacked as it was a sleepless night. I rest in the afternoon.

22 April 1915

Today is my 12th wedding anniversary. I would never have thought I would be spending it here. I don't have the heart to make any attempt to celebrate. Tonight I have to go back with the workers to the trenches. At five o'clock the work is cancelled.

23 April 1915

I am on orderly duty all day. It has been raining without let-up since yesterday. There is to be no trench work again tonight, because they are expecting an attack. We will see.

24 April 1915

Yesterday's expected attack took place tonight. The cannons started to roar at nine thirty and did not stop until two o'clock this morning. the Boches attacked Domjevin, Saint-Martin and Domèvre. There were no dead or wounded on our side. But the enemy suffered considerable losses. The wounded are brought to us at Domjevin and five prisoners are taken to Ogéviller – well set up fellows who don't look as if they are starving.

25 April 1915

Last night at eleven, we left for Saint-Martin to provide reinforcements. Two of my colleagues are in the trenches. It will be my turn tomorrow. A wounded German prisoner is brought in and we treat him – a bullet through his shoulder. He is a handsome fellow – a wholesale grocer from Dresden: good family, good education, and perfect discipline. We have one dead man from a bullet through the eye – a father of four from the 6th Company. In the afternoon, comrade and I had to take a Dragoon with a thigh wound, to Herbéviller. The heavy shelling continues ferociously. We were spotted on the road and had to take cover from the shells four times.

26 April 1915

At ten o'clock last night, and again at one in the morning, the bombardment was so savage, we received orders to take cover in the cellars. It was terrifying. The house rocked on its foundations. Today I'm in a veritable molehill – a little underground village. There is less danger here than outside. We are well sheltered – it's a good thing since the shells are dropping very near us. In spite of everything, I am so exhausted, I sleep.

27 April 1915

Return to the village. The relief last night was difficult because we were targeted by the shells. Just as are having supper we have to take a wounded man with a sprain to Herbéviller. The afternoon is not too bad and we play the piano. At about four, the Boches fire incendiary shells on Herbéviller and set fire to a house. We put it out in two hours – then complete calm until nine o'clock, when there is another ferocious bombardment. We turn in at eleven. At two o'clock in the morning another very fierce bombardment, but we don't go down to the cellars. Too bad. We will soon see. An hour later, all is quiet again

28 April 1915

A more or less passable day. Three bombardments during the day and two during the night. No victims. Our men know how to give like for like.

29 April 1915

The Boches fired 124 shells on Herbéviller. The incendiary bombs started fires in three different places. We are obliged to take cover at Ogéviller. Two light infantrymen are wounded. One is pierced through, above the heart; the other, was hit in the lower back as a result of a shell explosion. Shelling as usual in the evening and at night.

30 April 1915

Another fire at Herbéviller. Tonight I am on duty in the trenches. Infernal shelling all day long.

1 May 1915

In the trenches. The Boches have set fire to Fréménil. They are shelling the trenches on the front line. One dragoon is killed and another wounded. In the evening we collect the dead man. It is a terrible sight. He is buried in rubble; only the head is visible; the eyes are pulp and the mouth and chin are missing. We gather the remains from eight in the evening to one o'clock in the morning. No abdomen. We put the guts and body parts more or less in place. Our spades cut into a leg, or half a leg. We load it all and the mud onto a stretcher – it is a hideous mess. We cover it with a sheet and set off for Ogéviller where the remains will be buried tomorrow at seven o'clock. It is truly the most appalling sight.

Tonight there is a storm and great claps of thunder; it is nothing compared to the cannons.

2 May 1915

Intense shelling on Ogéviller with heavy, long-range artillery – 210. A woman is killed – blown to bits by a shell. Another woman and her little daughter are wounded. A so-called German victory.

3 May 1915

Shelling all about us, but no appreciable outcome. In the evening, there is a fairly violent storm. I take the medical report to Ogéviller. It is very hot.

4 May 1915

At eleven o'clock in the morning, a fierce bombardment is now much closer to us. A couple of metres away, we gather up pieces of shrapnel as big as one's hand. The evening and night are calm.

5 May 1915

A quiet day today – too quiet. What lies behind this?

6 May 1915

An even quieter day than yesterday. One wonders if this is not the prelude to a fresh attack. But no, nothing happens.

7 May 1915

It has happened. At five o'clock, the centre of town is bombarded. We had been warned in the morning. I had to wait half an hour before taking the medical report to Ogéviller. At five o'clock I went to get our supper. Two bombs fell right in front of me. To get from the infirmary to the kitchen just a hundred metres away, I had to take cover in a barn four times. But there were no casualties.

8 May 1915

Another bombardment in the afternoon but less intense than the day before. I went up to the molehill. At nine thirty, two artillery and cannon attacks, but without casualties. In the afternoon, one of our planes flew over the German lines eleven times and every flight it made one of our marine cannons set up in the Railleux forest, fired on the German lines on the Avricourt railway line. We do not know yet the outcome.

9 May 1915

I spent the day at the molehills. A quiet day and fine weather. I rest in the sun. No bombs. In the evening at eight thirty, I go back down.

10 May 1915

An almost calm day. There are few bombs and they don't fall near us. Wonderful weather. The Boches fire steadily at one of our planes, which flies superbly well above their lines.

11 May 1915

Similar day to the previous. Eighteen shells on Herbéviller. Beautiful weather. One man wounded.

12 May 1915

The bombardments continue but are not excessive. In the evening I go to the molehills for 24 hours. It has been a passable day. In the afternoon we have a musical session of piano and songs.

13 May 1915

I am at the molehills. Yesterday at nine thirty at night, the cannons roared fiercely and we thought it might be a real attack. Nevertheless, the night was more or less quiet. Tomorrow we are going to Bénaménil for four days rest. The weather is still fine.

It is Ascension Day today and an open-air mass was held in the Venkel woods, and said by the chaplain to the 17th Light Infantry. Fichel, an artillery captain, 32 years old and a great fellow, was present. He commands the 75 batteries. He was called out during mass. He went off to give orders and then returned. A second later, our 75s were firing uninterruptedly on the Boche. All the while Captain Fichel took communion. Then he assisted the chaplain, and then went off to see the outcome of his orders.

14 May 1915

I came down from the molehills last night. At midnight there was some furious shelling from our side. We waited for the call that was sure to come any second, for there would certainly be some damage. This is what happened. The Boches wanted to retake Reillon. We let them advance and then we bombarded the village and destroyed it. There was little or nothing left and those Boches who were not killed, must have fled. No one man from our side was hurt. This evening we leave for Bénaménil for four days' rest.

15 May 1915

We arrived at Bénaménil last night at midnight. Here, we will have a complete rest. I went into a pine forest to write in peace. To improve the state of my stomach, I eat at my own expense – eggs and green vegetables.

16 May 1915

It is Sunday. Still resting. I went to High Mass taken by the chaplain to the 12th Dragoons, and it was played and sung by many of my mates. Almost all afternoon I lie on the grass and sleep.

17 May 1915

It is raining incessantly and we leave tonight for the trenches. A storm in the afternoon. At six thirty in the evening, we leave Bénaménil. After walking for three and a half hours in the rain and with mud half way up our legs, and after losing our way twice in the fields, we came to a trench next to the 300th. Slept on the ground wrapped in my blanket. We can see the Boche in front of us.

18 May 1915

A quiet day in the Vého trench. A bombardment in the distance. At nine o'clock at night we left for Domjevin and Blémerey. Three hours to do ten kilometres – constant stops. We are spotted in the rocket lights – then cannons and guns. Completely done in we get back at one in the morning. Bed at two o'clock. Had a good sleep.

19 May 1915

Up at seven o'clock. The rounds at eight. We can only occasionally hear the cannons in the distance. In the afternoon, a little music with Pousot (a fellow stretcher-bearer – a singing teacher in Paris). In short, a day of rest. In the evening after dinner, more music and singing until ten o'clock.

20 May 1915

A quiet day and there is hardly any shelling. The chaplain comes in the afternoon to forewarn us that the Colonel of the 17th Light Cavalry, is coming at four thirty for an hour's music. He has asked us to give a little concert. We immediately put our heads together and a concert is organized. This is the programme:
Sidi Brahim, Le Chant du Nautonier, Valse Arabesque, Vision Fugitive, Le Veau d'Or, Le Clarion, Camarade, La Petite Agathe, Le Petit Paquet

First the choir and then at the end, we have the choir and the ten officers present singing along with us at the top of their voices. Then everybody stands, cap in hand, and sings the Marseillaise. Thanks from the Colonel who then sends us two bottles of Amiot champagne, which we drink immediately. In the evening, I go to the molehills, but once there I receive orders to go on my own, to Aid Post 5. It is a dangerous area. I am in quite a large shelter next to the Lieutenant. In front of me is the trench where the soldiers are: then the barbed-wire fence – and the Boches. I turn in at ten thirty. In the middle of the night I am woken by a fierce fusillade, and a few insignificant answering shots from our side. However, we are sure a massacre is taking place at Domèvre-sur-Vezouze. There will almost certainly be casualties over there. A few cannon bursts but nothing significant. Overcome with fatigue, I sleep.

21 May 1915

I am woken at four in the morning to have coffee. I sleep again until eight o'clock. A grey sky which clears a bit. Very little artillery. A more or less quiet day. No food. Without the intervention of a comrade, the lieutenants orderly, who offered me his officer's leftovers, I would have gone the whole day without eating. You can't take anything for granted in a war. I have written and read a lot. I turned in at ten o'clock. At this hour, a little light artillery but nothing important.

22 May 1915

Woken at four twenty for coffee. A quiet night with no incidents – just a few shots fired by the advance guards. I go back to sleep until six thirty. The weather is superb with brilliant sunshine. It is so hot in the afternoon, I'm obliged to stay in my shack. A violent cannonade in the afternoon. They are bombarding Saint-Martin below us. I leave the trenches in the evening. When I return at nine thirty, I learn that we have an injured corporal machine gunner with a shrapnel wound above his ankle. All is quiet in the evening.

23 May 1915

Woken at seven twenty. The doctor charges me to inspect the barracks and to make sure that everything is clean. I do the rounds and again at ten with the doctor. It all went well. Some gunfire in the afternoon. At three o'clock we fetch a wounded light cavalryman. The third finger of his left hand has been completely severed. He is in terrible pain. He was hit by a bullet from less than ten metres away. One of my friends, a telegraphist, tells me that Italy mobilizes tomorrow. It is a quiet evening.

24 May 1915

Up early after a peaceful night. I do the rounds of the barracks and give orders which are carried out well. At ten thirty another visit with the doctor who is satisfied. At that moment the telegraphist informs me that Italy has declared war on Austria and is on the march. So last night's news was true.

An unusual event took place this evening. To celebrate Italy's mobilization, General Varin ordered that the church bell at Saint-Martin should be rung for twenty minutes, along with all the bells in the surrounding villages, and at the same time the men in the trenches fired a salvo across the German trenches and cried, 'Long live Italy. Long live France!' followed by a deafening rendition of the Marseillaise in the face of the enemy. We could hear it from three kilometres away, so the Boches must certainly have heard it full on and it must have had an oddly demoralizing effect. We must certainly consider it a diplomatic victory that we managed to make a German ally defect to our side.

Of course, as might have been expected, we were gratified by a few shells, but without causing any damage. In the evening we learn that the day before yesterday, our regiment lost two men and one wounded; then yesterday, a nurse was killed, a man wounded, and another from the Dragoons.

Elsewhere, yesterday, they set fire to Herbéviller and Fréménil, and we set fire to Aménoncourt. We don't know what damage we may have inflicted on their men, but what with our salvos and the firing of our cannons particularly our heavy marine cannon, they certainly must have had some casualties. By evening, everything was relatively calm again – just few gunshots every now and then. Contrary to expectations the night too was quiet and we were undisturbed.

25 May 1915

Another quiet day – hardly any shelling. I spend my day reading and writing under a tall Ash tree in the garden. In the evening a little piano.

26 May 1915

A peaceful morning. Herbéviller is shelled in the afternoon but there are no casualties. Then Ogéviller is shelled, killing two soldiers and a civilian and wounding a civilian. The shelling started again in the evening, but less intense and without effect. A fairly fierce fusillade during the night which made us think there might be an attack, but nothing happened.

27 May 1915

This morning I took the medical report to Ogéviller. It has been badly damaged from yesterday's shelling. In spite of a minor bombardment, I managed to stay safe and sound in Vého. We gave a little concert with songs this afternoon. The weather is overcast and stormy. No doubt it is going to rain. The night is quiet.

28 May 1915

A quiet day. I copied a delightful little berceuse which I have sent to Marg. An interesting vocal and instrumental concert in the afternoon. Very little shelling during the day. Tonight, I am going to Aid Post 5 for 48 hours.

29 May 1915

I am at Aid Post 5. I got up at four thirty to let some Dragoons, who had spent the night on reconnaissance, get some sleep. We have been showered with 77s all morning. My Lieutenant's orderly just missed being hit. The afternoon is quiet. This evening there is to be a big reconnaissance right up to the German lines. I have been told to stand by. By midnight everything is still quiet and nobody has called me. I sleep in the shelter along with an warrant officer from the Dragoons.

30 May 1915

Second day in the trenches. A little shelling. Spent the day on duty and reading. In the evening I go back down, without incident.

31 May 1915

A more or less quiet day. Concert in the afternoon.

1 June 1915

After the rounds, a comrade and I took a wounded man from the 6th Engineers Regiment. It was very hot. We stayed in Ogéviller where we ate a good lunch. We returned at two thirty. Then I wrote and rested in the shade. There was little shelling. However, we fired quite a bit from our side – particularly the 75s. No damage suffered by us.

2 June 1915

Fairly intense shelling on Domjevin and Vého, but not on us. In the afternoon, rest and a little writing in the garden. In the evening I go up to Aid Post 5, where I am given a warm welcome by the sergeant major of the 31st Dragoons. There is a heavy reconnaissance, and while waiting for things to happen, we chat very amiably together. We turn in at one o'clock in the morning. A short while later, a fierce fusillade, but a little further away. Apart from that, we were undisturbed.

3 June 1915

Woken up at three, then at four. Up at seven o'clock. I helped the sergeant major, and then helped my lieutenant to construct a table and bench. That took care of the afternoon. In the evening at nine thirty, I went back down and had dinner as soon as I arrived. Played cards until eleven o'clock. Bed and a very quiet night.

4 June 1915

A fairly quiet morning. At four o'clock, a full concert given in the presence of the colonel of the 31st Dragoons (An American – Waddington), the lieutenant colonel of the 8th Dragoons, and many other officers, nurses and stretcher-bearers. The programme as follows:

Aubade du Roi d'Ys, Le Chant de l'Alouette, Le Canon, Valse Arabesque, Le Cor, L'Allusion, Brigitte, Hérodiade Vinon, Tipperary, Pauvre Fou, Missouri, Les Forgerons, A une Femme, Stances de Lakmé, Le Chant du Nantonier, Le Satyre de l'Escalier, La Puce, Les Enfants, Le Crucifix, La Marseillaise.

When it is over, the Colonel offers us beer and asks if we would give another concert the following Monday to which General Varin would be invited.

5 June 1915

A fairly quiet day. Very little heavy artillery – almost nothing in fact. Bad news, which has yet to be ascertained. The Russians have been thrashed at Przemysl. We must wait for this to be confirmed.

6 June 1915

A fairly calm morning. At ten o'clock, I washed in the river and ten minutes later, a few shells fell in the spot where I had just been. It is Sunday – glorious weather. In short sleeves, write in the garden. It is hard being here in these circumstances in such weather. Quiet evening and night.

7 June 1915

A fairly quiet morning, except for a brief, but quite fierce shelling on the Bois des Haies d'Albe. No damage. It has been as calm as a millpond since lunch. We can hear nothing. I write and read in the garden where it is very hot in spite of a little breeze. In the afternoon – a full concert with General Varin and Colonel Waddington presiding. Very successful. The programme as follows:

Sambre-et-Meuse, Dors Bébé, Conférence, L'Allusion, Berceuse, Le Chant du Nantonier, On Entend le Canon, Air de Joseph, Calme en Mer, L'Alouette, Les Enfants, Les Blés, Tipperary, Le Tango, Position Intéressante, Il y a des Espions, Aubade du Roi d'Ys, Hérodiade Vinon, Ballade de Chopin, À une Femme, Le Canon, Le Codicille de Me Mauser, Les Ombres, Le Crucifix, La Marseillaise.

At the end of the concert, we are offered beer. General Varin tells us that the King of Greece's illness is due to a knife wound inflicted by a Greek partisan. He also tells us that Romania will soon mobilize. He thanks each one of us with a pleasant word. He had come not wanting to stay longer than fifteen minutes, but stayed for an hour and a half – indeed to the end of the concert. He left in the hope that the concerts would resume. A quiet evening, but about eleven o'clock, there is a violent fusillade coming from the Bois Des Haies d'Albe towards Domèvre. Fifteen cannon shots from our side immediately bring everything to a halt. Then our 75s follow, and then all is quiet.

8 June 1915

This morning three of us went with our wheeled stretcher to Ogéviller to collect a sick man. The temperature was at least 50° and the road was in full sun – twelve kilometres there and back. We had a good lunch at Ogéviller, during which there was a storm, which made hardly any impression on the dust on the road. We returned at three thirty. An uneventful evening. There was a violent storm, during the night, which at the time, I thought impressive, but compared to the cannons it was a mere whisper. The rest of the night was quiet.

9 June 1915

This morning I was woken at six by a comrade – my old corporal who tells me he has just been made sergeant. I am pleased because he deserved the promotion. While making the rounds I set to work with four massages and frictions, then an iodoform dressing. The afternoon is quiet. I read and write in the garden as it is very muggy. Tonight I'm going to Aid Post 5.

At seven forty-five, I leave with Mr Roger who eight days ago, was staff sergeant, but who has now been promoted to sub-lieutenant. He is a charming fellow, whom I could call a real friend. He is replacing sub-lieutenant Couhaud, who two days ago, went on a blinder to Lunéville and returned at three o'clock in such a state that he was unable to march to the trenches. A fine example. A comrade and I are in the shelter, and Mr Roger comes over and chats until ten thirty. We turn in at eleven. It is a quiet night.

10 June 1915

At three twenty in the morning, I give up my place to some dragoons who have spent the night outside. The rest of the day was spent in this way – turn and turn about. We were shelled quite a bit, but not vey close, and we replied in kind. The weather is very oppressive and I think it's responsible for an agonizing pain in my right leg. I rest a little in the afternoon to make up for the shortness of last night. There is a violent storm at six. The sky is ablaze with flashing light. I spent an agreeable moment reading and writing. It is ten thirty and I go to bed.

11 June 1915

It was a good night and quiet. I got up at five o'clock. Even at that time, it was already very hot. At about eight, the Boches started to snipe at us again, and the shells were no higher than two metres above our heads. Fortunately, no one was hit. It is unbelievably hot and heavy. My kidneys and my thighs are extremely painful. To pass the time I read a lot and write.

At nine o'clock, I leave Aid Post 5. At ten having read a little, I was about to go up to bed when a young sub lieutenant was brought in suffering horribly from a burn to his hand, which he had incurred while trying to set a fuse in the trenches. With the doctor, we bandage it. As a result of this, I went to bed at eleven thirty. A quiet night.

12 June 1915

A quiet day. I rise at six and do some sewing and tidy my belongings. After lunch, I write all afternoon. No shelling for the entire day. At eight that evening one of our heavy cannons fired from the Bois des Railleux, but we don't know the outcome. Calm for the rest of the night.

13 June 1915

Today it's Sunday. I went to seven o'clock mass. It was said by a young chaplain whom we know and who is attached to the Dragoons and is actually on tour of duty with us at Saint-Martin.

14 June 1915

Quiet morning. After the morning meal, we pick cherries. Doctor Salles accompanied us to the 120 batteries to take photographs of us. At four o'clock, I bathed in the river. It was wonderful. In the evening I was stung on the wrist and my arm swelled up. I hope it doesn't turn nasty. Quiet evening. Quiet night.

15 June 1915

This morning my arm is swollen. I can't think what it is. We were witness to an air battle. It was fascinating. The weather is cooler. There is quite a fresh breeze and it is extremely pleasant in the garden where I am reading and writing. It seems that new forces have amassed on the Vého side – mostly from the Colonial. We are to attack from here any day now. Anyway, at the moment, calm reigns. In the evening, we are told that there will be a parade – since then, nothing. It is a very quiet night.

16 June 1915

This morning after the rounds, we were visited by the Senior Medical Officer with five-stripes to his name, and who has come to inspect the barracks, the trenches and the infirmary. He seems satisfied. At one o'clock, our cannons fired a round of about twenty shots at the enemy. And now they are retaliating. The shells are coming over us but are landing far away. We give like for like. But they have just attacked Blémerey – one wounded. Then at Ogéviller a woman and six horses have died, and another woman wounded. For our part, it seems we set fire to Igney in the afternoon. This evening a few gunshots and then a quiet night.

17 June 1915

Yesterday, a comrade (Dupas) and I made a room for ourselves in the infirmary. It is much healthier and quieter and we slept well. At about seven, a taube dropped a bomb on our lines but happily, without result. In the afternoon I read and write in the garden. And then we have dinner in the garden. In the evening I go up to Aid Post 5. At first all is calm then in the middle of the night a sharp artillery exchange, which from the sound of our guns, has obliged us to retreat. And then almost immediately, our cannons start firing on Des Haies d'Albe and repulse the attack. Then everything is quiet again.

18 June 1915

The rest of the night passed well. Woken at two in the morning. But I only get up at seven. At eight a taube flies over our lines and drops a bomb 100 metres away from us in a small wood. Fortunately, there are no casualties. It must also have dropped one on Domjevin because it is ablaze over there. Our cannons, from quite close by, roar furiously. But there is no retaliation. At about ten, it is more or less quiet again.

In the afternoon we are subjected to a bombardment, especially those at Aid Post 6 to our left; and a little copse where an artillery observer is positioned. But no casualties are signalled. Our artillery immediately reduces the enemy to silence. The evening is so-so. The night is quiet.

19 June 1915

Up at five thirty. About seven o'clock we are shelled again; then a shell explodes at the foot of the observation post, and finally it is Aid Post 6's turn. Suddenly we see an arm or a leg flying up from the post's trench. A second later, there is a call from the command post to say that six men from the 217th have just been killed at Aid Post 6. This is what we have just witnessed. Our cannons roar, and then suddenly are quiet again.

At ten we are told that we will not be relieved tonight, instead we will be reinforced by another company, as the intention is to attack tonight and to take Chazelles. It seems the company's offices have loaded the trucks in anticipation and are ready for every eventuality. Let's hope it all goes well. All afternoon, our artillery provoke the enemy with their spasmodic sniping. But there is no response.

Seven o'clock. The men are ordered to stand at the ready in the trench. There is no question of sleeping. Nine o'clock – there is an unending salvo, from the direction of Reillon and Leintrey and the Côte 303. Ten o'clock – the same fusillade on the Bois des Haies d'Albe. The cannons are firing shot by shot. It is hell on earth. Four batteries of 75, 90 and 120 are fired all at the same time. It is like an immense, unending storm. The fusillade continues. Bullets and shells whistle about our heads. Sheer butchery.

20 June 1915

At one in the morning, the Germans counter attack. We repulse them with two bayonet attacks and artillery, which has not let up. We can hear the cries of the Germans and can sense they are weakening. Two o'clock, and the battle is flagging a bit. Day is breaking. At three o'clock, our cannons stop for a while. We now know that there is one dead from the territorials, and one wounded from the 81st. From the 217th, only the captain is wounded, but the 223rd has many wounded. As we have succeeded in taking Côte 303, Reillon and Leintrey, the enemy is now returning fire. They are shelling Saint-Martin. A shell falls on some sleeping artillerymen killing three and wounding five. In fact, we thought there was practically nothing ahead of us and we were very mistaken. It has been a hot affair. Six hours of shelling and the enemy are still at it. We are not returning fire or very little; only the 75s are being operated, and for all the interest they are arousing, one can only imagine that they are not reaching any targets.

At midday the enemy counter-attack with steady determination. At two, our artillery returns fire aggressively. Then we can hear the machineguns. At four, the enemy come back in force, and with renewed vigour, counter-attack again and again and retake part of the Côte, which we had vanquished the night before. We have many casualties. Four thirty – the shelling continues furiously. Five o'clock – the 6th infantry-cyclists arrive to retake the trench in a bayonet attack, mercilessly stabbing the Boches one by one.

Six o'clock – two more of our companies arrive as reinforcements. They cross the re-conquered trench at top speed and take off down the road to Gondrexon. For the moment the Boches have been pushed right back. Eight o'clock. We now occupy the Amienbois, the Rémabois and Gondrexon. We will have to leave this village temporarily because we do not have sufficient manpower to hang on to it. We have exceeded the goal, but what carnage – we had to make two more bayonet attacks to get there.

In the evening we received the sad news that Petit, the nurse attached to the 5th company, was killed yesterday at Herbéviller while he was picking up an injured man. He had been with us since the beginning of the campaign. He was a delightful comrade. The cannons have more or less stopped.

21 June 1915

The night has been relatively quiet; there was a little gunfire and a little shrapnel from the Boches. We retaliated but our artillery was much farther away. Our men are on the fringes of the Rémabois strengthening their numbers. The Boches are spraying the old trench as much as they can. We have recovered a 75 cannon which is now returning fire steadily. At midday all is quiet. I learn that last night, Saint-Martin was heavily shelled. Three artillerymen killed and five wounded. One has been completely eviscerated but he only died fifteen minutes later. Another had an open head wound and was killed instantly. Another has no less than 29 wounds. It took an hour and a half to apply the bandages. I am relieved at nine o'clock and more than happy to get back to the village for a bit.

22 June 1915

Last night I went to bed at ten thirty and slept a bit. At midnight we are woken. The battle has recommenced with renewed fury. We have taken control of Gondrexon and part of Leintrey – but again, at what price. At about ten o'clock, the enemy bombards Herbéviller and Ogéviller. One of our men (5th Company) is killed at Herbéviller by a shell. At Ogéviller, a dragoon and six horses have been killed. They are attacking the far end of the village to prevent our reinforcements reaching our lines, but it is a useless exercise as apparently, we have what we need.

Our senior medical officer, Mr Chênebis tells us that he has received a letter, which he considers to be official, with the news that a peace agreement is to be signed in July – that is, next month. If only he proves to be right. He is not a very easy-going man, but he is serious and he says nothing lightly.

One of our batteries of 120 is firing all four of its cannons furiously and without let-up. So something is up again. Fifteen minutes later, things calm down a bit. It has been raining since ten o'clock this morning. It makes a bit of a change. It is quieter. We consolidate our positions.

23 June 1915

It has been a good night. Many attacks have been repulsed from the Domèvre side. Our troops have got as far as Gondrexon and have consolidated their position in the village. A little more and we will soon have pushed the Boches back to the borders of our side of the lines. It is much quieter this morning. There is little cannon activity. The weather, of course, has changed and is perhaps hampering operations a bit. At midday, there is another storm, the second since this morning, and it is raining continuously.

We have learnt that the poor quality of our shells was responsible for our blowing up a marine cannon and a 120 cannon. It is a great shame. But why is it that those in the legal profession are in our factories and are responsible for the manufacture of these weapons? Why is it not the professionals in the field who would be better equipped for the task? But it is not for me to judge. I am an observer and that's all.

The cannons have quietened a little. It's a relief. Twenty-seven shells have just been fired and fallen onto our 120 batteries. Eight of the shells have not exploded. How useless they are – even worse than ours. They must have bought them from the Americans. Midnight – in the distance, there is a heavy fusillade of cannons and artillery. The Boches are counter-attacking on the Bois de Rémabois. They're setting themselves up for a thrashing. At one thirty, all is quiet again.

24 June 1915

It is the day of St. Jean – my sister and my nephew's feast day. I am writing to them for the occasion. I was unable to do it last night because of the attack. It is a little quieter now except for the odd blast from the 75s which the enemy ignore. At one o'clock they get their revenge and bombard Domjevin. The shells are whistling over my head as I write in the garden. Our 75s retaliate very successfully. At five, there is an impressive air raid with five aeroplanes flying overhead. Then everything seems to calm down.

25 June 1915

At one forty five, I am woken by an infernal racket. I go into the garden to see what it's about. The Boches are spraying our trenches with shells and our men are replying. And then the artillery starts going at it hammer and tongs. The Germans are counter-attacking for the seventh time, and seven times they have been repulsed and we have held our positions. A huge number of their men are dead. And we have suffered considerable losses too.

On the rounds with Doctor Salles, I have been making a study of one of the men who has tapeworm. It is an extremely interesting subject, if a little messy.

At two o'clock we receive telegraphed news. In four days time there will be an all-out offensive strike. It's about time. Everyone is war-weary and would like to see the end of it soon. Right now, everything is quiet. During the evening a little artillery and cannon, but insignificant. Another Boches counter-attack at midnight where the Boches failed completely. The rest of the night is calm.

26 June 1915

This morning we have been bombarded at Saint-Martin, on the Moulin side, by their 77s. Absolutely no harm whatsoever has been done. Now it is our turn and the 75s and 120s are firing on their batteries, for we have discovered their positions. Half an hour later, it is more or less quiet. In the afternoon they spray the trenches of Aid Post 5 with shrapnel – where I'm going tonight. In the evening there is a fine air raid above the enemy lines. The enemy fire on the planes but are far from their mark. I go up to Aid Post 5. Everything is more or less all right. At about nine, a heavy fusillade breaks out in front of us. It is a strong Boche reconnaissance. It is dispersed in short order, by our 75s. The night is fairly good. A few cannon bursts and that's all.

27 June 1915

Up at six. The Boches are spraying Aid Post 6 with shrapnel. We fired eight shells yesterday which did not detonate. These are 77s with aluminium casings. Really, what a farce! From time to time our 75s reply irritably and then immediately stop. It is relatively quiet in the afternoon. At spaced intervals, the cannons blast shot by shot. The same thing during the night.

28 June 1915

It's a long time since we've had such a quiet morning. If it weren't for the trenches, one would have difficulty in believing that we were at war. It seems we may have to return at the last minute this evening – perhaps even, to Ogéviller to organize and set up a new service. If this is so, it will be a great pity, as we have become used to Saint-Martin, in spite of the constant danger. We will know this afternoon what has been decided. At four, several shells fall about us. They are 77s. One of them doesn't detonate. At nine thirty I leave Aid Post 5 for Saint-Martin. We are definitely not going to Ogéviller tonight because we've been warned of an attack at ten o'clock. Our troops are going to find a way to control Leintrey and Rémabois. At exactly ten, they fire an uninterrupted hail of shells on the enemy. But this time, unlike the last, they retaliate and with some strength. At two in the morning both sides stop. We are able to sleep undisturbed.

29 June 1915

This morning at reveille everything is quiet. We find out that our troops, who should have numbered 6000 for the attack, were only a battalion of 1000 men. They were so heavily shelled they were unable to come out of the trenches and as a result, the expected attack did not take place. So it is back to square one from this side. The weather is oppressive. The cannons have stopped their concert and everything is quiet. The attack will start again tonight. At eleven, the cannons roar a bit and then stop. The night is quiet.

30 June 1915

The attack did not happen and no one knows the reason. There must be enemy forces ahead of us. However, this is not what the last lot of prisoners say who have been interrogated. These men are happy to have been taken and would like to see the war end. They have had enough and can't stand their Colonel whom they say is a coward who does anything to keep out of harm's way. Apparently, he had asked to be moved to the back lines but had been refused. He hides from our artillery attacks, which is very damaging to their side. It rained until midday and the weather is very muggy. Not one cannon shot. Everything is extremely quiet. In the afternoon, I went fishing with a few comrades to kill time. The evening and night are dead calm

1 July 1915

Very quiet morning – just the occasional cannon blast to bring it home to us that we are at war. How peaceful compared to last week. Oh God! When will we be finished with this? At four thirty, a dogfight opposite us but without conclusion. Then immediately afterwards, a fierce cannonade to which the enemy respond, which indicates the prelude to an attack. Ten minutes later – nothing. Followed by a completely uneventful evening and night.

2 July 1915

It is beautiful weather with a light, fresh wind. Not one cannon shot. There is no war – we are in the country. It stays like this all day. In the evening, the doctor came up to Aid Post 5, to look at the positions. We were waiting for him and then we stayed chatting with him and drinking beer until half-past midnight. Everything was still very quiet.

3 July 1915

It was still quite quiet this morning until seven o'clock, when a German plane flew over and dropped two bombs just above and to the left of Herbéviller. I do not think there was any damage. The afternoon is dead quiet.

4 July 1915

At ten this morning, heavy bombardment on the village. We had one dead man from the 81st Territorials and five wounded from the 4th and 12th Dragoons. With the shells raining down on us we went to collect these poor men and dressed their wounds. We took huge risks. Their wounds are severe. What a job. A little earlier, it seems that we made an impact on Cirey and Avricourt. So this was their revenge. At about twelve thirty, our work done, we have lunch.

The afternoon is more or less quiet. Wading through blood, we washed down the infirmary and changed blood-spattered shirts. The captain of the 81st, a really good man, came to pay his respects to his fallen soldier. He knelt by him and then kissed him. In the evening I go up to Aid Post 5. We are again violently bombarded – pretty well everywhere.

At ten, my sergeant comes to find me and tells me his brother has been wounded. I go with him in a hail of shells, and find his brother and a dragoon, both of them wounded. I quickly bandage them and then set about getting the brother to the post. We have barely gone 20 metres when we are sprayed with shells again and have to make our way backwards with the wounded man to the shelter. We can't go more than two metres at a time without having to throw ourselves to the ground. We wait a while for the shelling to subside, and then reinforcements arrive and our comrades take the injured men away. At one in the morning, I get a bit of rest.

5 July 1915

It has been more or less quiet since this morning. My buttock still hurts. If I'm not too disturbed, I will try and get a bit of rest this afternoon. I was able to rest for about an hour. At four o'clock, a plane flew over our lines, trying to spot our cannons 155, which are doing them a lot of harm at Avricourt. Once again they have set fire to Ogéviller. Then they shelled Saint-Martin. Seven men were wounded, fortunately, not seriously. Our trenches were shelled four times during the night, but there were no casualties.

6 July 1915

More or less quiet since this morning, except our 155s are still bombarding the enemy and inflicting a lot of damage. A plane flew over again to find them but we have them well hidden. Return cannon fire but not on us. The weather is stormy and it is difficult to distinguish between cannon and thunder. At nine we come down from Aid Post 5. At eleven a terrifying storm. I learn that, during the day, the shelling has killed nine men at Fréménil. The night is more or less quiet.

7 July 1915

At reveille, I go into the village centre and see that three quarters of it has been devastated by the shelling. There is a dreadful wind. There is an eight-day furlough. The first detachment of men leaves tomorrow morning. I think it will soon be my turn. No shelling near us since the day before yesterday. At the moment all is quiet.

8 July 1915

Once again, those who should have been going on leave are still here this morning. It is very likely that in a couple of days we are all going to the back for six weeks and the whole regiment will take it in turn for an eight-day respite. But this is only hearsay and nothing is official yet. There has not been one cannon shot since this morning. It seems strange, but a blessed relief.

I spoke a little too soon. At three, we are told that a man has been killed at Des Haies d'Albe. He is brought to us and we must do what we have to do. Just as he was going back in the trench, he was hit by a bullet fired by a German standing opposite him. He was ripped apart from shoulder to shoulder. His captain (Major Legaut – 7th Company) wept and embraced him, and closed his eyes and mouth. We have taken him to the church and he will be interred tomorrow morning. The rest of the day and the night is quiet

9 July 1915

At nine o'clock this morning we go to the funeral of the soldier who fell yesterday. His captain gave a simple but moving speech. Everything is quiet. We have lunch. We have hardly finished when at eleven thirty, we are bombarded by ten large shells. We have one wounded man. Shrapnel through the left shoulder has made a gaping wound of about 15 centimetres long. He is in dreadful pain because the shrapnel did not exit. At three, he and another man, who the night before received slight injuries to his right side, were taken away in the medical wagon. At four o'clock, a store of 20,000 cartridges blew up at Aid Post 6, caused by a German shell. There were no victims. At ten o'clock, there is a violent fusillade and cannonade. The Boches are attacking Côte 303. The cannons fire for two hours without stopping. Then little by little calm reigns.

10 July 1915

A big commotion at eight o'clock – another bombardment. But no, some artillerymen have set off an unexploded 77 from last night. Tonight, we have to go to the shelters in the Rognelle woods, about 500 metres from the Aid Post 5, where we will stay for 48 hours. I don't know if I am going or not. I will know later. At eleven thirty, a comrade and I receive orders to go. We get there at night and are lodged in filthy wooden huts, which were built to house 30 men not 120. Many of the men sleep outside. I sleep on the hard ground. All is quiet.

11 July 1915

We are in the middle of the woods and willow. No shelling. Everything is more or less all right. I am dead tired after a bad night. We don't know how long we are here for. I might be replaced tonight. The commanding officer arrives at Saint-Martin this afternoon and will put up at the infirmary. At four thirty, the mess orderlies were spotted and the Boches immediately fired shells at them. But nothing untoward is signalled. In the evening I go down to the village for twenty-four hours to get some rest. It is a quiet night.

12 July 1915

I had a good and restful night. The weather is horrible and it is going to rain. It is very windy – typical of the Lorraine climate. Not much cannon activity this morning. This evening I go back up to the woods. Tonight we are going to have a hare, which was caught in a trap, and which somebody brought for us. It is a real treat at this time.

At quarter past seven, I am getting ready to leave when we are bombarded on the road to Blémerey. I wait forty- five minutes before leaving. Thanks to the kindness of a few comrades, I sleep that night in a genuine Neanderthal hut in the middle of the woods. A hut made of branches and reeds, where I slept very well. A little cannon fire during the night.

13 July 1915

Rain and yet more rain. We don't know where to put ourselves. A little shelling that goes over our heads. After dinner, I sleep a little in my hut to kill time and to relieve my boredom. I hope to be relieved tonight at eight thirty. In the evening we are relieved and prepare to return to Saint-Martin. Three hours in belting rain. Very happy to get back inside where it's dry. It is a good night and I sleep well.

14 July 1915

National Day. Who would have thought we would still be here at this time. It hasn't rained since this morning. A lot of wind and sometimes it's sunny. It lifts one's spirits a little. No shelling to speak of – a few odd shots from time to time and that's all. Tonight I'm going either to Aid Post 5 or 6. Let's hope it all goes well.

15 July 1915

We spent the night at Aid Post 5 with four stretcher-bearers from the 223rd. It was a quiet night. Rain on awakening and it hasn't stopped since. The morning has been quiet but since midday, there has been quite a bit of firing from the artillery and not very far from us. At four thirty we spot thirty or so Boches, rifles at the ready, advancing on our lines. We realize this is an attack, and we immediately get ready. The battle rages furiously at two steps away from us. At eight, we are relieved of duty, but we know it is our duty to remain. We stay until three thirty in the morning. At one thirty, the attack is even more virulent and the machine guns are giving their all. I cannot bring myself to describe here the outcome. At three thirty I go back to the village to get some rest.

16 July 1915

The battle is followed by relative calm. Tonight I am going again to Aid Post 5. Let's hope it will be all right. I did not go to the post but to the trench shelters where I was on call until ten past eleven. The wind is dreadful. Not much from the cannons.

17 July 1915

The night was taken up by a real tempest. At six in the morning, the rain was coming down so hard we had to stretch tents over our hut. There is a lot of rain again during the day. At five, the cannons were thundering to such an extent, we thought another attack must be imminent. But nothing came of it. At eight, I go down to the village for 24 hours.

18 July 1915

I ate at nine, when I returned. I had a good night. I spent all morning cleaning myself up. It seems that the class of 1899 will leave us in two or three days to reinforce the reserves. There is talk of a rest, but we don't know when. Tonight I am going to the trench shelters in the woods at Raguelle.

19 July 1915

I spent the night in a Neanderthal hut, where I was extremely cold. At seven thirty I went on the rounds with Doctor Fayot. It was in the open air and in the middle of the wood. I then went down to Saint-Martin to fetch the necessary medicines, and taking advantage of the errand had lunch in the village. I have learnt that the class of 1899 is leaving this morning for Saint-Clément to rejoin the 222nd Reserves. It is a sad parting for many, for they have fought side by side for a year. I also learn that we are to leave Saint-Martin tomorrow to go to Aid Posts 11 and 14 for four days. Then four days somewhere else and so on until 5 August. At twenty-five past twelve, I am told that we leave tonight rather than tomorrow. At three o'clock the lieutenant asks me to find out and report to him on the state of the sick. He tells me that the company will go to the trenches tonight.

The orders are so contradictory, it's impossible to understand what is going on. The weather is superb. It does one good after these last few days. Six thirty in the evening – I have never experienced a moment such as this. The class of 1899 are leaving. My comrade Schumpff is leaving too. I kiss him on both cheeks as if he were my brother. Officers and soldiers are weeping, indeed weeping bitterly. Lieutenant Payen makes a short speech but is so overcome with emotion, he cannot continue. All the while the Boches were firing as much grapeshot over our heads as they could. No, I will never forget the emotion one feels when taking leave of one's brothers-in-arms. In the evening, I had the pleasure of dining with Schumpff near me, and he even slept next to me.

20 July 1915

Sainte Marguerite – my wife's feast day. Odd sort of feast this year and to be so far from each other. This morning I rose at four to see off my good comrade Schumpff. Then with tears in our eyes we parted. Then life carried on as usual. In the afternoon I pack my things as we leave tonight for the trenches at Vého for four days. Let's hope for the best.

21 July 1915

I did not go to the trenches last night, but to Vého itself. Seven of us, knapsacks on our backs set off at eight in the evening and arrived at about midnight. We got lost in the woods, which was not at all amusing. After a short rest, we spent the rest of the day constructing a shelter to protect us from the shelling, because the village is far from being spared. I think there are only four houses still standing. Indeed we were gratified by a few shells during the afternoon. At three o'clock, we are told that there is one dead and one wounded at Aid Post 10. It is an extremely dangerous area. We went to collect the wounded man, but there was a counter-order because he was not at all seriously hurt and asked to be left in the trenches. We will go later tonight to fetch the dead man. At five o'clock, we are advised that we are to make a gas attack in order to retake the blockhaus opposite. At six, the artillery fire – it is quite dreadful and it so it goes on until ten at night. At eleven, since everything has quietened down, we go and fetch the dead man.

22 July 1915

The result of the battle last night: there are dead and wounded, but we did not retake the Blockhaus. It appears that the enemy are entrenched in shelters that are six or seven metres deep. So if that's true, there is nothing to be done. This evening, I have to go to Aid Post 12. Let's hope all goes well. There is a bit of a wind, but it is lovely weather. I go up to Aid Post 12 at eight o'clock. It is a trench shelter large enough to rest. My post is far from the company. I sleep well protected – a little stuffy, but not cold. It is a quiet night.

23 July 1915

At reveille, I explore the area a bit. Very pretty countryside, but dangerous. Below me is the forest of Parroy and the line: Lunéville, Deutsch-Avricourt, Dientz, and then Emberménil and above, a large forest where the Boches are. A connecting trench tunnel where you have to bend double so as not to be seen, leads to the company. It has rained without stopping since this morning and the mud comes above our shoes.

Some superior officers from the 20th Corps come to look over our trenches. They will no doubt take our place tomorrow. It seems their imperative now is to take the Côte d'Igney. It would be good if they would wait until we have gone. We have an artillery observation post just in front of the security entrance. Not much going on with the cannons this morning but a little shelling again on Vého and on the labourers opposite us. Rain all afternoon. At eight in the evening, our artillery and cannons attack without notice. It lasts for about two hours, but it is not a bold attack. The cannons are less vigorous than usual and only fire shot by shot and the artillery fusillade is not very strong. I think it may be a diversionary tactic to allow them to attack elsewhere. Tired, I turn in as the cannons have stopped their booming.

24 July 1915

I don't get up until eight thirty, as I am exhausted. The weather is more or less fine, but one can sense that it is going to rain again. It seems there was no outcome to last night's battle. Where is the point of killing men and wounding others? The cannons are firing shot by shot and are spaced between fairly long intervals. This evening we are meant to be going to Ogéviller for four days. We leave at eight thirty and we have a narrow escape. As we get to Vého, a large shell is fired into the middle of the company. We all throw ourselves to the ground . . . the shell lands without exploding, behind a hedge 20 metres away. We immediately set off again at a quick march and without further incident arrive at Ogéviller at quarter past midnight at our old infirmary.

25 July 1915

Got up a bit late. Had a much needed wash. Rounds. For these four days, I am detachment nurse under Doctor Fayot (a difficult man). He shouts all the time. But in spite of this, he's not such a bad sort. All is quiet here. There are still a few civilians around and it does one good to see a few people. It has rained for almost the whole day. In the evening, a comrade and I look for something to eat and find a good woman who fed us. We play cards, and then turn in.

26 July 1915

Up at six this morning. Coffee and milk at seven. The rounds at seven thirty. It is all satisfactory. We make our own arrangements for our mess meals and take them with a good woman who also gives us wine, vegetables and salad, which restores us bit. But the best restorative is to not hear the cannons in the distance. This mental rest is even better than the physical. If only it would continue in this way. We eat well in the evening and turn in immediately afterwards.

27 July 1915

A quiet night. At reveille, the rounds. At eleven o'clock, we treat ourselves to a good rabbit lunch, which boosts the morale and sets one up a bit. The weather is oppressive and it rains constantly. We rest. Overall, a quiet day.

28 July 1915

We are warned that we leave tonight for the woods. Fortunately, the weather is fine. The day goes by without a hitch. At seven at night, knapsacks on our backs, we leave for the woods. We get to a rather sparse wood where we leave our bags and go four kilometres farther on to the front line trenches – one step away from German-occupied Leintrey. Our men labour to enlarge the connecting tunnel. We supervise. While they work we receive two shells that don't explode.

At two in the morning we leave the area and have three hours rest in the woods, where we have the sky for our roof and the earth as our mattress. But in spite of everything, overcome by fatigue, I sleep.

29 July 1915

I am woken at seven thirty. I have a really bad toothache which is giving me a lot of trouble. The weather is fine, but we have had little rest. We hunt around to see if we can make our sleeping arrangements a little more agreeable. After lunch everyone has a siesta and the same thing in the evening.

At ten o'clock, there is some shelling in the Bois Jeanne d'Arc and some men are wounded. Fortunately, the weather is superb. A quiet afternoon. I still have toothache. I am not going to work at the trenches tonight. Only two stretcher-bearers need to be on duty. At nine o'clock, I sleep.

30 July 1915

It wasn't a bad night and I slept well. I am nicked by the lieutenant for not having gone to the trenches last night. I have to go tonight. I still have toothache, but it's not as bad as yesterday. The good weather is still holding. This morning there is a fairly fierce cannonade in the surrounding area. It is quieter this afternoon. At seven thirty we go with the men who will work on the trenches in a very dangerous spot with the Boches just two or three hundred metres away. I stretch out in a field in the open air, where I am very cold. At three in the morning, we return. At four we sleep. There were vigorous cannonades throughout the night.

31 July 1915

Up at eight. Four hours sleep. It is not very much. The rounds and then a meal. There is a little cannon fire. The weather seems a little irascible. However, it is not raining. It hasn't rained and the sky is clearing. At seven thirty, we leave for work in the trenches and the same scenario as yesterday – stretched out on the ground waiting for two in the morning. At three we return. We have coffee and sleep for a bit.

1 August 1915

Time is passing. We have had nearly a year of war and we are no further ahead than we were at the beginning. How much longer will this go on for? The rounds, then a meal. This evening we will be billeted at Reillon for four days. I don't know if I will go to the trenches. Very little cannon fire since this morning. The weather is getting up a bit. There is a wind blowing and it seems likely to stay. At seven thirty, knapsacks on our backs, we leave for Reillon and at the double. We get there at eight thirty and we are immediately dispatched to the second line's trench. My comrade and I are a little further away in a shelter made of a few planks. There is a little straw on the ground. We are sweating buckets, but wet as we are, we manage to sleep all the same.

2 August 1915

One year ago the country was mobilized. At two o'clock there is a hellish storm. Water is pouring into the shelter. We will look for another in the daylight. A little further away, we find a sort of nest, with a little straw, dug into the ground, where there is less rain – a nest where I wouldn't put my dog for fear of finishing him off. It is raining incessantly and we stay there flattened to the ground and frozen. The trench is one we took back from the Boches six weeks ago after a successful attack from the Côte 303. I am due to be relieved tonight and go to Reillon for 24 hours. That will be no bad thing. We can't move here. Immediately below us are Leintrey and the Rémabois which are completely occupied by the Boches. You can't put your nose out without being spotted. Quite a bit of intermittent shelling all about us. And from time to time there is a rapid burst of machine- gun fire from the Boches, but I'm not sure from which direction. If only the weather were fine. At two, word has it that a comrade who has been with us since the start of the campaign has been killed by a shell in the Boué woods. The news is confirmed this evening. At eight thirty we are called and four of us, led by the lieutenant, leave to fetch his body. It is a dangerous area and the Boches are just 300 metres away. We proceed in silence. We find the poor fellow who died while he lay asleep in his shelter. Shrapnel had gone through his thigh, cut the iliac artery, and perforated his intestines, causing internal and external haemorrhaging. But he is unchanged. We get him out of his hole with great difficulty, and have a lot of trouble transporting him, because he is heavy and the road is long and extremely slippery. We arrive at last sweating profusely. The doctor makes his report and then we help the captain and the lieutenant make an inventory of his belongings. At last we eat and then sleep. It is one in the morning.

3 August 1915

I get up at seven thirty with a headache. We take care of our fallen comrade and dig a hole for his grave and put him in a coffin. He will be buried at four this afternoon. It has rained all morning. At four o'clock, with the rain beating down on us, we buried our comrade in a cemetery made in a garden about 500 metres away. Six of us carried the coffin. I was at the head. It was extremely heavy and smelt strongly. Our captain gave a short and sensitive speech, and then six minutes later, it was all over. It was a quiet night, and we were able to get some rest.

4 August 1915

One year since war was declared. God it has been so long. The rain which fell all night has stopped. It is fairly quiet and the day has passed without incident. Many planes are flying over the village. At dinner a little shelling but not on us. A quiet night

5 August 1915

It isn't raining, but the weather is heavy. Apparently we leave tonight for Fréménil or Ogéviller for four days rest. But we don't know for certain. Not far away the cannons are firing a bit. At nine o'clock we leave for Ogéviller for four days. Once again, much-earned rest. It is long, tedious march. We halt for supper at Domjevin at ten thirty. We arrive at Ogéviller at one in the morning. The journey was without incident, but we are exhausted. We sleep.

6 August 1915

I rise at seven. We have changed the location of the infirmary, and we are in a very clean house. At eight, Doctor Lemoine takes me in the car to do the rounds in Fréménil. It is interesting and it is very kind of him. In the afternoon, I write peacefully in the garden. At midnight we are abruptly called out. There is an attack. Where? At Vého and Reillon, in exactly the place where we were two days ago. We go back to bed at two.

7 August 1915

The remainder of the night was uneventful. We are told that the Boches have tripped over themselves. I go again with the doctor to Fréménil. We are going to gather medicinal herbs and plants, which occupies us until six thirty. The evening and night are quiet.

8 August 1915

It is Sunday. The few peasants who still remain, respect it. They clean up and in their Sunday best go to mass. This morning, I asked the captain for fulough for the first days in September, which he has granted. He told me to remind him of it again sometime during the month. It is fine weather but a little heavy. It is quiet. It is a good day. In the evening, I am a little feverish, due no doubt to the hot, ever-changing weather. Before sleeping, I have a glass of hot wine and four lumps of sugar.

9 August 1915

I feel a bit better but I'm tired. It is very hot – at least 50 degrees in the sun. This evening we leave Ogéviller for Saint Martin and will take up duty in the Bois Des Haies d'Albe. At the moment all is quiet. Departure at seven thirty. A stressful journey as it is so hot and muggy. After a hard march we get to the Bois des Haies d'Albe. The captain of the Dragoons and commander of the post informs us that we must follow a reconnaissance party at twelve forty-five. We leave punctually with 15 men. A sergeant and staff sergeant lead the patrol. After three hundred metres, they lose their way in the woods, and two hours later, we return without having achieved anything. Not a very successful exercise.

10 August 1915

We sleep at three thirty in the morning and don't get up until ten. Shortly afterwards, there is a rather violent storm and the rain comes into the shelter and continues in this way all day. We are given notice that the reconnaissance will take place again tonight and that we are going along too. We get some rest in our shelter on a bed of manure. At quarter past twelve we leave. This time, we find the way but not before the sergeant misses it – twice. The reconnaissance is made in good conditions. We waited at the edge of the woods but there were no incidents. At four o'clock we return and sleep.

11 August 1915

I get up at eight. The weather is making an effort to clear up. There is a little sun and we take advantage of it to dry our things. This evening we leave for Herbévill; nobody is quite sure whether it is for two days or four. There is a little cannon fire and artillery from time to time, but nothing out of the ordinary. What a job. When will it end? We leave at eight for Herbéviller for four days, and after eating en route at Saint-Martin, arrive there at ten o'clock. At last I can sleep on a decent bed and mattress.

12 August 1915

Up at seven. The rounds. I then take the reports to Saint-Martin. On my return, I am told that my comrades and I have received official congratulations from our superiors, which goes something as follows:

> *"Congratulations to stretcher-bearers Besnard, Dupas, Verport, and Chêne for the devotion to duty shown when accompanying a reconnaissance patrol for two nights running to enemy lines. The sub-lieutenant adds his personal congratulations to those of the captain commanding the post."*

For once, we really deserve it. It is a fine day. I wash cap and clothes. A little cannon fire in the distance, but it is quiet here. Nothing untoward in the afternoon. In the evening, a cup of tea and a game of cards.

13 August 1915

Up at seven and it's raining. The rounds at eight. Nothing untoward. In the afternoon I spend my time writing. It is quiet. In the evening, a comrade and I go with about 30 men to work on the trenches about 500 metres from Domèvre. It is raining so hard and is so dark, one can't see further than two metres. The men can't even dig or drive the stakes in.

So at ten we return and get back at ten forty-five. We have been in the pouring rain for three quarters of an hour and we are cold. I am more than happy to get to bed at midnight.

14 August 1915

Strong sunshine follows the rain, but it is very windy. I've given myself colic from eating too many mirabelles – about 150 – over two days. All is quiet. A good afternoon and evening.

15 August 1915

A feast day today. One would never think it. It rained for part of the night and again this morning. It still is, more or less. We leave Herbéviller at six this evening and will spend 48 hours at Des Haies d'Albe. We leave at six for the woods. Marching is hot work and the road is rough going. We get there at eight and go to bed.

At ten thirty an uninterrupted and ferocious fusillade and cannonade. There is an attack on Aid Post 4 (we are at 2), then on Reillon. Next to us we have a battery that did not stop firing from ten until three in the morning, and then everything calmed down.

16 August 1915

Up at five thirty for coffee. It is very muggy. First we get rain, then the sun. At nine o'clock, I go for a meal in Saint-Martin about three kilometres away. It passes the time, but the road is really bad. The weather is mild. More cannons firing in the middle of the night, but much less than the night before;

17 August 1915

In spite of everything, it wasn't a bad night. Up at five thirty for coffee. It is a fine day. Tonight we are going to Fréménil to rest for four days. At eleven o'clock the Boches fire fifteen shells on Herbéviller, but there was no damage. We reply forcefully and not far from us, one battery alone fires off 29 shots in 30 seconds. Right now, it is quiet. At ten, we wait on the outskirts of Fréménil for an hour and a half. We are bombarding Avricourt and they fear reprisals. We go to bed after midnight.

18 August 1915

Another bombardment at two. At six o'clock we get up. We are fed up with this vile job. Fortunately, the weather is good. I go to the river for a bit, and rest and write. The evening is quiet. I turn in at eight thirty. A little cannon fire during the night.

19 August 1915

Up at six thirty. Not much to do. The rounds at nine o'clock. This evening we will accompany the men to work on the trenches at Leintrey. This afternoon I find a huge meadow and write in peace on the banks of the river. At seven, we leave for work on the trenches at Aid Post 10A.

One hundred and fifty metres above Domjevin, there is a sick man. A comrade and I take him to Domjevin. On the way, we come across one dead man and four wounded from Aid Post 16. We are bombarded all night, but fortunately, there are no casualties. We return at four in the morning, and have coffee. I go to bed.

20 August 1915

I get up at seven. The rounds, then lunch. In the afternoon, I go again to the water's edge again in the meadow. There is still a little shelling. The evening is quiet and I gather strength by getting a good night's rest.

21 August 1915

Up at five forty-five to accompany a comrade who is on furlough. We watch him go, a little heavy hearted, but he is so delighted, we are pleased for him. The afternoon is quiet. At six thirty in the evening, we leave for the Reillon trenches where we are very late. The Boches shelled our trenches all night. This is becoming truly depressing.

22 August 1915

I have slept very, very little. The shelling is still going on. On top of this it keeps raining and the water is coming into our shelter. Forty eight hours of this in the damp. Very windy this afternoon, but less rain, which is a good thing. The shelling has hardly stopped. At eleven this evening, there is heavy fire.

23 August 1915

Persistent, heavy fire particularly at three in the morning. Up at seven forty-five having had very little sleep. A dense fog which clears at nine, and is followed by a nice hot sun. I write in the orchard in the shade of a plum tree. It is wonderful weather, and we can rest. At eight o'clock , I am relieved and go down to Reillon for 48 hours.

24 August 1915

I had a good night's rest. After the rounds, I go to Domjevin to do some shopping. While there, I learn of an unfortunate accident which befell a squad of grenadiers. A grenade exploded in the trench and there are four dead and many wounded. The dead are atrociously mutilated. No one from our company was hurt. It was a stupid accident. The bombarding continues. It is beautiful weather. The evening is more or less uneventful.

25 August 1915

The comrades are going to the funeral of the men killed yesterday at Domjevin. They wake us up and we are obliged to get up early. Everything was going more or less as it should when at ten o'clock, the surrounding countryside was bombarded. Fortunately, there are no casualties. The bombarding around us and on the trenches continues all afternoon. It's a little windy, but it's beautiful weather. At nine, work on the trenches, but I am not going as it's not my turn. I make the most of it and go straight to the bois Sans-nom. On the way my corporal-nurse and I encounter an artilleryman who has crushed his finger in the breech of his 75 cannon, which he was firing on Avricourt. The corporal bandaged it by the light of the moon. We arrive at nine thirty and at ten we go to bed.

26 August 1915

Up at seven. It is a beautiful day. There is quite a bit of cannon fire all around us. The rounds and then a meal. It is very hot in the afternoon and we rest. It is a little quieter. At seven thirty, we go to work on the night trenches at the rectangular woods near the Bois Zeppelin. The moon is so bright, one would think it to be full daylight. It is not very favourable as we are a little too visible to the Boches. However as they are working opposite us about 450 metres away, they leave us more or less undisturbed. We return at four in the morning, and everything went as it should.

27 August 1915

Up at eight. I haven't had much sleep. It is a beautiful day. There is not much sound from the cannons, and we are more or less undisturbed. I am whacked. I'm going to try and get some rest. I write outside. This evening, work on the trenches. We leave at seven thirty for the Bois Zeppelin by the light of a superb moon. There are no incidents. Fifty metres away from us there is a dead German lying in a bomb crater, where he has been since July 15, the day our side attacked. He is partly dried out and foul-smelling.

Further on, in a bundle of barbed wire, another is lying on his stomach. A stake has been driven through his buttock. Why this lack of respect? He was the enemy it's true, but he was a human being and a brave one too, for he fought and he fell in the front line. We should really find some kind of burial ground for these poor men. At five to two we leave again and at that exact moment, our cannons fire on the enemy. They reply in kind and shrapnel whistles over our heads. We leave as fast as we can and get back at four.

28 August 1915

Bed at five, and up at seven forty-five. Little rest. The morning is tolerable. After lunch, I go off to sleep – two hours. It is fine but very humid. Tonight, work.

29 August 1915

My comrades returned at three in the morning having narrowly escaped some heavy shells. Quarter of an hour later, a violent storm breaks and at midday it is still thundery. Everything around us is flooded. This evening we leave for Bénaménil, but apparently, we are still going to work on the trenches from there. This is taking it too far, as all the men are completely exhausted. Right now it is quiet. At two thirty, a comrade and I leave in advance. On the way, we find a car and get to Bénaménil early. The men are going to work on the trenches tonight, but without us. Tonight, I sleep in a barn.

30 August 1915

I slept well in spite of the fleas. We have found a nice woman who has made us a casserole. Horrible weather today. It is raining without let-up. There is nothing to do to today but to rest. Tonight there is night work, but not for us. At eight there seems to be an attack in the distance but there is no follow-up.

31 August 1915

Up at seven. Those on furlough leave at eight. We are all envious. The rounds – there are 65 men sick from exhaustion and all approved. In the afternoon I go in search of a kepi and return by car. It makes a change. It is a fine day and all is quiet. We eat in comfort in the evening and then go to bed bed. The artillery clatters not far from us.

1 September 1915

A cold night, which has given me the runs. At reveille it is bitingly cold and there is a thick fog. But it is shortly followed by a fine day, when the sun rises. I go off to see a corporal-nurse, who is also a dentist, and who treats one of my teeth. Good lunch. It is quiet. An incident at Lunéville. A plane dropped some bombs – 40 dead and 60 wounded. We have an uneventful afternoon and evening.

2 September 1915

Up at six. Our corporal-nurse (Debout) is going to Remiremont for a few days to learn about poison gas. In the meantime, I will take his place. This morning the rounds – there are 37 sick men. Tonight we leave for Aid Post 16, but in my role as nurse, I am hoping to stay at Vého with two other stretcher-bearers. A little rain every now and then and a lot of wind. At six we leave for Vého. At nine I sleep in a filthy mess of rat droppings.

3 September 1915

Up at six forty-five not having slept, needless to say. At eight o'clock the rounds. I mustn't forget that I am now a nurse. The morning is so-so. At midday, I was asked to send to stretcher-bearers to fetch two wounded men between Aid Posts 16 and 18. They are brought back to us. Doctor Lemoine and I dress their wounds. One has been wounded in the head and thorax, the other has been wounded in the shoulder, the hip and the foot. I stay to look after them. It is no fun. They are suffering horribly and their cries of pain are continuous. A morphine injection has helped them a bit, but not for very long.

In the meantime, the whole area is being bombarded over and over again. No more wounded have been reported up to now. It is raining. At six o'clock, I leave my patients to have dinner. My head is pounding from the cries and moans of those poor men. I eat and then sleep. More cannon fire. My headache is so bad I have to get up at four to take an aspirin. It is pouring with rain.

4 September 1915

I get up at seven and take another aspirin. It is still raining which at least has stopped the cannons. The rounds. It is fairly quiet for the moment. The evening is so-so – the night, more or less quiet.

5 September 1915

Up at six. The rounds. The weather has cleared a bit, and the cannons immediately start up. At eleven, we have to take shelter in the cellars. No damage. The afternoon is more or less tolerable. In the evening we drink tea with Doctor Lemoine, a passable evening.

6 September 1915

At three thirty in the morning we are woken by extremely heavy shelling. Then everything is quiet. Up at seven. The rounds. Everything goes more or less as it should. At two we start to shell fiercely and the enemy retaliates. We have to go down to the cellars while 88s fall so close the shrapnel actually reaches us. More shelling at five. My corporal-nurse has returned. In the evening we drink mint tea with the doctor.

7 September 1915

At three in the morning, our side start shelling with fury. Impossible to sleep. I rise at six thirty. The rounds. It is a beautiful day, but the shelling continues on both sides. No problems so far and everything is more or less as it should be. In the afternoon, I read and write. The doctor joins us for coffee in the evening, and stays to chat until ten thirty.

8 September 1915

At two thirty in the morning, the shelling from our side is so intense, that I go outside to see what is happening. The Boches have only fallen back a little. I go back to bed and get up at about seven. The rounds last a bit longer than usual. Lunch is barely over when the Doctor takes me with him to take photographs.

The cannons are firing furiously at every second. At four the whole area is bombarded. The infirmary and other houses are not spared. I just had time to find shelter in a cellar. A shell fell two metres from where I was. A wall, the paving stones – what was left of them – and the shutters were blown to pieces. That's what it means when you look death in the face. I had the feeling that the entire house was falling on my head. A hundred yards away a machine gunner from the 217th is killed by a shell. At last it dies down a bit and at seven we leave for the trenches at Aid Post 16A. We take over without a hitch.

9 September 1915

A more or less tolerable night. The shelling was not very heavy. At nine it starts again and a comrade and I have to fetch water for the others. We set off. On our return we have to take shelter in a little copse for over two hours, as the shelling is continuous and dangerously close. We risk being killed at least twenty times. We finally make it back to the post. There is furious shelling from both sides. All this in beautiful weather. More shelling in the afternoon, which calms down in the evening.

10 September 1915

At one, our side start bombarding again. There is little response from the enemy. From six to eight we continue to attack fiercely from the Bois de Pailleux. At eight, all hell is let loose. The shells rain down on us and our trenches are torn apart. Our shelter is cracking but is still standing for the moment. There are many dead and wounded among the 87th. The Boches fire less intensely in the afternoon, but then it is our turn to start the offensive. We are to be relieved in the evening. I hope that it will not be too difficult. At ten the relief. We trip over shell craters at every step, but in spite of that, we make it to Vého and then Domjevin. I have a good supper of vermicelli soup with the cook and the quartermaster sergeant. Then exhausted, I turn in at half past midnight.

11 September 1915

Up at seven. My nerves are on end and I am numb with fatigue. The rounds. In the afternoon I accompany Captain Planson to take photographs for Doctor Lemoine. Apparently, we are to go to Bénaménil tomorrow for three days. It is beautiful weather.

More shelling at five. We go back to the cellars. There are no casualties and all is well. At midnight a Boche attack and another attack at three in the morning.

12 September 1915

At reveille I learn that there are several victims from the two German attacks, which nevertheless, were repulsed. At eleven, departure for Bénaménil. I stay behind to load up the medical wagon and don't leave until two. We get there at three and we are blessed with more or less comfortable lodgings – alone in a garage. We return to our nice Madame Genet who cooks our dinner. Tonight we have a gigot of lamb and fried potatoes. The shelling continues but it is now far away.

13 September 1915

Up at six after a more or less good night. It is a relief to not hear the cannons except at a distance. In the afternoon, I read and write in a little garden. A good supper this evening and a good night.

14 September 1915

Up at six. We clean the infirmary for inspection by the senior medical officer. At four, we are presented with a wheeled stretcher. At six, we leave for the Sans-nom woods and put our knapsacks on the stretcher. It is all right on the road, but going across fields is another matter. It is hard going through the mud and ruts. At one point we get lost and find ourselves enmeshed in barbed wire. We are caught in the rain. Soaked to the skin and with great difficulty we finally reach our post. I am to replace my corporal-nurse Debout, who is going on duty with Doctor Desvignes at Reillon. We turn in and despite still being soaked, we manage to sleep.

15 September 1915

Up at six thirty. We managed to sleep in spite of the rain which has hardly stopped. It is very humid, but for the moment it is not raining. The rounds at eight o'clock. At eleven thirty, I go to Domjevin to do a dressing and to find medical supplies. In the afternoon I write outdoors, but it is not warm. The noise of the cannons is continuous and it is really tiring. There some moments of respite. At four – a big commotion. A shell falls not far from the ridge, and then two at the same time fall among our men in the woods. Miraculously no one was even hurt. Only a mess tin was pierced, a haversack ripped and a greatcoat riddled with shrapnel. Once the shock was over, the men went back to their positions. The trench workers don't leave until ten. There is to be an attack from our side, which starts at eight. It is not very forceful and there is little reciprocation. Worn out, I go to bed. In the middle of the night, a rat jumps onto me and then onto my comrade next to me.

16 September 1915

Up at five thirty as I have been unable to sleep since the workers came back. It is very foggy and chilly. The rounds go as they should, then lunch. Not far away, the cannons are firing. It is more or less quiet in the afternoon. Work in the trenches, but I am replaced as I am still on duty as nurse. I turn in at eight, a little feverish from the heavy weather.

17 September 1915

Up at five fifty. I feel better today than I did last night. The rounds at nine. There are many battle-exhausted men. Lunch. It is not raining but the sky is very grey, which clears a bit in the afternoon. It is now fine and pleasant. At three, an inspection by the senior medical officer and I am the only nurse on duty to greet him. Of course, sir doesn't find much to his liking, although the barracks are not dirty. The evening is more or less tolerable.

18 September 1915

Up at ten to six. It is going to be a nice day. The rounds at nine. Not far from us the cannons continue their infernal racket without a break. Tonight, we are going to Reillon. At six thirty we leave. It is really hard work crossing the fields with the wheeled stretcher. En route we hear that only four men will go on furlough instead of nine. This seems to indicate that things are about to happen. We have barely reached Reillon when it is bombarded. We are called in haste. A huge shell has injured five people near the church. We find them and bandage their wounds. At eleven we turn in, but the bombarding continues more or less the whole night.

19 September 1915

Up at six. The rounds. They are still shelling. Going out is difficult. Up to now there are no wounded. The afternoon is very little quieter. In the evening, more shelling. I have a boil on my buttock which is extremely painful – so much so, that I had a restless night.

20 September 1915

At six, we are woken by the cannons (ours). The Boches don't reciprocate until about ten when they lob incendiary shells and set fire to five houses in front of us. They will no doubt still be burning tomorrow. My boil hurts and is making me a little feverish. This evening; I am going to Côte 293. It is windy but it is a beautiful day. We get to the shelter at Côte 293 without any problems at six.. We have quite a good night except for a heavy bombardment.

21 September 1915

Reveille at six. It is a superb day. Our shelter seems adequate, but we are under fire all the time. There's an announcement to say that we are to attack Avricourt and that we are to be careful as there are likely to be reprisals. Half an hour after the attack the reprisal was to set fire to Vého, and rain us with shells. This morning we watched as 21 white aeroplanes fly towards the enemy. One would have thought they were seagulls. The Boches fired at them, but none of them was hit.

This evening we learn that Saint-Martin has been bombarded. There are dead and wounded. At night there is some quite heavy shelling. The rest of the night is quiet.

22 September 1915

This morning I rise at six. I have not slept well because a few days ago, I caught cold and I have a very sore throat. More shelling. Domjevin is burning and Vého has been heavily bombarded. Tonight we leave for four days rest at Ogéviller. We are not relieved until nine in the evening. In the meantime, we watch Vého being shelled, and Reillon and then Ogéviller itself. At nine thirty we leave by the light of a full moon but the way is hard going and tiring. We arrive at midnight. We have a meal (we haven't eaten anything since ten this morning) and then at two in the morning we go to bed. We have a comfortable house, but it has also been visibly damaged by the shelling. There is a huge hole in the wall of the barn.

23 September 1915

Up at seven. A good sleep for what remained of the night. The rounds at eight. At eleven o'clock, we meet up again with our nice woman who makes us lunch. It will be a good one. I write in the afternoon. Everything seems more or less quiet. Please God let it last. In the evening our hostess is ill. So we make our meal ourselves as we are in a fairly comfortable house where there is a cooker. We had a little family party in the evening.

24 September 1915

We had a good, undisturbed night. The rounds were a bit late this morning. The weather is very oppressive. Our hostess is better and gave us a good lunch. It is quiet this afternoon and I write. We spent the evening chatting and then went to bed at ten. At half past midnight, I am the first to wake to a drum roll. I get up and the village is in an uproar. There is a fire at Buriville, a little village about 1600 metres away from here. We hastily dress and offer our services. But there are troops at Buriville and they do not need us up there. We go back to bed.

25 September 1915

I had a short sleep until six thirty. There is watery sunshine, which heralds rain. The rounds. For lunch, we feast on beans we have picked from the garden. I write in the afternoon and it is raining. We are obliged to stay indoors. It is all more or less quiet. A pleasant afternoon and a good night.

26 September 1915

Up at six, then the rounds. At lunch we have an apple tart with a good bottle of Mercurey. At three o'clock, still with the wheeled stretcher, we leave for Des Haies d'Albe. On the way, they read us a bulletin from Joffre who announces that we are now in a position to advance. It is of some comfort. We are lodged in a shelter big enough only to kneel or lie in. A lot of artillery fire, but the night is more or less tolerable.

27 September 1915

Woken at six. Rain fell all night and this morning there is no let-up. There is good news. In the Champagne region, we have taken 18,000 prisoners and 34 cannons. A first offensive and it was a real coup. Everyone is pleased. I go for a meal and return soaked. Every now and then, bullets whistle all about us.

The rain continues the entire day. We go to bed early.

28 September 1915

Up at six. The weather is improving a little. At eight in the morning, it changes. There are still bullets whistling about over our heads. In the evening a captain from the dragoons sends me on an errand to the machine gunners trench. In the pitch dark, I wade through the woods for half an hour and then finally find my way.

Good news – more prisoners have been taken. At eight the Boches seem to attack – a lot of cannon fire and some artillery. But after an hour it all calms down, and I go to bed.

29 September 1915

A good night. At reveille, there is a violent wind which smells of rain. I go for a meal to warm me up. At two thirty, there is a telephone bulletin to say that three of our divisions have once again broken through enemy lines in the Champagne region. In the middle of the woods, we sound the bugle and raise the flag to announce the victory.

A good evening until we are woken and ordered to go on a reconnaissance patrol with the Dragoons. We go and return at one in the morning. It all went well.

30 September 1915

I get up at eight, after a short sleep. We are told that we are going to Reillon for four days. We ask ourselves why. We leave at five fifty. A comrade and I are behind the supplies wagon with our wheeled stretcher. We do at least 15 kilometres on foot and we arrive at nine twenty, covered with mud and dropping with fatigue. I eat a bit and at eleven, go to bed.

1 October 1915

Up at seven, a little more rested. We learn that last night, one of our reconnaissance patrols took seven Boche prisoners who it seemed, gave some interesting information. It is fairly quiet in the afternoon, so I can write. There are no bulletins during the day, which is annoying as we don't know what to think. There is work on the trenches tonight, but we are not going. It is cold outside now.

2 October 1915

Up at seven. There is a heavy white frost. A bulletin tells us that in the last few days we have captured 109 cannons. That is very good. At six o'clock tonight, we are going to Aid Post 14. It is beautiful weather and fairly quiet. It has all gone well.

3 October 1915

My feet have been agonizingly cold. At five in the morning, I could no longer stand it and pulled on some socks. This morning we hear that we are to go Fréménil tonight for two days. A few shells come our way but they are still fairly far off. It is extremely cold in the afternoon, and it is pitch dark and icy cold when we get to Fréménil.

4 October 1915

We froze all night. We are in an attic with broken panes. Rest. The weather is fine and we are relatively undisturbed.

5 October 1915

Another very cold night. At half past midnight we go up to Aid Post 6 with the wheeled stretcher. It is a disgusting road. They sent us and another comrade to Aid Post 6A by mistake. We get back to 6. A wonderful shelter. There is some shelling.

After dinner we chat for a bit. Far, far away we can hear the cannon booming loudly, and we have no illusions about what might be happening over there. It is coming from the direction of Argonne. At nine we go to bed with an army of mice. In spite of everything, we sleep. We are in the very front line. It is quite comfortable in the shelter and my corporal-nurse and I have metal bunks to sleep on.

6 October 1915

Up at six. It was a good night. In the distance, the cannons are still firing fiercely. As we eat, a few shells are fired not far from us.

One of our comrades (Chêne) received a letter this afternoon from one of his brothers-in-law who in the last few days has been fighting in the Arras region. He recounts a few things that the newspapers keep well away from us. This is the gist of the letter:

> 'Saturday morning they are taken to the trenches, and at twenty-five past midday, they attack. They fly through the first trench, without any losses; they suffer a few losses in the second and many in the third. But at that point the Boches surrender. And then suddenly, our 75s start firing on their own men, which meant our troops couldn't advance, and the enemy seeing this, rallied their forces and turned on them and forced them back to where they had started and we suffered some heavy losses as a result.'

This man actually lived through this story. It is written in a very simple way, and no commentary from me is needed. The weather is grey and gloomy. We take up shovel and pick to strengthen our shelter, which is hard labour. I forgot to add that our comrade's letter dates from when his brother-in-law left for the trenches – 25 September. They were carrying grenades and many exploded wounding about 20 men.

It is pitch dark in the evening and not far off we can hear the boom of the artillery, but we are not disturbed.

7 October 1915

It was a quiet night for us but that wasn't the case everywhere else. The Boches taking advantage of the dark night, advanced close to our lines and as they went past the listening posts, two of our men were almost taken prisoner, but they got away and rejoined their comrades in the morning – thank goodness. The cannons are still thundering loudly in the distance, and we still have no orders, which is unsettling. Every now and then, we are shelled but relatively little. However, the artillery is making itself felt. We have to be very careful as our trenches are being quite heavily bombarded. We turn in at nine thirty.

8 October 1915

Up at six. There is a dense fog which slowly dissipates and gives way to some fine sunshine. Four torpedo shells fall near our flanks, but they don't explode. As it is a fine day, visibility is excellent and it is a shot-for-shot duel. Then at two o'clock, the Boches suddenly make an all-out attack on a front line of nearly two kilometres long. We are sprayed with huge shells and poison gas shells, and the artillery joins in. At three thirty, we have a wounded man (Minne) who has injuries to his left arm, his left thigh and a very bruised back. A comrade (Dupas) and I go and look for him. We run 1500 metres from where we are completely unprotected from the shells and gunfire, but we are untouched. Coming back we have to wait for a long moment as the shells are really raining down. Finally, we make it back. It is impossible to go through the tunnels with our stretcher. As it is also impossible as well as being forbidden to take a stretcher patient across exposed ground, we take it in turns to carry him on our backs. It is hard labour. We get back at last, completely out of breath. It all quietens down a bit, and then at midnight there is a fierce exchange of artillery, which fortunately does not disturb us.

9 October 1915

Up at seven. We hear that, thanks to the mustard gas, the enemy have retaken the Bois Zeppelin and part of the Bois Boué. It is very disheartening. Since this morning, the cannons from both sides have been firing without stopping. At two, our cannons are thundering so loudly that we assume we must be counter-attacking. It would be good if we could recover lost ground. They go on firing until eight, but we can't hear any artillery. Then everything calms down a bit and the cannons and the firing is reduced to shot for shot. At nine thirty, we turn in.

10 October 1915

Up at seven. The news is that last night we retook Bois Boué in a bayonet attack, but not Bois Zeppelin. We are told that there are a number of men are hors de combat, I don't even want to write it down, it seems so unreal. We have not yet been relieved this evening, because apparently, there will be another attack. At three o'clock, the enemy launch a number of shells on the Bois Jeanne d'Arc that kill two of our men and wound four others. These are closely followed by eight shrapnel shells. Two hundred metres away, four men, from the 6th Company are wounded. We fetch them and Doctor Lemoine and I dress their wounds and we take them to Blémerey. We are relieved at six and go to the infirmary at Blémerey. The whole area has been thoroughly shelled. We talk for a bit and then go to bed at ten thirty.

11 October 1915

Up at seven. We were woken many times by intense shelling. At eight, we have to dig a grave for two of the men from the 333rd, who died last night from their injuries. At four we became undertakers and bury the poor fellows. At five thirty, just as we were sitting down to eat – a bombardment. We have to take shelter in a cellar three times. The same thing at ten past midnight.

12 October 1915

We get up at seven thirty. We slept badly because of the bombardments. The rounds then lunch. At about two, the Bois Jeanne d'Arc is bombarded, and then the batteries near us. Grey weather and rain threatens. The afternoon is more or less tolerable. In the evening, at nine thirty, we had just turned in – another bombardment on the batteries and on the village. On the third explosion, we go down to the cellar and spend the rest of the night there.

13 October 1915

Up at six. The rounds and then I go to the mess. There is still spasmodic shelling. It is very heavy and at two o'clock, there is a terrific storm. I think we are going to Aid Post 5 tonight. At five o'clock while we are at dinner, there is another bombardment and we have to go down to the cellar. At six, we set off to take up our duties at Aid Post 5. We lose our way and have to wade through mud and barbed wire. Finally we arrive. Shelling all night, but we still manage to sleep a bit.

14 October 1915

Up at six. It's a fine day, which lifts our spirits a bit. It is more or less quiet in the afternoon. We are told that we will attack sometime during the evening.

15 October 1915

Up at six. The attack did not take place. In fact, it was even very quiet last night. We are told that it has been put off until tonight. At midday, the enemy attacks us in the rectangular woods, which is about two kilometres away from Aid Post 5. The artillery on both sides is infernal. We hurry to get water to fill all the equipment as we fear a gas attack.

An amusing incident this morning. At Des Haies d'Albe, two Russian prisoners, who were working for the enemy and on their front lines, escaped and came over to our side to hide. They had been prisoners for seven months, and were extremely pleased and proud of themselves to have escaped.

At three thirty, the cannonade flags, but picks up again in the evening and doesn't let up. At five thirty just as we are finishing dinner, a shell lands on our shelter and it is violently shaken. Then, the smell of sulphur and phosphorous seep into the shelter. We are frightened it is poison gas, but it is nothing like that. A 150 falls into the trench next to us, but doesn't go off. This is becoming very unamusing.

The cannons roar all night without stopping. At six we are told that we have retaken the Bois Zeppelin and without great loss. We turn in at eleven, but are wakeful all night.

16 October 1915

Up at six. The cannons are still thundering, but less intensely. We are told that only part of the Bois Zeppelin was retaken. In fact, nobody really knows anything very much, and we just have to wait. According to the men, the business at Gerbéviller was nothing compared to last night. The afternoon is quiet. After dinner we play cards and at ten, we turn in. At eleven, I am woken again by the cannons hellish cacophony. A huge battle is taking place near Rémabois, about three kilometres from Reillon. It is quite simply, appalling and I am overwhelmed by the horror of it all. Cannons, artillery, rockets – the full orchestra. It goes on until one in the morning, when we finally get some sleep.

17 October 1915

An hour later at two in the morning, I am woken again. The enemy are counter-attacking – the same scenario as before, and the same concert from hell. Back to sleep at three and at eight I get up. The battle is still raging but a little less violently. We know absolutely nothing about the outcome, but our positions from where we are firing our shells seems proof that we must have advanced. Still, we don't know anything for certain. A village in front of us that we set fire to is still burning – it is either Gondrexon or Aménoncourt. I go off to Aid Post 4 to see where the enemy is positioned. In front of us, our 75s have set Chazelles alight. The cannons start up again with renewed intensity. In retaliation the enemy have set fire to Reillon. Soon there will be nothing left. At six, we are relieved and go down to Blémerey. We chat a little and then go to bed.

18 October 1915

Up at six. Not much information on yesterday's attack. What we do know is that the infantry (the 50th) were engaged in close combat using knives. The savagery doesn't bear thinking about. The Boches launched a huge number of 210s and apparently have taken out a number of our men. The sky is grey and overcast, no doubt this is the reason for less cannon activity. It is even almost quiet. Everything was all right until eight o'clock, when without any warning, the Boches make an artillery attack and take us by complete surprise. Finally, the cannons roar thunderously. In the middle of the night, there is a similar attack but less fierce. We go to bed at ten.

19 October 1915

Up at six. The rounds. We learn that the two attacks yesterday were repulsed. At midday, we are told that we leave this afternoon for Fréménil for two days.

20 October 1915

Up at seven. I was in pain all night and still am, from enteritis. It must be due to the temperature because it is so cold that it feels as if it is going to snow – not fun. But at least here, we hardly hear the cannons, which is an enormous relief. This afternoon I go to Ogéviller. I have really bad diarrhoea during the night.

21 October 1915

I get up at seven. I am still in pain from the enteritis. Doctor Lemoine suggests I stay with him at Fréménil, but I prefer to go with my comrades to Aid Post 6, which we get to at quarter past three. The weather is fine. At three forty-five, we leave. On the way we picnic at La Roquelle then settle into our shelter. We turn in at nine thirty.

22 October 1915

Up at six thirty. It was fairly quiet last night. Still at about seven one of our men came to us as he had been hurt last night by a shell at the listening post, but it is only a bad graze to his shoulder. My enteritis is a bit better but I still don't feel too good. There is a cannon near us that has not stopped firing. It is disturbing, because it could lead to other things. After lunch, our time is taken up by fetching and carrying water. The evening tolerable.

23 October 1915

Up at six thirty. There has been a heavy frost – there is even ice. We learn that Doctor Desvignes is to leave us to go behind. He is replaced by Doctor Girard, whom we haven't yet met. We construct a latrine. At about eleven, the weather clears up and the sun comes out. The cannons on both sides take advantage and start firing spasmodically.

The afternoon and evening are taken up with reading and writing. We turn in at nine.

24 October 1915

Up at six thirty. A heavy fog covers the entire plain, but it is a little less cold. Good news. The captain in on furlough and from tomorrow, one man a day will go on furlough. As for us one will leave every four days, which is not a day too soon. At four, one of our comrades (Chêne) takes his belongings to Ogéviller because he is due to go on furlough tomorrow morning. Quiet afternoon and evening.

25 October 1915

Up at six thirty. Everything is fine until ten when the Boches bombard our trenches. We don't take long in retaliating. This evening, we are to go back to Fréménil. The sky is heavy and it is going to rain. At six thirty, we leave. The road is more than hard going as the ground is icy and is very slippery. Many of us get left by the wayside. We go to bed at nine o'clock.

26 October 1915

Up at six after a good night. The wind is violent and it is very cold. The rounds. Doctor Lemoine tells me that his wife and mine have met and we are both delighted. I go to Ogéviller in the afternoon to find medical supplies. The cannons are still thundering in the distance. We have a good mess where we are very comfortable we – chat a little and then bed at nine thirty.

27 October 1915

Up at six. A milky coffee taken chez Mademoiselle Juliette (at least sixty years old). The rounds then lunch. In the afternoon, I write and go for a short walk with my corporal-nurse (Debout). Bed at nine.

28 October 1915

Up at six thirty after a good night. Coffee and milk – the rounds – then lunch. It is almost the good life here, as we are more or less undisturbed. The afternoon goes by and we turn in at eight thirty.

29 October 1915

Up at seven. The rounds at eight. Lunch at midday, as we are leaving at four to go up to Aid Post 6. At eleven there is a bombardment of large calibre shells about 200 metres from the village. The enemy is looking for one of our large cannons hidden in the area. For the moment the shells are falling in the fields. The villagers are in an uproar. We leave at four for Aid Post 6 to replace the 6th Company who had another man wounded yesterday. We get there without incident. At eight thirty we are called upon to unload the palisades from the lorries. A bit of a ruse as it is not our job. Still, we can see that it has to be done quickly and there is no one else to do it. We turn in at nine thirty and have a peaceful night.

30 October 1915

A bit lazy this morning and we don't get up until seven thirty. It is a fine day. I have a meal at nine. There is fierce firing, but in the distance. In the afternoon I read and write. The evening passes pleasantly.

31 October 1915

Up at seven. At ten there is a little shelling. At midday, Sub-lieutenant Couhault comes to ask us (very politely) if would do a little work for him. It consists of constructing two screens in a place which is very visible to the Boches. We try, but have to put the work off until it is dark as it is a little too unprotected for comfort. It is a quiet night.

1 November 1915

All Saints Day. A hellish wind and rain. A little shelling. We stay in the shelter all afternoon, as it is extremely cold outside. Shut in, we pass the time reading and writing and turn in at nine o'clock.

2 November 1915

Up at six thirty. I am taking my kit to Blémerey. It is All Souls Day today; it seems almost as if there a tacit truce has been declared, as we can't hear the cannons. It is raining and there is a very cold wind. This evening we are going down to Fréménil again for four days. At about two there is a little firing from the cannons, but nothing much. At six, only the stretcher-bearers leave Post 6 for Fréménil. It is pitch dark, and the road very slippery from the rain; walking is difficult. We arrive dripping with sweat. We turn in at nine o'clock.

3 November 1915

We had a good night. Up at six thirty. We go back to our good cook and have coffee. The rounds at nine thirty. They are bombarding not very far from us. It is a cold, grey day. At dinner we learn that tomorrow, we are going as reserves to the shelter at Aid Post 6 – what a bore. We go to bed at nine thirty.

4 November 1915

Up at six thirty. We have a rapid meal and at nine forty-five we leave for the shelters at Post 6. As nobody knows where to put us up, the doctor gives orders for us to go to Blémerey, but then they find us room in a large shelter with some NCOs. We chat with them for quite a while and then turn in at nine.

5 November 1915

It was very cold last night. I got up frozen to the marrow and walked backwards and forwards to warm up a bit. In the afternoon, I stayed wrapped up in the shelter. A few cannon shots but at a fair distance. It started to rain in the afternoon and didn't stop all evening and all night.

6 November 1915

Up at six thirty. It was not so cold last night. We've been told that the 97 and 98 conscripts are to be deployed. An hour later, they only need 48 men to a company. An hour after that it is 48 men to a whole regiment. In any case, the stretcher-bearers will not be relieved. Horrible weather and a lot of mud. This evening we have to go up to Aid Post 6. At five o'clock we go up to the post alone. We eat when we get there. A pleasant evening. Bed at nine thirty.

7 November 1915

Up at seven fifteen. What a peaceful night. It is wonderfully sunny today. It is Sunday. At about four thirty, we are bombarded but there are no casualties. In the evening, we can hear an artillery and grenade battle going on over on the Zeppelin side.

8 November 1915

Up at six thirty. We had a good night. At about nine thirty another bombardment but without incident. I go for a meal. At five, more shelling. Bed at nine.

9 November 1915

Up at seven after a good night. Heavy shelling in the Ogéviller direction. Bright sunshine. A good afternoon. We turn in at nine.

10 November 1915

Up at six thirty. I go to fetch coffee. It is raining and there is a very cold wind. Some large shells fall not far from us. In the afternoon we stay holed up in the shelter. In the evening, we go down to the shelters at la Roquelle. At five o'clock, we are relieved. We go to bed at eight thirty.

11 November 1915

Up at six thirty. I was really cold last night. It has rained without stopping since this morning. We are obliged to stay inside. A few isolated shells. A little sun this afternoon, but it started to rain again and it hasn't stopped. It is a meaningless, shut-in life. After dinner this evening, a little reading and then bed.

12 November 1915

Up at six thirty. It was not so cold last night. It is Saint René's Day – my feast day. Once again, it won't be much fun this year. It hasn't stopped raining, and there's a raging wind. We are so cold that we go to bed early.

13 November 1915

Up at six. There is a veritable cyclone of wind and rain. We can't put a nose outside without being half thrown to the ground. At ten, my four comrades present me with a bottle of Moulin à Vent for my feast day. I can't think where they could have found that. It seems that furlough is still being delayed. It is outrageous. No cannons today. At nine as we are about to turn in, we are bombarded by eight huge shells, which fall very close to us. The rest of the night is without incident.

14 November 1915

Up at six. The wind has died down completely, but it is snowing with large, heavy flakes. It is very cold. We are going up to Aid Post 6 tonight. It seems that we are going for a sixteen-day rest at Ogéviller – if only that were true. A little cannon fire not very far away. At four forty-five, we go up to Aid Post 6. It is an uneventful night, but there is a lot of artillery and grenade activity.

15 November 1915

The entire countryside is covered with snow. It is beautiful, but it is bitterly cold. The cannons are firing quite a bit, which plays on our nerves. The sun comes out a bit in the afternoon. This evening we are going to Ogéviller for a rest. At four forty five, only Debout my comrade and I leave. The other two have gone on ahead with the wheeled stretcher. We have about a two-hour walk. At the beginning we go cross-country until Saint-Martin and it is extremely heavy going. I carry a stretcher over my shoulder all the way. Half way there, we are caught in the snow, which whips into our faces for the rest of the way until we reach Ogéviller at six o'clock.

A big surprise is awaiting us. Our comrades have found us a house (with Toussaint, the postman), where our hostess feeds us and gives us two bedrooms for the four of us. (Our comrade Verport, went on furlough yesterday) In the evening we dine on a bacon omelette and salad in a beautifully warm room. Afterwards at eight thirty, we turn in. I am sharing a room with Debout. Oh what bliss to be able to undress and to get into a bed. It is so comfortable, I sleep like a log.

16 November 1915

Up at seven fifteen. I am so comfortable, I can hardly tear myself from my bed. At seven forty-five, our hostess sets up a foot bath for me. At eight, a milky coffee. At eleven thirty, we have hearty lunch still in the warmth. The cannons are firing quite loudly, but they seem quite far off. This evening after dinner, we don't waste any time before going straight to our comfortable beds.

17 November 1915

Up at seven. A good, peaceful night. It is completely white outside and it hasn't stopped snowing. We stay indoors in the warmth all morning. After a good lunch, we remain indoors. The cannons boom in the distance. I spend the afternoon reading and writing. At dinner tonight, our host, M. Toussaint, tells us story that took place at Fort Manonviller, which if one is to believe him, was betrayed to the enemy. He tells us that on 22 August, the enemy entered Ogéviller and took him and thirty others and imprisoned them in a barn. All the while, not a shot was fired from either side. In the evening of August 23, the enemy fired on the fort and took it without firing another shot. There was no return fire at all from the fort. That is quite a story, but one told by a very reliable witness. But what to make of it? I don't dare offer my opinion on the subject. At nine we go to bed.

18 November 1915

Up at seven fifteen. I had to get up at five to put a kitten that was annoying us, outside. The sun is shining and it is a beautiful day. Good lunch. In the afternoon, I write in the warmth. In the evening after dinner, we have a game of cards with Monsieur and Madame Toussaint. We turn in at ten.

19 November 1915

Up at seven fifteen. It is a fine day but cold. Good lunch. I go with my comrade Debout to Hablainville in the afternoon, to look over our future barracks. Our hostess has a touch of flu, which is a blow. She really is quite sick tonight, so we make dinner ourselves. We go to bed at nine o'clock.

20 November 1915

Up at seven forty-five. Madame Toussaint is a bit better, but only gets up in the evening. We cook ourselves a good lunch. At twelve forty-five, we all go to the infirmary to examine men who were wearing masks against mustard gas. It was not too bad, but it went on for quite a long time. In the evening, our hostess is up and about and after dinner we play Forty-one. We go to bed at ten thirty.

21 November 1915

Up at seven. I go to the infirmary to sweep and light the fires. We are going to celebrate St Cecilia's day (all the stretcher-bearers are ex-bandsmen). We have a good lunch and only leave the table at three o'clock. Then we dine again at six thirty. Then after a game of forty-one, we go to bed at ten thirty.

22 November 1915

Up at seven forty-five. Breakfast, then on duty at the infirmary. Lunch at midday. There is talk of redeploying the conscripts. I hope to God this does not happen. In the afternoon, in the Reillon direction, the cannons thunder so loudly, that we fear an attack. But by evening it has calmed down. We play cards and go to bed at ten thirty.

23 November 1915

Up at seven. Lunch at ten thirty. At one thirty, we leave for Hablainville about 3.7 kilometres away. We are billeted in a house and are all in one room. Instead of a comfortable bed, we sleep on stretchers once again. We eat frugally and turn in at ten.

24 November 1915

We make our own meals. In the afternoon we go 1500 metres into the forest to cut down a tree for firewood. The cannons are firing in the distance; nevertheless, they are very loud, and it goes on for some time. In the evening we have dinner and then go to bed at ten.

25 November 1915

Up at seven forty-five. I must have caught cold, because during the night I became quite feverish. We potter about until after midday, when we have lunch. All the while, the cannon fire is quite loud. There is a thaw in the afternoon, and it feels quite mild.

After a good dinner, we read until we are called out to attend to a sick man. Debout and I go. The patient is in the throes of an asthma attack. We administer morphine and treat him until ten thirty. We go to bed at eleven thirty.

26 November 1915

Up at seven forty-five. There is at least ten centimetres of snow on the ground. I go on an errand to Ogéviller for the doctor and return in bright sunshine but accompanied by the roar of cannons, not far off. Good lunch. Not a bad afternoon but it is snowing and freezing over.

27 November 1915

Up at seven. There is at least fifteen centimetres of snow outside. fortunately, we have a good fire going here. The cannons sound from a distance and we can hardly hear them. Nothing untoward in the afternoon. We go to bed at ten.

28 November 1915

Up at seven. It's Sunday and it's bitterly cold. At eleven last night it was minus 15°. This morning it is minus 10°. Apparently two men died at Des Haies d'Albe – one from congestion and the other from frozen feet. At ten thirty nothing out of the ordinary. We go to High Mass. Captain

Boué tells me that I am leaving on furlough on Tuesday, and asks if I will take two German rifles to his house. I accept the errand with pleasure. There was some cannon fire this morning, but the afternoon was quiet. A good dinner in the evening and bed at ten.

29 November 1915

Up at seven. There is a weather change. The snow has melted and it is very mild. Tomorrow, I'm on furlough. We dine well on sauerkraut. The cannons are still firing a little. Captain Boué calls me over this evening and gives me an aluminium ring and instructions to visit his wife. I go to bed at ten thirty.

30 November 1915

Up at four thirty. I leave at six with two comrades. It is filthy weather – rain and wind. When we go through Ogéviller, I take charge of Captain Boué's two rifles (at least 20 kilos). We get to the station at Bénaménil where we are called and leave at nine forty-five. We get to Lunéville at about eleven. At the main station, we are told to meet up again at six thirty in the evening. I'm at the station at six. We are handed our furlough papers then at nine we board the train. At Blainville our furlough papers are taken away from us and then handed back at eleven thirty. We finally leave for Paris at midnight.

1 December 1915

I slept a bit in the train. The countryside is dismal because of the rain. Then once again we see the Marne and Champagne battlefields. The nearer we get to Paris the greater my impatience (seventeen months since I saw my family).

Finally, at three fifteen, we disembark. There is a crowd of people in the street, but nobody is there to greet me since no one knows I am coming. I go straight to the Galeries Lafayette, to find my sister-in-law Yvonne and to get the keys to the house. Then I quickly go to my captain's house at 7 Rue Parrot, to deliver the rifles and the ring, but I only see his mother. And then I go home where my wife is overcome by my sudden appearance. I'm not going to describe it here. It is wonderful to be home and it makes life worth living. Then I go off to see my mother where everyone welcomes me with open arms, and then to my sister Marie and the same thing there. Finally, I dine at home and once again savour the good things of life at home. I go to bed at eleven.

2 December 1915

My wife and I spend the whole day visiting friends. We are invited to lunch or to dinner everywhere we go. I have to refuse many invitations just to have a little time for myself. I'm not going to linger too long on how I spend my time on furlough. The only thing I have to say is this: Paris is horrible. It is swamped with shirkers. Life here is at a heightened normality. The women are entirely convinced that the men are fighting just for them, and they are so chic that I have to admit I am choked with a jealousy that squeezes my heart painfully when I think that, all too soon and in spite of my disgust, I will have to leave this enchanted city.

3 December 1915

Normal day. Visited friends.

4 December 1915

Same as yesterday, except we lunched with the Delapraz and dined with my sister Marie.

5 December 1915

Lunch with the Bakx, and then a big family dinner at my mother's, where we all get together. So far we have not gone to bed before midnight.

6 December 1915

At last a whole day at home with my family. I wake up late and don't even dress. I potter around all day and go to bed at about ten

7 December 1915

Stayed at home this morning, then lunch in Joinville. This afternoon, I say au revoir to my mother and my sisters as my furlough is over. We get home at six. Aymée comes to us for dinner. I get to bed at midnight as usual.

8 December 1915

Up at eight. Vonvon has given up a morning's work at the Galeries, to be with me until I leave. A quarrel with my wife, which I deeply regret. However, all is well when we separate, but in tears of course. I hug my little Nysette tenderly. At eleven fifteen I leave. Vonvon comes with me to the metro at the Gare de l'Est, and we are in tears when we say goodbye and promise to see each other soon. I find my brother-in-law Georges at the top, and we stay together for some time. Then, I hug him like a brother and we separate. At half past twelve I am in the train, and we leave at one. A journey of little interest. All I can think of is my family and I have a sleepless night.

9 December 1915

I arrive at six thirty, spend the morning at Lunéville and then hurry to catch the local train to Bénaménil. I get to Fréménil at nine. I am warmly welcomed by all my comrades. I am told we leave for Des Haies d'Albes at eleven. What a journey. Mud up to our ankles and an impossibly hard-going route. I am unbelievably homesick. We get to our shelter which is letting in the rain. At eight I am still thinking of the family and my heart is filled with a black rage that I have to do the job I am doing at the moment.

A fellow here, who is completely reliable, told us an interesting story. Apparently, in the Zeppelin woods the Boches and the French are fraternizing in an extraordinary agreement. The trenches have become completely untenable because of the rain and subsidence. So everyone is on the edges of the trenches and there has been a tacit cease fire, and both the enemy and our leaders have agreed that no one will take the offensive. Many of our men went over to the Boches trenches to talk. If this is really so, dear God, what are we coming to?

10 December 1915

I wake at eight and my first thought is for my family. What awful weather. It is still raining and didn't stop all night. I get up and go for a meal. Mud half way up my legs. It is shameful to think of those men having to hold position in these conditions. We are huddled in the back of the shelter and we can't move. We have to sit because there is no room to stand. Oh, my office, my beautiful bedroom, and my dining room, where are you? I am hugely resentful that I have to be here in the cold and the rain, when I think how comfortable I am in my own place. Oh, wide boulevards and fashionable skimpy short skirts, I'd give anything to be near you. But alas – duty is duty and I can't, indeed I must not, shirk it. I just hope that some fine weather will not be too long in returning. In the afternoon, it is raining so hard and the wind is so strong, that I stay put in our miserable shelter. At nine o'clock, knocked out and dazed with fatigue, I stretch out on the straw and sleep, in spite of everything.

11 December 1915

It is still raining and windy. I get up at eight, not knowing what to do. My back is breaking from the lack of straw. Oh, my beautiful bed, where are you? Rain and mud – the day drags on interminably. Disgusted, I turn in at eight thirty.

12 December 1915

Up at eight. Rain and more rain. At ten, I go for a meal. The mud comes up over my shoes. I return in a shocking state and go barefoot for two hours while my socks dry out. The whole day is spent squatting in the shelter, and not being able to go out. There is quite a bit of cannon and artillery fire from both sides. I am trembling with cold. I can't stop thinking sadly about home – what a change between one Sunday to the next. It is even colder tonight. It seems as if the weather might change.

13 December 1915

The weather is clearing, but there is a fair amount of ice. Tonight we are going back to Fréménil for four days. It is so cold that we make a small fire in the shelter. At four we go back down, wading through mud half way up our legs. We get to Fréménil at six thirty after a hard and exhausting trek. We eat chez Mademoiselle Juliette. At nine thirty, we sleep in a barn opposite, where it is not warm.

14 December 1915

Up at seven. At eight I'm on duty with the artillery medical corps. It all goes as it should. Bright sunshine, which warms us up a bit. They are talking again about deploying the conscripts. It's really frustrating not knowing what is true and what isn't. It has yet to be confirmed. At one o'clock, with one of the others, I return to the artillery medical corps. It is a satisfactory session. In the evening we eat in the warmth and turn in at ten.

15 December 1915

Up at seven. How cold it is. I couldn't get warm at all last night. The temperature has gone down to minus 12°. At eight, I am still on duty with the artillery medical corps. At eleven, there is a panic on. The area has to be evacuated, as we are to attack enemy territory. Everyone leaves, but after an hour or so, nothing happens, and we return. I am on duty with the artillery again at one thirty. We wait in vain until two thirty, as there is no session this afternoon. There has been no thaw during the day. In the afternoon I write a bit in the warmth which does me good. Bed at nine thirty.

16 December 1915

Up at seven. Since four this morning, I've been unable sleep because of the cold. I'm not on duty anywhere, so I wander about aimlessly all day. I return to write, and the day passes moderately well. I turn in at ten.

17 December 1915

Up at seven. Very overcast, but it's less cold. We have lunch at eleven. At two o'clock we go up to Aid Post 6. It is a horrible road and what with the wheeled stretcher, we are exhausted when we get there. There is so much noise from the cannons around us that we wonder if an attack is not imminent. When we get back to our shelter, we find that with the last lot of rain the roof is leaking everywhere and we have to stretch canvas tents over it to keep dry. However, we make a hole for a chimney and light a good fire. We eat at six, and then write. We turn in at ten.

18 December 1915

Up a six thirty. I go to get the coffee. The ground is partly frozen. When I get back, I do a little digging, to warm up. The sun rises and it is going to be a fine day. At lunch we eat next to a good fire. The cannons are roaring and the Boches are returning fire. We make a roaring fire in the evening and are too warm at night.

19 December 1915

Up at six. I go for coffee and a meal. It froze hard last night and my fingers are numb with cold from carrying two pails of water. It is sunny when it gets light. Visibility is so good that the cannons are thundering on both sides. We are called urgently at three thirty. a man is down with congested lungs at the fourth trench of Post 6. Debout and I hurry over there. It is not that serious, but we have to call for another stretcher to take the man to Blémerey. I get back to my post at six. We eat and the turn in at eleven.

20 December 1915

Up at six fifty. I go for coffee. It froze solid last night and it is not warm this morning. A little shelling in the morning. In the afternoon, an artillery exchange. We eat at six. and eight it starts snowing. We turn in at nine thirty. The Boches are firing heavy shells on our positions.

At ten thirty we are called out. There is a wounded man in the first trench. It is a dragoon who was at the listening post and who was hit full on. His stomach is an open wound, his thighs are riddled with shrapnel and a hand is partly torn off. We take him to Blémerey, but he dies on the way. At eleven fifty, our work finished, we go to bed.

21 December 1915

Up at seven. It is snowing without let-up. It is white everywhere and it is not warm. Tonight we go down to Blémerey for four days. Only a little cannon in the afternoon as visibility is very poor. We stay in the shelter to keep warm. The afternoon is passable. We go down to Blémerey at five in heavy snow. Happily, a nice fire awaits us. We eat and go to bed at ten o'clock.

22 December 1915

Up at six thirty. I go for the coffee. Horrible weather – it has rained and now there's a thaw. We are bogged down. It is disgusting. The rounds at eight – longer than usual. Then lunch. In the afternoon we stay in the warmth and write next to the fire. Bed at ten thirty.

23 December 1915

Up at seven. Awful weather. It is pouring. There is a little shelling. The rounds go on for a long time. At nine thirty, I make my way through a disgusting mire to get a meal. Lunch at eleven. It is still raining in the afternoon and we stay indoors in the warmth. At dinner we have a heavy discussion about religion. After dinner, we read a bit. Bed at ten thirty.

24 December 1915

At one thirty in the morning, we are called out to a wounded man at the first trench at Post 6. Two of us go for a dragoon, who has the beginnings of frostbite to his feet. We rub his feet with camphorated oil for an hour and a half, and then go back to bed at three. Up at six. I go for the coffee. It is foul weather – wind, incessant rain and mud. The rounds, then I go for a meal and the weather hasn't changed.

At one in the afternoon we are bombarded, otherwise, a passable afternoon. In the evening we treat ourselves to a tasty dinner. At eight thirty, Doctor Lemoine and Doctor Bellion come round and stay for two hours to have cake and good wine, topped off with coffee and a Mirabelle. We have a very amusing evening and the good doctors become real comrades. But I can't help myself thinking of my family and resenting the fact that, for the second year running since the start of the war, I will not be sharing this beautiful religious festival with them. I feel more like weeping than laughing. We go to bed at eleven fifty. Midnight strikes and I think – it is Christmas.

25 December 1915

I get up at seven thirty. I am feeling a little under the weather. It is a more or less fine day. There is not a single shot from the cannons. At eleven, it clouds over and it starts to rain again. It seems that God is not in the mood to celebrate today, and he is right. In the afternoon, we go up to our shelter at Aid Post 6 for four days. We make our way with the rain beating down on us and wading through mud up to our ankles. It is a sad evening for a festive occasion. The cannons are roaring very close to us and as they are firing on our trenches, we fear that at any minute we will be called out. Very fortunately, nothing happens and we turn in at ten.

26 December 1915

Up at seven. I go for the coffee, and I'm in a black mood as nobody else could be bothered. More rain and wind. It's enough to put anybody in a foul mood. Perhaps it is precisely because it's Christmas that I am so fed up. We patch up the shelter a bit by putting slates on the roof in the hope that it will leak a little less. I don't feel like doing anything. In the afternoon, we do a little sawing for firewood. We eat at about seven and at eleven o'clock, we go to bed.

27 December 1915

Up at six thirty. This morning it is my turn to make the fire. The weather seems to be clearing up a bit, but it is still very windy and muddy. I cut up wood to give me something to do. A few kilometres away, the cannons are roaring and we watch the explosions. What a way to spend time – it's insane. The afternoon drags on, and God, how long it is. We turn in at ten. At midnight we are called out to a man from the 168th, who is sick from exhaustion. He spends the night at the Aid Post.

28 December 1915

Up at six thirty. I go for the coffee. It is still raining and it is unbelievably muddy. A year ago today, I sprained my ankle. It would have been better if I had done it this year. The day drags on with heavy cannon fire on both sides. It is so wearying. There are no letters today. I hope we get double the normal number tomorrow. The air around us smells of gunpowder. We go to bed at ten.

29 December 1915

Up at seven. It is barely light when the cannons start up. Tonight we go back to Blémerey for four days. An artillery exchange in the afternoon. Later at the Bois Sans-nom, there is one dead and three wounded from the 87th. We have only just arrived when a comrade and I are called out to Aid Post 6 to collect a man from the light cavalry of the 6th who has frostbite to his feet. It is pitch dark and we have to wade through mud. The minute we get back, I go to bed. It is ten o'clock.

30 December 1915

Up at seven. The rounds at eight. Nothing out of the ordinary. A quite fierce bombardment which doesn't reach us. The day goes by as usual. Bed at ten thirty.

31 December 1915

Up at seven. It is very foggy, which dissipates from one minute to the next, and becomes a lovely day. In the afternoon, the Boches fire heavily on the woods. It goes over the village and happily, does not land on us. We don't celebrate in the evening, but we stay up fairly late. We go to bed at eleven.

1 January 1916

The start of another year. I hope we will be spending the end of it at home with the family and that the war will have ended. All I ask is that God spare us throughout this coming year. I get up at seven and go for the coffee. All the comrades shake hands and wish each a happy new year. How miserable to be spending it at Blémerey – a town emptied of its population and now, completely devastated. Not a sweet little child to kiss – no family member to confide in or to wish that all their dreams for the coming year come true.

The mess has pulled out the stops. We have pâté, potatoes, champagne, ground coffee and cigars. During the meal, the Boches, don't forget to send us their good wishes in the shape of shells, which fall generously about us and reach the town and we are ordered to go down to the cellars. And then it is all over, and we eat in relative peace. Some of the comrades come over to drink champagne with us. Everything goes more or less smoothly in the afternoon until about three o'clock when the Boches bombard us again, and once more we have to go down to the cellars. It is unbelievably tedious. Finally, a more or less peaceful evening. We turn in at ten. But I am burning up with resentment to think that at this moment, in spite of the war, Paris is having fun and many families are enjoying their little festivities without a thought for those at the front. This is not the case with my family, as I know everyone feels my absence and they are not having much fun.

2 January 1916

Up at seven. It's a vile day. After the rounds, we eat a hasty meal as we leave for Ogéviller for 16 days to rest (or so they say). They are still talking about deploying the conscripts. I wonder if there is any truth in this – who knows? But it is very upsetting. The Boches are shelling the woods close by. We are waiting to be relieved by the stretcher-bearers from another battalion. At four thirty, Doctor Lemoine accompanies us to Ogéviller, where a nasty surprise awaits us. Our place with the Toussaint has been commandeered by the NCOs from the 2nd Platoon. A bunch of louts who we don't even want to talk to. With some difficulty we find an empty house with a little straw just for the bedding. The house has been very badly shelled, and we have to be careful. We go to bed at eleven thirty.

3 January 1916

We were so tired we have slept well in spite of everything. Up at eight. We find a nice woman who cooks for us. In the afternoon we organize our lodgings. In the evening I write until eleven o' clock.

4 January 1916

Up at seven thirty. I am on medical rounds as I am replacing my corporal-nurse Debout, who is going on furlough. A two thirty we accompany him to the end of the road. He is very happy to be going, naturally. I then do the dressings. In the evening we have invited a comrade for a hot toddy and a game of cards with us. We turn in at ten.

5 January 1916

Up at seven. I go for coffee, and then at eight, the rounds. At one, I have my two teeth seen to, and then bandage a cut on the right hand of a young girl of sixteen, who is amazed when I refuse her offer of twenty sous. I am busy all day. In the evening, after dinner, we read until ten thirty, when we go to bed.

6 January 1916

Up at six forty-five. A light persistent rain. The rounds at eight thirty. What a bore as the rain is continuous. The day drags on. In the evening after dinner, we make fritters to celebrate the three kings and Epiphany, but we forget to insert the kings. Bed at midnight.

7 January 1916

Up at seven thirty. It is very windy. After the rounds the captain asks us to give a concert for the fifteenth. I'm not sure what we will come up with because there is nothing to hand here. At three thirty all of us, stretcher-bearers and nurses, are called to the infirmary where Doctors Lemoine, Bellion and the chief surgeon, Fusiller, are there to wish us all the best for the new year. They have laid out a spread of petit-fours, a Boucher white wine, tea, marc de Bourgogne, and also cigars. It is a pleasant get-together and does a lot to bridge the gap between our bosses and ourselves, which is perhaps what I find the most pleasing.

The cannons are very loud and just a few hundred metres away, but we can't tell exactly where they are coming from. We go for supper and then turn in at ten thirty.

8 January 1916

I get up at seven forty-five. The cannons hardly stopped last night and they are still at it. The rounds at eight thirty, then lunch. I do a few dressings in the afternoon, and then go back to have my teeth seen to.

I don't know what has possessed us all, but we are all extremely down in the dumps – every one of us is sick and tired of this war, which has been going on for far too long. In the evening after dinner, I read a little and the turn in at eleven.

9 January 1916

Up at seven thirty. I go for my coffee, then the rounds. A few shells go overhead, but happily, don't land here. No change to the same monotonous routine. The day drags on into the evening. Bed at eleven.

10 January 1916

Up at seven thirty. Vile weather, because it's going to rain again. The rounds at nine, then lunch. A fairly quiet afternoon. I read a bit in the evening and turn in at eleven.

11 January 1916

Up at eight. Same old monotonous life. A fine, persistent rain is falling. I read and write in the afternoon – same thing in the evening.

12 January 1916

Up at eight. There was a freeze last night, so it is fine day today. The rounds, then after lunch at one, we go to Réclonville to rehearse for our concert which will take place in Ogéviller on Sunday. We haven't managed to find any instruments in the area. I have caught cold and I have a sore throat. I'm going to make myself a gargle. Tired, I go to bed at ten thirty.

13 January 1916

I'm up at five because in my role as nurse, I'm going with some men to target practice. In all we have 36 kilometres to do. Fortunately, I find a way of going most of the way in a vehicle. The rounds at six. At seven thirty, target practice is cancelled. A piece of luck as I am not well. There are white patches in my throat and it is painful. Rehearsal in the afternoon at Réclonville for a concert that we are giving on Saturday and Sunday at Ogéviller. My comrade Debout returns from Paris at six. He brings me good news from my family and a parcel from Yvonne, my sister-in-law, which give me a lot of pleasure. In the evening, I am tired and turn in at ten thirty.

14 January 1916

Up at seven. I do the rounds to bring Debout up to date. I show Doctor Lemoine my throat – alum gargle – it's serious and I have to be careful. At one in the afternoon a general rehearsal for the concert tomorrow. We are really working hard on this and it promises to be good. Then we have dinner and turn in at eleven o'clock.

15 January 1916

Up at seven. Our last rehearsal is at eight thirty, as the concert is at five tonight. I think it is going to be quite good.

Apparently, a parliamentary delegation has arrived. There has already been a lot of talk about it. What happened is reprehensible. One of the three members stopped off at Bénaménil to see his brother, and he didn't think there was much point in coming as far as this; the other two came as far as the bridge at Ogéviller, had photographs taken of themselves on the bridge and then left. They didn't go further afield than that and didn't talk to one soldier. So these are the wonderful men who we pay to write pretty reports on events they have not even seen. I don't want to continue with this.

A very successful concert at five. Here is the programme:

> La Marseillaise
> Le Bienvenue by the orchestra
> Chanson faite dans les Tranchées sung by Zidor
> L'Enfant de Paris sung by Nectou

Les Trucs de Boîtadoux sung by Poirier
Balade du Roi d'Ys sung by Nézeloff
Valse Arabesque au piano played by Parrot
Noël de Pierrot La Fanchette sung by Lambert
Vas-y Léon sung by Brasser
Les Orphéonistes sung by Victor
Parvenu à la Fenêtre sung by Philibert
Colette et Colay Polka by the orchestra
Chanson du Nord sung by Legros
La Traviata sung by Poursinez
La Grenouille à Nicolas sung by Rousseau
J'arrive du Congo sung by Rousseau
Hérodiade sung by Nézeloff
L'Anglophobie du Kaiser sung by Jacqueney
Chanson du Midi sung by Bromer
Faust sung by Philibert
Le Sabotier sung by Lambert
Le Concierge Récalcitrant sung by Lambert
Le Crucifix sung by Nézeloff and Jacqueney
Dordoche et Mais Voilà sung by Müller
Rêverie d'Actualité sung by Maudit
Lettre du Kronprinz à Son Père sung by Maudit
Chœur des Alliés sung by Mr Duval CO of the 2nd Batallion of the 37 R.F.G.
Film – organized by the Foyer du Soldat

When the concert is over, the Commanding Officer thanks us with a very moving speech, and then offers us biscuits and champagne. We have dinner at eight thirty and turn in at ten thirty.

16 January 1916

Up at seven; I have a bit of a headache. At ten thirty, I have my teeth seen to. We have another concert at four this afternoon. In the mean time I write. At five the concert starts, and is perhaps even more successful than that of last night. Players and singers are a lot more confident. For a change, I play the violin in the orchestra. When it is over we are again offered champagne. Our commanding officer certainly knows how things are done. We dine a little late and turn in at eleven o'clock.

17 January 1916

Up at seven. There was a freeze last night and it is extremely cold. At two, there is a lecture at the infirmary given by Doctor Lemoine on poison gas. At four, I have a visit from my friend Schumpff who is still with the Motor Transport Division. I can't think what is stopping me from joining him – perhaps I will, who knows? News: we were meant to be going to the trenches tomorrow, but this has just been countermanded; instead, we are going to Flin or Vathiménil the day after tomorrow for a ten to fifteen-days rest. We are delighted. They have been talking about this for a long time. I pass the time in the afternoon, by reading and writing. We go to bed at ten thirty.

18 January 1916

Up at seven. It is definite. We are going to Flin tomorrow. We prepare all day for the departure. Apparently we will be there for ten days. After lunch, I spend my time rolling cigarettes. In the evening, I turn in at ten thirty.

19 January 1916

Up at seven, and we get ready to leave. To be more precise, we are going to Ménil-Flin. At ten fifty-five, we set off in good order under the Commanding Officer. The road is quite heavy going as there is a lot of mud. We go through the Mondon forest and arrive at Ménil-Flin at one thirty. We are billeted on the postman where we will eat. Then my comrade Dupas and I find a wonderful room for two, for ten sous a night. At nine thirty, I undress and go to bed and taste the sweet luxury of being between clean sheets. I sleep like a log. At exactly midnight we are suddenly woken by four huge explosions We wonder what it can be. I go back to sleep.

20 January 1916

I get up at eight. The whole village is in a state excitement. The explosion we heard came from a Boche aeroplane, which, while flying over looking for a suitable spot to bomb, had developed engine trouble and had came down about a kilometre away. Everyone, including me, goes to look. The plane is nosed into the earth; its wing is torn, and the petrol lead and silencer are broken. The two pilots have fled. A little while later, the commanding officer tells me that they have been arrested at Saint-Clément. He goes over to have a look too. I forgot that the postman told us an odd story. During the mobilization, he was in a frontier village. He watched as the Germans entered and they were ordered to fall back to Verdun. There, he witnessed the 23rd Midi artillery company, abandon arms. All the officers were executed on the spot, and the men were forced back to their posts by at least 200 policemen. But it was too late because the Boches marched by just at that moment. So – some true facts from a man who actually saw what happened. Wonderful! I turn in at ten thirty.

21 January 1916

I had a good night. At three, I am woken by a rat. I look for it, but don't find it, so I go back to bed until eight. In the afternoon we fetch wood from the Mondon forest. I've been told that on Monday or Tuesday, we are to give a concert here, which will be followed by a film. The cannons are loud but in the distance. In the afternoon, I saw up wood for something to do. In the evening we play Manille and then turn in at ten thirty.

22 January 1916

Up at seven fifteen. At eight thirty we rehearse for the coming concert until after ten, and then at two, we have another rehearsal, and another at four. After dinner, we have a game of Manille and then go to bed;

23 January 1916

Up at seven thirty. At eight I go to mass at Flin. At nine thirty, we rehearse until ten thirty, then another rehearsal after lunch at four. It is a fine, sunny day, and as mild as spring. It is pleasant here and we just wish the war would end.

The latest information is that we have to go back up to La Rognelle next Saturday, and yet nothing has been fixed so far. I write a bit after dinner. And then we are taken with the fanciful notion to go fishing for frogs. Apparently there are a lot in the ponds next to the fields. One of our comrades tells us that he catches a lot by lighting a candle on a plank on the edge of the pond and the frogs come of their own accord, and all one has to do is to gather them up. At eight thirty, we tramp across the fields. It's beginning to freeze and it's cold. We tried the experiment twice – needless to say we didn't catch any. We return at the double and I go to bed at ten, as I have a bad cold.

24 January 1916

Up at seven thirty. I feel lousy, as if I have flu. Rehearsal at eight thirty. In the afternoon we get the news that on Saturday, we are to return to the trenches for two months. Another rehearsal in the afternoon, then I go back and go to bed as I have a temperature and I can't stop coughing.

25 January 1916

I had a bad night. I coughed all the time without stopping. In the morning, my comrades come to see me and Debout has brought Dr Lemoine with him, who gives me a thorough examination. There is nothing on my lungs, just tracheitis. He advises me to stay lying down for the day. But I can't do that and I get up. I feel dizzy. But of course, I don't go to rehearsal today and in the afternoon I stay in the warmth. At nine I go up to bed.

26 January 1916

I get up at ten. Thanks to a morphine tablet, I slept a little and at least I coughed less. In the afternoon I go the rehearsal, because I don't feel so bad. The concert seems to have gone well. In the evening we have a game of Manille and we kill a rabbit to eat tomorrow. I turn in at eleven.

27 January 1916

Up at seven thirty. Rehearsal at eight thirty. Our photographs are taken. I'm dizzy and am still not up to scratch. The concert at five followed by a film. Not too bad all told, but a bit long. In fact, it goes on until nine. The room was packed with about 400 people. When we come out we dine on a nice, well-cooked rabbit. I turn in at eleven thirty.

28 January 1916

Up at eight. It is rather foggy and gloomy and a fine light rain is falling. Everyone is a bit apathetic and grumpy because tomorrow we go back up to Aid Post 6 and that doesn't please anyone. Anyway, there's nothing we can do about it, so we have to put up with it.

My flu is a bit better. I go and visit one of my comrades, Grégoire, who is now a sub- lieutenant with the 8th Company. We use the familiar 'tu', which raises a few eyebrows. I stay half an hour with him in his room and then return for dinner and we turn in at 10 thirty.

29 January 1916

Up at seven fifteen. We get ready to leave. We eat at nine and at ten fifteen we are on our way. In a field, about a kilometre further on, we are reviewed by General de Riberpray. He makes us an unctuous speech and calls us his dear comrades – thank you we already knew that – sweet nothings as always. When these fine gentlemen practice what they preach, we might lend an ear to what they have to say. I know they have to say these things, but it seems ignoble compared to what they expect of the poor infantrymen.

Afterwards we continued our march through the Mondon forest in mud fifteen centimetres deep. It is really rough going. We get to Ogéviller where we rest up for an hour and then start off again for Blémerey which we get to by crossing fields. We finally take up our positions at Aid Post 6 in our old shelter. Nearby the Boches are firing fairly constantly, and it seems we must be very careful. The evening is tolerable, but we are very tired and turn in at ten.

30 January 1916

Up at seven fifteen. I go and fetch the coffee. It is not warm today. There is a bit of shelling all about us but fortunately, nothing reaches us. To pass the time we take turns all day to cut up wood, and in the meantime we write. We eat and then at about eight, the shelling intensifies for about an hour. It stops at about ten and we go to bed.

31 January 1916

Up at seven thirty. There is quite a bit of shelling all about us. We can sense a little agitation in the air. We should be relieved tonight to go down to Blémerey for two days. In the afternoon I go into the village to get hyposulphite and carbonate of soda against poison gas. The captain leaves tonight on furlough, lucky devil. In the evening we learn that a zeppelin has bombed Paris causing damage and casualties. We are extremely anxious for our families, particularly as we are not getting any information at the moment. I turn in at ten.

1 February 1916

Up at seven. The rounds at eight, and nursing duty. Not very far away, the Boches are bombarding us. I read and write in the afternoon. A little shelling in the evening, and then everything is quiet. I go to bed at ten thirty.

2 February 1916

Up at seven thirty. My tracheitis has returned. I coughed so much in the night that my comrades reported it to Doctor Lemoine, who wants to listen to my chest. After a thorough examination, he says it's nothing dangerous, but he wants to follow my progress and examine me every day when I go to do the rounds. I don't know what it can be, and of course, I feel extremely out of sorts.

In the evening we go up to Aid Post 6, and on the way, I learn that they are looking for drivers. I go immediately to the Commanding Officer's quarters and register. I don't know if I have done the right thing, but I am so disgusted by my present existence, that if I succeed, my attitude might change a little. Let's hope I succeed. There is a quite fierce cannonade at nine. We turn in at ten.

3 February 1916

Up at seven. It was a good night. I go for a meal at nine because I have to see Doctor Lemoine, but I get there too late and the rounds have already finished. I thought about the motor transport division during the night. Will I be any better off – who knows? In any case the Boches have been bombarding us since this morning and it is hardly pleasant. In the afternoon I go with Debout to the second trench to inspect the Vermoral sprayers (a sprayer with a pump action used to disperse poison gas in the trenches). At about three thirty we are quite heavily bombarded on la Rognelle and then a shell falls about thirty metres away from where are standing. At about four, all is quiet again. It is still quiet in the evening and we turn in at ten thirty.

4 February 1916

Up at seven thirty. It is a superb day and oddly, there is no shelling. But I spoke too soon. At ten they bombarded Blémerey. By one o'clock, all hell is let loose. Their Howitzers fire over one hundred shells on Blémerey, where one person has died and seven are injured. They were all 105s and they landed on the entire village. At four, things quieten down a bit and we go for a meal. No news from the motor transport division, but it's still early days. I go to bed at ten.

5 February 1916

A quiet night, but I was very restless. I get up at six thirty and go for coffee. It is reasonable morning. In the afternoon shelling from both sides but without mishaps. In the afternoon Dr Lemoine comes up to see how I am. We talk for a long time about this and that and then chop wood to kill time. A good evening and we go to bed at ten. I toss and turn a lot before falling asleep.

6 February 1916

I get up at six and go for coffee. It is very foggy which lifts quite soon. We see a dozen French aeroplanes coming back from a raid. They are magnificent. The Boches fire at them without hitting one.

More shelling in the afternoon on the La Rognelle shelters. At five fifteen we are relieved. We go back down to Blémerey for two days. We turn in quite early at nine thirty.

7 February 1916

At two in the morning my comrade Verport and I are called up to Aid Post 6 to pick up an injured man. It is a sergeant from the 6th Light Cavalry. He was on patrol and was hit point blank in the stomach. His liver and intestines are falling out and he is in agony. Dr Lemoine gives him two shots of morphine. He dozes off a bit. At five fifteen, a vehicle arrives to take him to hospital at Lunéville. He is still alive at this time. Only God knows what will happen. It is so sad to see these young people being cut down in this fashion. I don't go back to bed. At six I go for coffee and then the rounds at eight thirty. I have still been coughing a lot and Dr Lemoine examines me. He can hear a bit of a bronchial rattle at the top of my right lung. He gets Debout to cup me. I don't know if it has made much difference. A little shelling overhead, but, happily, nothing lands on us. More or less quiet in the afternoon. By evening I am very tired, and turn in at eight thirty.

8 February 1916

Up at six thirty. Because I was so tired, I had a good night. Perhaps it was the cupping session that did me good, for I coughed much less. We were meant to be going to Vathiménil for four days but we are told we are going for eight.

At eleven Dr Lemoine comes over and tells us that plans are completely changed, and that we are to stay another eight days here. Oh, the joys of this job. Still the same old contradictions. This is really the way to win the war. To think there are still some who stick to their illusions – God, the naivety of humans.

We take a wounded man to Reillon in the afternoon. The automobile picked us up an hour later. After that we are more or less undisturbed, so I take the opportunity to write. We have dinner and turn in at nine thirty.

9 February 1916

Up at six thirty. I go for coffee. I was still coughing a lot at half past twelve, last night. It is really tedious. The rounds at eight thirty. The Boches are firing a little and not very far away. A few shells fall on the village but no one is hit. At eight, a man is injured by a wagon. We fetch him and he stays with us for part of the night. We turn in at ten.

10 February 1916

I get up at six thirty and go for coffee. There is a change in the weather. It is very cold and there is at least ten centimetres of snow. A fairly quiet morning. It snows without stopping in the afternoon. It is now at least fifteen centimetres deep. At three, another bombardment on our batteries about two hundred yards away. We stay at the post in spite of it. At three thirty, my friend Schumpff who is with the transport company, and is passing through, drops in to see me. I tell him I have registered for the motor transport division as well. He tells me he will take care of it for me but that it will take at least two to three weeks. At four thirty, we go up to Aid Post 6 and get there without any trouble. A fairly quiet evening. We turn in at ten.

11 February 1916

Up at six. I go for coffee. It is very cold but in spite of this, it is thawing a little. There is a smell of gunpowder in the air, as the cannons have been thundering since early this morning, particularly from the Boche side. Between ten and eleven, the cannonade becomes even more intense. The trenches are collapsing from the shelling.

At about two, Dr Lemoine comes to the shelter to see us. I congratulate him very sincerely, for he has just been awarded the Croix de Guerre, which moreover, he has well deserved. He is moved by what I have to say, and thanks me. The artillery, which had died down a bit, picks up. How will this night turn out? In the middle of the night, there is a violent cannonade which keeps us on the alert for a good while. However, we are not called out. So all is well.

12 February 1916

Up at seven thirty. I learn that during the night the Boches sent out a heavy patrol as far as our lines and cut through the barbed wire. They received a warm welcome, as our men fired over five thousand cartridges on them. No doubt they will get their revenge. I go for a meal and the shells falling fast. The party has begun, and it is hell on earth until six in the evening. Our trenches are turned upside down and the communication tunnels are unusable. It is shambolic and everywhere is full of water. There is certainly going to be an attack. It can't be otherwise and there is every sign of it. So far there has not been a single casualty and I am dumfounded because the few men we have seen tell us that the shells were hailing down on them. Then at about six thirty, it is suddenly quiet. Would the Boche attack be curtailed? I fear the night will hold some nasty surprises for us. At nine fifteen I have to go out for an urgent call of nature. And all was calm until at that very moment, eight shells land not far from me. I leapt out of the way, but fortunately, they were further away than I thought. At ten – a sudden attack on Reillon. Machine guns and cannons let rip at the same time. It is diabolical. However, we are still not called out to any of our men. The attack lasts about three quarters of an hour. At eleven thirty everything seems more or less quiet, and at half past twelve, we take the opportunity to get some sleep.

13 February 1916

At four thirty, they start bombarding furiously again and very near the shelter. We jump up and stay on the alert. But nothing happens and at five thirty, it seems to have stopped. But we don't go back to bed. It is a tolerable morning, but the artillery are at it continuously. At four, I go for a meal and then immediately go down to Blémerey, where we are to stay for three days. I have hardly arrived when once again the storm starts its infernal concert. I get there in time to help a wounded man who has broken his ankle. I gave him a rudimentary bandage and send for Dr Lemoine, who when his work is finished collars me to talk about the transport division. He tells me I am making a mistake because of my weak constitution. Oh really? And how the devil did he know about this? Then what about declaring me unfit for service? The orchestra starts up again at seven. Will there be no peace to night? At ten we are about to go to bed when we are called out to fetch a wounded man. Two go. The injured party has a sprain, which keeps us up until half past twelve, when finally we can go to bed.

14 February 1916

Up at seven. I have slept well as I was really tired. The rounds at eight thirty, and there's a lot of work. Just as we thought there'd be a little peace in the afternoon, they shell the bottom end of the village, fortunately there are no casualties. In the evening it rains torrentially. At nine thirty, just as we are turning in, there is a furious cannonade from our side. It is terrifying and lasts for an hour. We finally get to bed at eleven.

15 February 1916

It was all right for the rest of the night. Up at six. I go for coffee, and then the rounds. The wind and rain are tempestuous, so we have a more or less peaceful day. We spend most of the afternoon dressing and bandaging wounds. Bed at ten.

16 February 1916

Up at seven. At seven thirty, the division's doctor – five stripes – pays us a surprise visit, and of course everything is wrong. The rounds are late. The weather is still vile. Tonight we go back up to Aid Post 6. Pray that all goes well. Quite a bit of bandaging and cupping to do in the afternoon.

At four thirty we go up to Security Post in inhuman weather – a tempest of rain and wind and mud half-way up our legs. You have to be French to accept this sort of situation. We finally make it to our post. There's a fire in the shelter and it is certainly needed to dry us off. We eat and it's not long before we turn in as we are exhausted.

17 February 1916

It was a good night. I get up at seven. It is raining a bit less but is still just as windy. There is still a little shelling, just to remind us. It is a passable day. At four, they bombard us again quite intensely. At five I go for a meal and then get away from it all as best I can. At ten we are called out. A cavalry officer has a wound to his left biceps. We pick him up from the first trench without mishap. We then play cards to cheer ourselves up a bit and at midnight go to bed.

18 February 1916

The rest of the night was good. I get up at seven thirty. The weather is still very threatening. We are relieved in the evening, and go to Herbéviller for four days. We leave at five with the rain beating down on us. Someone falls sick on the way and we have to carry his kit. It is really rough going. At seven we get to Herbéviller where happily, our billet isn't too bad. We make a fire to get dry, talk a bit and then turn in at ten.

19 February 1916

Up at six thirty. I go for coffee. It is still raining. We spend the day settling in more comfortably. We make our own meal, so we eat a little better. I read and write in the afternoon and go to bed at ten.

20 February 1916

Up at six. I go for coffee. We are meant to be reviewed by a general and some members of parliament. Then at midday, we learn that these gentlemen have not gone further than Bénaménil. All the while, the men have spent the whole morning polishing up in order to receive them. It's a disgrace.

It froze a little during the night and we have a beautiful day, and the sun is almost warm. It is horrible that we have to be here, particularly on a Sunday. There is a little bombarding in the afternoon but in the distance. A more or less ordinary day. Bed at ten.

21 February 1916

Up at seven thirty. There was a hard freeze in the night, but now it is very sunny. It smells of spring. At nine I have something to eat. In the afternoon, Boche and French planes are out in force, and they are being fired at from everywhere. No mishaps so far. However, the cannons are thundering determinedly quite close by. We turn in at ten.

22 February 1916

Up at seven thirty. The cannons have been firing heavily all night on the Zeppelin woods. This morning there is more than ten centimetres of snow everywhere, and it is not warm. In the evening we are going to Des Haies d'Albe for four days. That should be fun.

We get there at six. They have lined the whole way with wood so there is no mud. We settle in. It is the same shelter, except that the straw has been removed and we sleep on bare planks. At nine, the captain comes to see us and spends a little time chatting. At ten we go to bed.

23 February 1916

Up at seven. It was more or less quiet during the night. We hear the growl of artillery and cannon in the distance which has gone on for three days and nights without a break. It seems that the Boches, are planning a heavy attack on Verdun. It is very cold as it is 11° below zero. At nine, I go for a meal to warm up a bit. Saint-Martin and the Bois Vannequel are being bombarded. I visit the trenches in the afternoon. At nine, there is a fierce artillery exchange, and the same thing in the middle of the night, but no casualties, fortunately.

24 February 1916

Up at seven thirty. It is snowing heavily and without let-up. The cannons are still firing on Verdun. Apparently though, the Boches messed up this particular attack. At nine, I go for a meal. A fairly good afternoon. They have announced heavy patrols everywhere tonight. With that in mind, we go to bed at nine.

25 February 1916

Up at seven thirty. The night could not have been more peaceful. It is still very cold and it is snowing. In the afternoon, Sub-lieutenant Rogier, comes to be bandaged. He was moving to an advance position when a shrapnel bullet grazed the lower part of his right leg. I bandage him myself. While this is going on, he is told he has received the Croix de Guerre (not for this incident, of course), and in spite of his injury, can't conceal his pleasure at this news. In the meantime, there is still heavy fire on Verdun. At nine, we are told that we are holding our positions and keeping the enemy back. We go to bed at nine thirty.

26 February 1916

Up at seven thirty. There was a bit of a freeze, and now there is bright sunshine. Furlough has been suspended because the lines are blocked by troops being transported to Verdun. We have no fresh news from this side. What can be happening? For there is still very heavy fire in the direction of Verdun. We will be relieved this evening and will go to Ogéviller for eight days, which is no bad thing and will do us good. We are relieved at six and set off for Ogéviller in the pitch dark, and the route is very hard going. Once again the NCOs have taken our old lodgings. We find another base which consists of a large bedroom with no tiling or stove. So we are frozen all night.

27 February 1916

Up at six thirty. We froze all night. Fortunately we have managed to do a deal with an excellent woman who has given us a large room with a fireplace, where she allows us to stay all day, and where we can even try to get a little sleep.

A little gossip: it seems that a chaplain has bet a captain 45,000 francs that the war will have ended by the end of March. What a piece of luck it would be for him – and for us – if he were to win! The afternoon is passable. We are bombarded at about six in the evening, but not for very long. However, there is a casualty. At eight, I help load the injured man into the ambulance and to my astonishment it is driven by two very elegant Englishmen. What are they doing here when so many others such as myself have asked to be transferred to the transport division. Why have they taken our places? It is absolutely disgraceful. I go back disheartened and rather angry. At eleven thirty, I go to bed fed up. I forgot – a disaster at Aid Post 1 at Domèvre. A 210 shell fell directly onto the Command Post shelter. It has killed a captain, his orderly and two telephonists.

28 February 1916

Up at seven thirty. It has been a quiet night. A tolerable morning and afternoon. At six, I go with Debout to cup a poor old lady (Madame Robert). There is a dispatch. We are making progress in Verdun, but with unbelievable losses on both sides. In the evening after dinner, we play cards. At eleven thirty, we go to bed.

29 February 1916

Up at six thirty. The weather is springlike. There is heavy firing all around us. It seems there is a halt in the offensive on Verdun. So much the better if that is true. I spend the afternoon sawing up wood. The evening is passable. At ten we go to bed.

1 March 1916

The morning goes by as usual. There is heavy shelling at eleven.

Dramatic turn of events – at two o'clock I am told that I leave in an hour for Lunéville, and then on to Nancy the following day to join the motor transport division. I am beside myself with joy. Goodbye trenches but also – as the song so aptly says – goodbye comrades. We have pulled off a good one. Nevertheless, it is affecting. Who knows if we will ever see each other again. I have tears in my eyes but I have to admit, my pleasure overrides any other emotion. Who knows what this move will bring, but it has to be better than my present life. Ten of us leave together. At the pace of two pack mules, we finally arrive at Lunéville at eight fifteen at night. We are welcomed by the Hôtel du Cheval Hongrois, where we are to sleep.

2 March 1916

Up at five. At six seventeen, we take the train for Nancy, and the Drouot Barracks. After the formalities, we take a driving test. I drive extremely badly. But it seems that I passed all right. I eat at the canteen and the then set off to find a straw mattress to sleep on. It is regular barracks life here, but apparently, it is just for a few days. We are soon assigned to a section. So I am waiting to be assigned to another. I am quite exhausted. I hope things will improve. In the evening I eat at the canteen.

3 March 1916

Up at six. There is roll call at seven. I am on fatigue duty heaving coal. I go all the way through the town in a lorry, load up 3,000 kilograms of coal, bring it back and then unload it. It's a very busy life here. This morning I had lunch at the Brasserie Wagner – very good but a little expensive. What I really enjoy is looking at all the grand houses still intact and the elegant, little women in the streets. What I do find irritating is my impression that I'm being watched all the time as if I were a shirker. Anyway so what? It's about time I had a turn.

We continue unloading in the afternoon. In the evening I eat at the canteen and then go with some mates for a coffee in town. At nine, as we are in barracks, there is roll call and we go to bed immediately afterwards

4 March 1916

Up at six. I go for the coffee as I am room orderly. As such, I am also exempt from fatigue duty for the morning. I take the opportunity to shave and clean up. I eat at the mess, which is not bad. There is a dining room here and proper plates. This is almost a luxury for me. Fatigue duty in the afternoon, which is not tiring. It consists of carrying cords of wood from one room and putting them in another. At three, I am free and I take the chance to write. I have caught a really bad head cold. In short, the duties are quite hard but what a difference from my former activity – and no shells. From this point of view, my depression seems to have lifted a bit. After dinner, I go with some comrades to the Brasserie Wagner to play Manille. Then I turn in at nine thirty.

5 March 1916

Up at six fifteen. I'm on guard duty at seven. I go and it is interesting. At eleven thirty, I am called into the office and I am assigned to a lorry, and I am to leave immediately. It is quite a coincidence that the person who comes to find me is a notaire's clerk whom I knew in civilian life. As he is part of the administrative staff, I get him to send someone else in my place. I like it here and I am in no hurry to leave. But I think I will have to go tomorrow or the day after, as there are many departures at the moment. I just hope that whatever happens, I will be safe. I am on guard duty in the evening from nine until eleven, and then in the morning, from five until seven.

6 March 1916

I am relieved of duty and I am free for the rest of the morning. In the afternoon, I stack coke. The evening goes by, then after dinner, I go to the Wagner Brasserie. There are still no departures today.

7 March 1916

Up at six. At seven I'm on coke fatigue duty. I am really annoyed because I have discovered I have lice and I don't know how I can get rid of them here. I am free in the afternoon and take the opportunity to write. In the evening, Brasserie Wagner and bed at nine.

8 March 1916

Up at six. I am going to the touring-car driving school. The instructor is very brusque and he doesn't think I'm very good. It has to be said that I don't show what I am really capable of as I am in no hurry to leave this place. In the afternoon we are instructed how to reverse, which is not that easy. In the evening, the café and then bed at nine.

9 March 1916

Up at six. It is snowing solidly. I'm not on fatigue duty, and I have nothing to do. A secretary calls me to the Section 45 office (the section for the repairs workshop). He is a delightful fellow who tells me that my friend Schumpff has requested I work with him at the TM [Transports Matériels] at Marainviller. He has spoken to Lieutenant Jacotin (with Lieutenant de Crozal the CO of the mechanical transport base), who has promised to attach me to the 499. At three o'clock I am told I am detached to the 3rd Cavalry Division and I am to take a lorry to Lunéville. I immediately go to Lieutenant Jacotin, who puts a stop to my leaving and confirms that I will only be assigned to the 499. So I am still here and being left, more or less, in peace. In the afternoon, I write; in the evening, Brasserie Wagner and then bed at nine thirty.

10 March 1916

Up at six. I have nothing to do as I am not on fatigue duty. I make the most of it and write, as no doubt, I will be doing something this afternoon. Wrong. I have nothing to do again, which enables me to tidy my belongings. In the evening, the Brasserie Wagner and then bed at ten.

11 March 1916

Up at six fifteen. There are a lot of departures today, but I am still staying here. I go to the driving school, and discover I am not very good at reversing. Then I have a shower in the hope of getting rid of my lice. Sand fatigue duty in the afternoon. This morning some idiot made me sprain my right wrist while putting the auto into reverse. The student didn't engage the gear lever correctly. At the time, I didn't think anything of it, but in the afternoon, I went to the infirmary to get it massaged. It had to happen to me. In the evening, Brasserie Wagner. I go alone as one by one, all the comrades have left. No doubt it will be my turn next week. Bed at ten.

12 March 1916

Up at six fifteen. It is Sunday and we are confined to barracks which is a bore. This morning I have fatigue duty, but thanks to my wrist, I have been exempted. It rained a lot during the night, but has now cleared and it promises to be fine today.

At nine, I am dumbfounded. Two soldiers from the 37th arrive, and one of them is my ex-comrade and fellow stretcher-bearer, Dupas. He has just taken his motorcycle test. I am delighted to see him again. We spend the day together, and of course, we have lunch together at the canteen, then at six, we go to the Brasserie Wagner where there is a film showing. There are so many people, it is impossible to eat there. But I see my friend Bonet (Lieutenant Jacotin's secretary), who helps me out once again. There are four of us and thanks to him we can eat at the brasserie. I buy him dinner, which is the least I can do. Then we return and I go to bed at nine thirty.

13 March 1916

Up at six. I am room orderly, which gives me a little free time during the day. I only have an easy fatigue duty in the afternoon. In the evening, Brasserie Wagner. Bed at nine thirty.

14 March 1916

Up at six. I go to the driving school, and I do a bit better. We have a lesson in reversing in the afternoon. That is a lot better too. I haven't had a minute to myself during the day. Brasserie Wagner this evening. Bed at nine thirty and at the same moment, we hear bombs exploding outside. It was a Boche aeroplane flying over Nancy. It was welcomed by cannon fire. A little while later, all is quiet.

15 March 1916

Up at six fifteen. I have fatigue duty with the 45th. It is very hard work, as we are manually pushing automobiles. At ten thirty, I am called to the Heavy Vehicles Office to be told that I have been attached as second to a general stores truck. Apparently, this is the best job going. But it is not my thing and I go to Lieutenant Jacotin. He tells me that he picked me for the job because he needed someone he could rely on and with business know-how (sweet-talk). But since he had given me his word on attaching me to the 499, he doesn't retract. I don't know if I'm right or wrong, but I promised to join my mate Schumpff and I will do everything I can to bring this about. In the meantime, I get the post on the general stores truck assigned to my friend Dupas, who is delighted.

I'm on fatigue duty in the afternoon at the Staub piano factory from where all the equipment is being moved. It is extremely tiring. In the evening, I go as usual to the Brasserie, where my comrades upbraid me for turning down the general stores truck. Bed at ten.

16 March 1916

Up at six. I go to unload the merchandise from the Staub factory. It is exhausting as we are handling crates of 150 to 200 kilos. The same scenario in the afternoon. The Brasserie Wagner in the evening. Bed at ten.

17 March 1916

Up at six. Fatigue duty at the Staub factory again. Two comrades from the 237th arrive and are joining the motorized transport section. They impart some very sad news. At the Des Haies d'Albe listening post, Sergeant Necton (a good fellow) was killed by two bullets to the stomach, and two soldiers were injured.

The area is becoming extremely unhealthy and it was time for me to leave. In the afternoon, we are still working at the Staub factory. The Brasserie Wagner again in the evening, and bed at nine thirty.

18 March 1916

Up at six. Fatigue duty at the Staub factory. Nothing special. Fatigue duty at Staub ends in the afternoon. Brasserie Wagener in the evening and bed at nine.

19 March 1916

Up at six. I go to the driving school where I am getting better and better – and I am congratulated. It is Sunday. Some friends and I go out until evening. We have a long walk in the countryside and then go to a film at Wagner's. We then have a generous meal at a little bistro where thoroughly enjoy ourselves. Bed at nine

20 March 1916

Up at six. Barracks fatigue in the morning and fuel fatigue in the afternoon. At the end of fuel fatigue, I catch a finger between two cylinders and pull my nail off. I have it bandaged at the infirmary. Yesterday, I was almost sent off for the fourth time but they spotted the mistake and once again, I stayed behind. Brasserie Wagner in the Evening. Bed at ten.

21 March 1916

Up at six. I am room orderly and take the opportunity to rest a bit. My pinched finger is a bit painful. I tidy my things in the afternoon. Brasserie Wagner in the evening. Bed at nine thirty.

22 March 1916

I volunteered again for room duty, so I don't have to do any heavy work with my damaged finger. On top of which, I have caught a cold and I feel lousy. I rest in the afternoon. In the evening, we go to a little café we've been told about, and not far from here, which is frequented by a few delightful women. We have quite a good time. Bed at nine thirty.

23 March 1916

Up at six fifteen. I have a bit of a temperature and I feel generally lousy. I go to the driving school for more instruction, and the same thing in the afternoon. I have a tooth that has lost a filling. I go to the dentist who is well established and seems capable. We go to the little café in the evening, but I don't stay too long as I feel feverish and want to go to bed, which I do at nine o'clock.

24 March 1916

Up at six. I ask to be excused fatigue duty because of my finger. I sweep the Staub factory in the afternoon. I return at five o'clock. The little café in the evening. Bed at nine thirty.

25 March 1916

Up at six. I meet up with my civilian friend Bigerelle from the 37th. He is an art teacher – drawing and painting – at Auxerre. He's here with Mechanical Transport to paint – anything and everything. I get him to take me on so as to get out of fatigue duty. (The things one does to be left alone!). The same duties in the afternoon. The little café again in the evning. Bed at nine thirty.

26 March 1916

Up at six. It is Sunday. I'm on fire picket (letters A to K). In the afternoon, I find a way of ducking out. Wagner's is so overcrowded, that we can't watch the film. We have an aperitif opposite and then have dinner at the little café. We are given a little warning to be more discreet, as we have been spotted and reported for being a little too boisterous with the women. Bed at ten

27 March 1916

Up at six. Thanks to the painting job, I can still duck fatigue duty. Nothing particular to report today. We enjoy ourselves quite bit at the little café in the evening. Bed at nine thirty.

28 March 1916

Up at six forty-five. I am on guard duty for twenty four hours. The weather is vile and very windy. At about midday, there is a real tempest with an avalanche of snow, which is falling without let-up. Impossible to go out tonight which annoys me. I get up for guard duty from eleven to one in the morning. I manage to put it off for half an hour. Fortunately, it's not that cold. At one thirty, I go back to bed.

29 March 1916

I go on guard duty from five until seven. I still manage to be half an hour late. At seven, it finishes. At nine I have a good hot shower, which makes me feel a bit better. I am on fatigue duty this afternoon, fetching sand. It is quite hard work but it passes the time. In the evening, the little café where Géa from the little casino, who is part of our group, entertains us with a few songs. Bed at nine thirty.

30 March 1916

Up at six. I go to the driving school where I try out a new car – a Rolland Pillain. The instructor says I am outstanding. Fatigue duty (twice) in the afternoon, taking motorcycles to the Saint Jean station. The little café in the evening and bed at nine thirty.

31 March 1916

Up at six. I'm on potato fatigue. In the afternoon I pile up tyres. The little cafe in the evening. Bed at nine thirty.

1 April 1916

Up at six. It is a beautiful day. Some Taubes fly overhead. The cannons roar out, not far away. We think it must be on Lunéville. I go to the touring-car driving school, and I am declared a very good driver. In the afternoon, instruction on reversing, where I shine. In the evening, the little café and bed at nine thirty.

2 April 1916

Up at six. It is Sunday. I have permission to go out. Light fatigue duty this morning. We weed the courtyard. Everything is fine until ten fifteen, when I am called out on fuel fatigue. I am furious because it lasted until twelve fifteen. I only have time to shave and have a very quick lunch before going out. At four we go to the cinema at Wagner's and then have dinner at the little café. Bed at ten.

3 April 1916

Up at six. I peel potatoes, which is quite restful. This afternoon, I am called in to take a test at the 45th division's workshops. But I was named in error, and so I can take the afternoon off. The little café in the evening. Bed at nine thirty.

4 April 1916

Up at six. I am on potato fatigue again. In the afternoon, we have to manipulate a pump to empty a sump, but we are unsuccessful. In the evening we are made to change our room. It's annoying to find ourselves with new faces. However the men here seem to be fairly orderly and we are not too uncomfortable after all. The little café in the evening. Bed at nine thirty.

5 April 1916

Up at six. I thought I was on guard duty but I made a mistake. Fatigue duty this morning with the 45th, which is long but not very arduous. The same work in the afternoon and no harder than this morning. The little café in the evening. Bed at nine.

6 April 1916

Up at six. I'm still on fatigue duty with the 45th but it is much harder today than yesterday. I haven't even time to write. The same fatigue in the afternoon and just as hard. I just have time to shave before dinner. The little café in the evening. Bed at nine thirty.

7 April 1916

Up at six. I am at the driving school. The instructor has hurt a finger and I bandage it. Driving school again in the afternoon. The little café in the evening. Bed at nine thirty.

8 April 1916

Up at six. For fatigue duty, I spread slag in the courtyard. A comrade from the 37th arrives, and tells us that at Des Haies D'Albe, the 4th company lost eight men; nine were wounded; and eleven were taken prisoner. It was definitely the right time for me to leave the trenches.

The same fatigue duty in the afternoon. At two a Taube paid us a visit and dropped three bombs. One was just 200 metres from a gas factory, the other fell on a house and the third on the Malzeville plateau. We don't know what damage has been done. At three forty-five, I have a long hot shower, which is wonderful. In the evening, the little café. Bed at nine thirty.

9 April 1916

Up at six. It is Sunday. But as I'm on fire picket, it is just another day. Fatigue duty this morning is spreading slag in the courtyard. Rest in the afternoon and I write a lot. In the evening, dinner in town with friends. Bed at nine thirty

10 April 1916

Up at six. Fatigue duty is spreading slag in the courtyard. We can hear the cannons in the distance, and it seems strange. Fuel and slag fatigue in the afternoon. In the evening at nine forty-five, a Taube drops four bombs, two of which land four-hundred metres from us. At two in the morning, the cannons thunder loudly. Something must be going on in Verdun. It is quiet for the rest of the night.

11 April 1916

Up at six. I go to the touring-car driving school, and try a new car, an Alcyon. It is extremely difficult to drive, but I manage very well. In the afternoon driving school again, but it is raining and I stop quite early. The little café in the evening. Bed at nine thirty.

12 April 1916

Up at six. I peel potatoes. I see the lorry driving school corporal go by, and I am suddenly taken with the idea to ask him to take me on. He is very pleased to do so, and we immediately go off into the country. I drive for three quarters of an hour on a perfect road. It is certainly more interesting than circling round a courtyard in a touring car. It's the same thing in the afternoon, and I drive for an hour. We go as far as Neuves-Maisons and Chavigny. We do about forty kilometres through marvellous countryside. It is very interesting and instructive, to be able to drive like this on a main road. In the evening, the little café. Bed at nine thirty.

13 April 1916

Up at six. As I did yesterday, I go to the lorry driving school all day. But it's less fun today, as it's pouring with rain. Furlough which had been suspended has been reinstated. I must look into it. The little café in the evening. Bed at nine thirty.

14 April 1916

Up at six. Lorry driving school again, and the weather is still lousy. My lessons are going from strength to strength. School again in the afternoon. The little café in the evening. Bed at nine thirty.

15 April 1916

Up at six. Still at the lorry driving school and the weather is still foul. The same scenario in the afternoon. For a change, Brasserie Wagner in the evening. Bed at nine thirty.

16 April 1916

Up at six. At roll call at seven, things start to happen. I have been assigned to leave with the TM 77.* I immediately go to Lieutenant Jacotin and remind him that he promised me the 499. He tells me that this doesn't exist any longer and that as they need good drivers for the 77th, I must go with them. I find out a bit more. We are going to Chanteheux, about one and a half kilometres from Lunéville. I have to leave at twelve thirty. I hope all will be well. Before leaving I get the truth of the matter. The lieutenant did not want to tell me the real reason for sending me with the 77th. It seems I have shot myself in the foot. The fact that I asked to drive the lorries, when I was driving touring automobiles, was like biting the hand that fed me – and just as I was beginning to get used to this place and particularly that I wasn't in any danger – however, I must admit, that I was beginning to feel like a shirker and I would have hated myself in the end. Anyway, what will be, will be, and I have to follow my destiny. At one thirty, four of us leave in a small lorry for the 37th section auto park at Lunéville. Somebody is to fetch us from here and take us to Chanteheux. As it is already four o'clock, we phone and we are told that the 77th have left Chanteheux and nobody knows where they are. At six we eat and then walk for a bit as far as the château. We are astonished to see the TM 77 are there. We don't say anything. We go back to the village where we have a couple of beers and then thanks to the kindness of a comrade, sleep on straw in a hovel.

17 April 1916

Up at five thirty. I slept well in spite of everything. We have coffee at six and go to the auto park, where we wait for someone to fetch us. By eleven no one has arrived. We have lunch at the kitchens. At one we go back, and there is still nobody there – God, what disorganization! One of us decides to go and find someone at the château and he takes a lorry and accompanied by the section's quartermaster, we leave at three thirty and get there at four. Introductions to the section's lieutenant (Lieutenant Nartillet) who, would you believe, is extremely charming. He's a real joker – he will certainly become a mate. They lodge us in rooms with iron beds piled with straw. At five, we eat and then go into town. A comrade and I explore the town and then find a café. Furlough has been notified. Since I am just down from the trenches, perhaps it will not be long before I go. I go to bed at nine.

18 April 1916

Up a six. It was very stormy all night, but in spite of it I slept quite well. At eight, I have nothing to do so I go with the others to have a look round the auto park. At nine I'm pressed into straw fatigue. At ten thirty, I'm told that I am assigned as second to lorry no. 110-086-8 and we have orders to leave at twelve forty-five to go to the Dietrich factory for equipment to be transported to Einville. I drive back from Einville, and it all goes very well. I go to bed at nine.

19 April 1916

Up at six. I take my lorry to the mess in town. In the afternoon, we fetch a lorry load of sand. Everything is perfect. The café in the evening and then bed at nine.

20 April 1916

Up at six. It is my 38th birthday today. We are at the driving school all day, and I am told I am outstanding, particularly in the way I drive through town. A comrade and I have found a room to rent in town (20 francs per month). We turn in at nine.

21 April 1916

This morning I am at the mess. Everything is going well. In the afternoon, my lorry is taken out for a test drive. I organize it that I don't go, and have a free afternoon. I tidy my belongings and write a lot. The weather is improving and above all, it is warmer. The café in the evening, and then I go to my room to bed. Before sleeping, I read a bit and feel better for it. I sleep at ten.

22 April 1916

Up at five forty-five. I go to the barracks at six fifteen, but there are no orders yet for the day. I make use of the time and wash my lorry as it needs it. This takes me until ten o'clock. At one, I join the others on wood fatigue. We go into the Mondon forest via Thiébauménil and Bénaménil – towns which alas, I knew so well not so long ago. Fatigue ends at five thirty. I was married thirteen years ago to my beloved wife. How much has happened since then and who could have foreseen that we would be separated for two years by this war. People are so cruel and it is so unfair that because of a handful of imbeciles we should suffer so much for the things we hold most dear. But there is nothing one can do. It is perhaps the law of nature, but it certainly can't be a divine one; I can't believe God would permit that people tear each other's throats out in this way. When the day comes, he will certainly know just how to punish those who have deliberately acted against his will. I can remember every second of that happy day thirteen years ago. But I am confident that I will shortly be reunited with my family and enjoy all the pleasures we knew before. In the evening after supper, we wander round the town, and then go to the café. We turn in at ten.

23 April 1916

Easter day. My comrade gets up at five without saying a word. I wake at six twenty. I go to the barracks and learn we have a free day as it is a feast day. At ten, my comrade asks me to go with him to high mass, and I accept with pleasure. He tells me that he has already made his Easter communion. He really is a good fellow. There's a huge crowd attending high mass. There is beautiful music and a wonderful singer.

We go to barracks for lunch. A superb meal has been laid out. This is the menu: butter, radishes, ham, bread, boudin, lamb, salad, crêpes, red and white wine, coffee, and cigars. In the afternoon, we go for a walk round town. Then go out again and have dinner at the Hotel Cheval Gris, which was quite good, but expensive. Afterwards, a little time at the cafe, then we turn in at nine thirty.

24 April 1916

I'm on lorry guard duty from three in the morning until five. Fortunately, I have an alarm clock. I get up at two thirty. As it is a little early, I go back to sleep again and don't wake until four fifteen. I race off to the barracks. Nobody is in the courtyard. I find out that nobody at all was on guard all night. Nobody seems to be concerned. I go and look at the duty roster. There are very few who are off duty, and I am one of those. In the morning I go to the workshops to pass the time. After lunch, we go into town for coffee. Then I go back to barracks where I write and roll cigarettes. Afterwards we go to the park and have a game of football, and then to the airfield, to watch the planes on flight exercise, which is fascinating. In the evening after supper, we go to the café with friends, and then bed at nine thirty. At ten past ten, someone comes to tell me that I am on duty at five thirty tomorrow.

25 April 1916

Up at four forty-five. At five thirty, we leave for the civilian labourers' camp above Thiébauménil to pick up some men. At seven, we bring them to Lunéville. At nine thirty we take them back to the camp. From there we take their lieutenant to Saint-Clément, and then return to Lunéville. We have a bite to eat in our lorry at Lunéville in front of the Gare de l'Est, and then hurry back to the camp to pick up some men. From there we go to Bénaménil to pick up others and then take them all to Lunéville. We have a break until five. At seven we leave again to return the men to camp. Then finally, we return at nine at night. So, a well-filled day. I have been at the wheel for almost the whole day. I write a bit before going to bed at ten thirty.

26 April 1916

What a rude awakening! At five fifteen, I hear bombs falling on the town. I get up and dress without haste, because I think it is a plane flying over. At six, just as I am about to go up to the château, I hear two huge explosions which land on this side. My comrade and I immediately turn back and cross a large meadow. It is a very distressing sight. The Boches are firing 380s on the town and the two bombs I heard earlier, landed on two wings of the château. Half-naked men, women and children are fleeing in panic in every direction across the meadow still wet with dew. There is panic everywhere. A shell lands and explodes 150 metres from us. We throw ourselves to the ground and I see the earth spray upwards to over 100 metres. I wait an hour and then go back to the château. In the meantime the plane drops two more bombs. The château is a horrible sight. There is not a whole pane of glass left, or any of the shop windows opposite. There is not a lorry to be seen in the courtyard. We go round the town and find one of our section's lorries. It takes us along the Nancy road, where we find another. We wait there until little by little, we regroup. In the meantime, we give a lift to a pretty young woman fleeing the area and take her to Vitrimont. She is lucky to be female and able take advantage of the general chaos, because giving lifts is strictly forbidden. We hide her in the back of the lorry. The storm seems to be dying down. Under the lieutenant's orders, some will go for a meal at the château while the others will stand guard over the lorries on the road. I am one of these. Someone brings me a meal and I eat in the open air. I'm beginning to get used to it. And this is how we spend the morning – at the side of the road.

At twelve forty-five, I'm back on duty, which involves taking a few officers for field exercises. We wait all afternoon for them to finish and don't leave until six forty. We go to the château and find all the section's lorries reunited. Let's hope that everything will now return to normal. We spend a little time at the café, and then I go to my room to write and go to bed at ten.

27 April 1916

Up at five forty-five. At six, as I am leaving a Taube flies over the village. Is it going to start all over again? But no – one of our planes gives chase but it quickly flies away. I am not on duty today. This morning is given over to washing and cleaning the lorries. Then at one thirty, the group captain gives us a talk, which is pretty moronic. The lorries have to shine and to do that we have to polish the bodywork with paraffin. To think we have to listen to that – to do it – and not say a word; all the while knowing that there are some households who don't have enough to light a lamp, because it is so expensive. Anyway – it is quite right to call this the war of attrition in every respect. As I was free at three o'clock, I folded and tidied my laundry and then we went to the café for a while. After supper we went to watch a game of football in the park and then to the café again. I went to bed at ten.

28 April 1916

Up at four thirty. At five thirty I leave for the civilian labourers' camp. Return to Lunéville via St Clément at eight. At midday, another trip to the camp. At half past twelve, lunch at the camp in the middle of the woods. Return to Lunéville at two. At five we have supper at the château. At six forty-five, I leave yet again for the camp and return to Lunéville at eight. I am alone in the lorry and I drive through the town as night falls. I have never done so much. I just have time for a small beer at the café and then turn in at ten.

29 April 1916

Up at five thirty. The lorries are washed in the morning, as I am on duty tonight. The day goes by. At five thirty in the evening, we leave for Einville to load up with logs which we carry along the Serres Road to Hoéville. No headlights allowed along the road as the Boches are a short distance away – great fun! These great logs are to be used for mounting artillery. On our return, when we reach Einville we are allowed to use our headlights which makes driving much easier. I get back and go to bed at two in the morning.

30 April 1916

I get up at seven fifteen and hurry to the château as the lorries have to be washed. As we are quite tired, we get it over and done with as quickly as possible. After lunch, two comrades and I wander round the town and then go to the park to watch an interesting football match. And then we decide to buy dried sausage, head cheese, a tin of marinated mackerel, some little cakes, and three cans of beer, which we take up to our room and have a delicious meal, which didn't even cost very much. We spend a little time in the café. I go back to my room to write and go to bed at ten.

1 May 1916

Up at five thirty. At six thirty, I leave for Marainviller. At the village station we load up with logs and make two trips to Neuville-aux-Bois, where we can hear the cannons quite clearly as we are not from the Boche lines. We then go to Bénaménil where we picnic in a meadow. We have a little nap from which we are roused by a few drops of rain, and a few moments later there is a storm which lasts a good hour.

At half past twelve we leave again for the Mondon forest, where we load up with stakes, which we take to Blémerey – where I was posted for such a long time. I am distressed to see how changed it is in just two months. In fact, there is nothing left of the village at all. Two days ago, the Boches once again lambasted it with large shells. It's stupid, but I was really moved and almost happy to see my old stamping ground where I had such a bad time. Having said that, I have to admit that once we had unloaded, we wasted no time in quickly getting out of the place. We went back to the Mondon forest for another load of stakes, which we took to Bénaménil. Then half an hour later, I took the lorry back to Lunéville and got back at five forty-five. Supper, a walk round the town, and then bed at ten.

2 May 1916

Up at five thirty. An alert. We are moving and leaving Lunéville. We are to be ready by ten as we leave at midday for Bar-le-Duc and then, no doubt, for Verdun. We leave at one in convoy – 19 lorries. I take the wheel. Fifty kilometres along an excellent road. We arrive at five thirty at Gondreville where we sleep. My lorry is my bed, where I have to say, I am extremely comfortable.

3 May 1916

Up at five. We should leave at six thirty, but have to wait until seven. I drive as far as Brillon-en-Barrois, where we will be billeted. The road is very good, but I am dead tired as I have been at the wheel without a break. It promises to be very difficult here. It seems we have to do 150 kilometres without a break. We will see. We have coffee in the evening and then at eight thirty I go to sleep in a barn where there is a good pile of straw.

4 May 1916

We are woken at four. At four fifteen, we leave the Bar-le-Duc station. The lorries are loaded up with Shells (75s), which we have to take to the Ferme Frama. It is 75 kilometres from Brillon. We meet more than 500 lorries on the way and the ditches are lined with many broken-down vehicles. Some are virtually useless. The Ferme Frama is eight kilometres from Verdun. It is an immense field where all the shells are stocked. There are troops camped pretty well everywhere. Ambulances, loaded with the wounded, are tearing about all over the place. This is what the real war looks like – a truly horrific spectacle. The road is very bad. We take the empty crates back to the station at Bar-le-Duc, and then return to Brillon-en-Barrois ant five forty-five in the evening covered in dust and absolutely exhausted. The same scenario is scheduled for tomorrow. In the evening we have beer in an unpleasant café. Then I turn in at nine.

5 May 1916

Up at five thirty. There has been no order given to leave, but it will soon come. At twelve fifteen, we are on our way. We load 155mm shells at the Bar-le-Duc station and are on the road again for Frama. I am lucky to have a lorry in such good working order, because there are so many comrades who are stranded on the side of the road. It seems that things are hotting up at Verdun. The cannons have not stopped firing. We leave Verdun in haste at nine forty-five. At one forty-five in the morning, I am so dusty that I have to stop to wash my face in a fountain at Bar-le Duc. It takes some nerve at that hour in the morning. We get back at two thirty and I get to sleep at three o'clock.

6 May 1916

I get up at seven fifteen without having had much sleep. I get my lorry ready for the next departure. We wait for orders. Perhaps today, we will be staying put. At two thirty we leave precipitously. We load up at the Bar-le-Duc station and leave for Maison Rouge. We get there quickly, but wait a long time at the unloading station. I return at four thirty in the morning. I fill up with petrol and oil and at five, I go to bed.

7 May 1916

I get up at six thirty, unable to sleep longer – I have slept an hour and a half. We leave at eleven thirty. We load up at the Bar-le-Duc station and head off to the battery field at Billemont. It is horrible weather as it is raining without let-up. The road is so slippery that several times, the lorry almost turns round on itself. Coming back, I had to get down more than twenty times to relight the headlamp (we are allowed to use the light on the return trip). In these conditions the road is really hard going. But in spite of its state, I manage to drive at speed and at twelve forty-five, I am the first to get back. I get to bed at one in the morning

8 May 1916

I get up at seven twenty-five. I set to work on my lorry. By one, we still haven't received our orders – I just wish they could leave us alone today to get some rest. It seems that we are not going out before tomorrow midday, which turns out to be true. This gives us time to check our lorries over a bit. I have found my friend Schumpff here, who is with the 499th, and in the same area as us. He invites me over to dinner at his mess at six o'clock. I go, and seven of us have a good meal, which is over at nine, and then I go straight to bed.

9 May 1916

Up at seven. I slept well and I am well rested. I adjust the magneto and the carburettor. At midday we are ready and waiting for the order to leave, which arrives at one thirty. We load up shells at the Bar-le-Duc station to take to Ferme Frama. All goes well and I return at two thirty in the morning. I turn in at three.

10 May 1916

Up at six. I get the lorry ready and we wait for the order of the day. At quarter past twelve, we load up shells at Bar-le-Duc and then set off for the Billemont quarry. It is a long way. The munitions depot is located on a rise – and idiotically – in the middle of a bombardment zone. On our way back we step on it a bit and get back at one thirty in the morning.

11 May 1916

Up at six. I get the lorry ready. At eleven, we are told that we are not going out today. Perfect – we can rest. I write quite a bit in the afternoon and then go into a nearby wood to pick lilies of the valley. I turn in at nine, as it is likely that we will leave at seven in the morning.

12 May 1916

Up at six thirty. There are no departure orders. At eleven we are told we leave at one thirty. At quarter past one, we leave for Bar-le-Duc and load up 155mm shells (short) to go to Dombasle. It is a long and dangerous route as the countryside is being bombarded continually. We return at two fifteen in the morning. We are immediately told not to sleep because we are going to another billet, and that we will leave at six for Beauzée.

13 May 1916

And in fact, we do leave at six for Beauzée. We go at snail's pace and get there at ten. The area is completely devastated. There is nowhere at all to billet. We will have to sleep in our lorries. We are caught in the rain. We have a cold meal at midday. In the afternoon only eight lorries are required for service at the Beauzée station. Fortunately, I am not part of the convoy. I get the lorry organized, as I will have to sleep in it.

14 May 1916

We are woken at five. At six we leave to load up at the Èvres station. It is pouring with rain. I am fed up. We make two trips to Billemont – 160 kilometres in all. I return to eat at eight and turn in immediately afterwards.

15 May 1916

Up at five thirty. The rain buckets down all day. We go again to Billemont but just one trip. We return at six. I turn in at eight thirty.

16 May 1916

Up at five. At six we leave for another area. We go 5 kilometres away to Bulainville, where we will sleep in a large barn, which is a bit better. At ten we load up at the Èvres station and go to Frama. We return at six thirty. I go to bed at nine.

17 May 1916

Up at five. At six we load up again at Èvres to go to Frama. The weather is superb – delectable. We travel at speed. On our return we do not take the exact route, and to our great regret we are made to turn back again to Frama. We return at five fifteen. I fill up, then have supper and turn in at nine.

18 May 1916

I should be resting up today, but because four lorries have broken down, I have to go out all the same. Up at five thirty. Departure at six thirty. We load up as always at Èvres to go to Frama.

On the way, near Lemmes, we are witness to an accident. A lorry was sideswiped by the train. It is smashed to pieces and apparently, the driver has a broken leg. One has to be careful. We return quite slowly and so we only make one trip. I get back at five fifteen. Bed at nine

19 May 1916

My co-driver is tired out, and so he is staying to rest up and I go out alone. I am going to Frama, but as the train is three hours late, I only make one trip. When I return at six, my co-driver tells me he is leaving for TM 61. I am sorry, because he's a good fellow and he has been very helpful to me. I will now have to make the trips in my lorry alone and that is going to be doubly tiring for me. I go to bed at nine.

20 May 1916

This morning, we are only leaving at nine. The cannons have been firing fiercely and there is no let-up this morning. At this hour, with any luck, we will probably be making only one trip. I go to Maison Rouge and return at four o'clock. At five we are made to load up again at Fleury station to go to Billemont. It's crazy – this is endless. My petrol tank has a leak. I tell my lieutenant, and he tells me to take the lorry to the workshops tomorrow morning.

21 May 1916

We stayed the night at Billemont. I returned at five fifty-five in the morning. I am so fed up that, instead of taking the lorry to the workshops, I go and wash in the river. I prefer to do that than to sleep. In the afternoon, I still don't feel like working on my lorry. Instead, I sleep at the side of the river, then return. Supper and bed at nine thirty.

22 May 1916

Up at six. I do not leave my vehicle until five in the evening. So now it is completely tuned. I have news: after a request made to my lieutenant on Saturday, I understand that I am to leave on Friday on furlough. If only that were true. Tonight my lorry is not yet ready to leave. It will have to wait until tomorrow. Bed at nine.

23 May 1916

Up at six. There are no orders to leave. Apparently a train has derailed and no one knows when we will leave. At four in the afternoon, we get orders to load up at Bar-le-Duc. I go on my own as I no longer have a co-driver. I am the last to arrive at the station and there is nothing left for me to load. Nevertheless, I am ordered to go with the convoy to Frama, to rescue anyone who breaks down. On the way to Vadelaincourt, I receive another order to return, which I don't mind at all. I get back at three fifteen in the morning. I fill up and get to bed at four.

24 May 1916

I get up at eight. I get my lorry ready as we leave tonight at five forty. I go to Carrières and return at five in the morning. I am not expecting to go out during the day because I am exhausted and with good reason.

25 May 1916

I have not slept. There are orders to leave at one in the afternoon, but a comrade takes my place in the lorry. However, I am completely depressed the whole day, as I thought permission for furlough would be here today – and it isn't. I am bored. I go to bed at nine.

26 May 1916

Up at six. Departure at eight. It is vile weather as it is raining continuously. At Èvres station, I bump into my brother-in-law Edmond, who is an NCO with the light cavalry. I am delighted to see him and we hug each other like two brothers. I make a trip to Frama and a second to Carrières. Between the two, I hear that my furlough has been approved for tomorrow. I don't care about anything else; now I am happy.

27 May 1916

I return at five in the morning. I prepare my lorry and someone else takes it over at six thirty. Then I concentrate on myself. There are about ten of us going on leave. At two we are at Bar-le Duc, but we don't take the train until one in the morning.

28 May 1916

We get to Gare de l'Est in Paris at ten twenty. I leap into the metro and I am home by eleven where I get the sort of welcome you can imagine. I'm not going to spend too much time writing about my leave as I have other things to do. I go and see my mother, where I find the whole family gathered together. At seven we go back home and have a family supper. I go to bed at ten.

29 May 1916

I get up a bit late. I had a good night's rest. Visited people all day. Tired. Aperitif at Galeries Layfayette. Bed at ten.

30 May 1916

Up at eight. Lunch with Vonvon at Galeries Lafayette in the middle of a gaggle of women. It's a bit too much all in one go. Dinner with my mother in the evening. Bed at eleven.

31 May 1916

Up at seven. Lunch with the Bakx. Stayed at home in the afternoon. Bed at ten.

1 June 1916

It's Ascension – a feast day. After mass, I collect my daughter from her boarding school. We have lunch at home. In the afternoon we visit Madame Lemoine, the wife of my doctor from the trenches. In the evening, dinner with my mother.

2 June 1916

Up early to do a bit of gardening. At midday, I fetch my wife at Nestlé and we have lunch with the Delapraz at the Taverne de Namur. In the afternoon, I wander around the Galeries Lafayette and then go home. In the evening the Delapraz come to the house.

3 June 1916

Up very late. Lunch at Joinville. I visit M. Morret again to say goodbye, and then my mother. We have dinner with my sister Marie in the evening.

4 June 1916

A sad day. I have to go and my furlough is over. It has been too short and has gone too quickly. My wife and Vonvon accompany me to the station. I make the return journey with a friend.

5 June 1916

Arrive at Bar-le-Duc at one in the morning. A lorry takes us from there to Beauzée and then we're on foot from Beauzée to Bulainville. It is raining without let-up. I get a hearty welcome when I get to the barracks. I rest in the afternoon, and I am depressed.

6 June 1916

I am called into service. I busy myself with my lorry and I notice that the carburettor is leaking, which I report, and am then declared unavailable for service. I stay at the barracks where, I am thoroughly bored – what a drag!!

The rain is still tipping down. In the evening some comrades go boar hunting. I go with them, but without a rifle. A little boar goes by at a few metres from me, but I have nothing to shoot it with. I go to bed at nine thirty.

7 June 1916

Up at seven. I finish tinkering with my lorry. At one o'clock, I load up at the Fleury station to go to Billemont. I am the first to return at ten twenty-five. I go to bed at eleven.

8 June 1916

I'm not going out today; someone else is taking my place. Turn and turn about. I stay at the barracks and look after my own affairs. I am still extremely depressed. I go to bed at nine thirty.

9 June 1916

Up at seven. I work on my lorry. At one, I set off for Maison Rouge. I return at eight and go to bed at nine o'clock.

10 June 1916

Up at six. At eleven fifty-five, departure for Billemont. The itinerary has partly changed as part of the way has been bombarded. We came back at top speed at nine. Bed at nine thirty.

11 June 1916

Up at seven. It is a feast day today, and I am not going out. I spend my time writing, darning my socks and rolling cigarettes. Bed at nine thirty.

12 June 1916

Up at six thirty. I tinker with my lorry. At ten thirty, I go the office and sign up to take an officer's exam within the auto service. I have no idea what the outcome will be. I just pray to God that He will at least allow me to pass the sub-lieutenant's exam. Departure at midday, and I make a trip to Billemont, and return at nine fifteen. Bed at nine thirty.

13 June 1916

Up at seven. I get my lorry ready, but I don't go out and get a day of rest. I spend the day tinkering. Bed at nine.

14 June 1916

Up at six thirty. I am a bit nervous as I have been authorized to sit the officers' exam. In the afternoon, I go to Frama. On our stops, I do a bit of revision for the exam. Return at nine and I go to bed immediately

15 June 1916

Up at five, which is really four, as today, the clocks have gone forward an hour. At seven, I go to the village next to Nubécourt to sit the officers' exam. There are sixteen contestants for five places. We are in a small classroom. We have dictation, a French composition, and a theoretical and practical question on mechanics. I seem to have managed quite well and discover that I am just as good as many of the other examinees. I rest a bit in the afternoon. Bed at nine.

16 June 1916

I get up at six and go to Nubécourt at seven. I learn that I have been unsuccessful in the officers' exam. I was certain of it, because when I left this morning I was told that Captain Barthez (a pig), who commands the auto section, came to dinner last night with our lieutenant whose cousin sat the exam with me. He told him, when talking about me, that I would make up the fourth in this game of cards. In fact, I came eighth out of the sixteen contestants, and as I said, there were only five places available. I think it is shameful to see this sort of favouritism, particularly in war time. It is quite obvious and it is disgusting. I hope after the war, we will be able to talk a little more freely, since we will not be subjected to the iron rule of these inexperienced whippersnappers.

At ten thirty, I take the wheel and go to Frama. It is a beautiful day. In the evening I'm on lorry guard duty from nine until eleven. I go to bed immediately afterwards.

17 June 1916

Up at seven thirty. There was talk of our leaving this place, but then news comes that on the contrary, we are to stay here and to expect a big attack, so much so, that we will be in service for 29 hours at the wheel at a stretch, with six hours of rest in between. We will do what we can. I am at rest today, and a colleague goes in my place. Before leaving, he reports that the back left wheel seems to be in danger of coming off. He is told that there is nothing wrong with it and he leaves. At eight thirty at night, I learn that he has broken down in front of the field hospital at Lemmes, with the said wheel missing. It's the third time this has happened to him, and yet it is not his fault. Bed at ten.

18 June 1916

Up at seven forty five. My lorry and my colleague are at the Bar-le-Duc automobile park. Rather him than me. In the meantime I am immediately consigned lorry 16. I get it ready, but I don't go out. In the afternoon, a bit more cleaning, then I read and write. I go to bed at ten.

19 June 1916

Up at seven forty-five. I accompany my colleague as far as Nubécourt, while he takes the lorry on to Bar-le-Duc. Afterwards, everyone is put to cleaning of all the back parts of the lorries, as there is a review at three o'clock.

A big commotion at two fifty. A Boche plane flies over and drops six bombs quite near us. Two people are killed and eight wounded. And I thought we were safe here. The rest of the day is quiet. I go to bed at ten.

20 June 1916

Up at seven. I am on duty and take lorry 16 and go to Billemont. A Boche plane flies over the munitions depot, but is chased away by our own planes. I return at eight and go to bed at ten.

21 June 1916

Up at seven. At three in the morning, another Boche plane flew over but was immediately seen off by our planes. I am at rest today. At eight o'clock at night, our men return in a state of shock. They were fiercely bombarded at Carrières. All the vehicles have been hit by shrapnel. One of the men was wounded in his left thigh and another was hit in the head, but fortunately nothing serious. Bed at ten.

22 June 1916

I prepare my lorry as we are going out today. Departure at eleven. I go to the Èvres station, but three of us return at two o'clock because nothing remained for us to load. Two more lorries have broken down. And they think they can put us to work intensively, with these sorts of tools. A passable afternoon. Between eight and ten in the evening, I go up to the heights to lie in the grass and breathe a little fresh air, which does me good. I go to bed at ten.

23 June 1916

Up at seven fifteen. I am not going out today. I have nothing to do. It is a beautiful day and very hot. I am on lorry guard duty between nine and eleven. I go to bed at eleven thirty. At midnight there is a violent storm, which clears the air.

24 June 1916

Up at seven. I get my lorry ready. Departure at half past twelve. We don't leave the station at Fleury until four, as the train is late. I go to Frama and while I am unloading, a beautiful boar comes in sight. Everyone gives chase, but of course, no one catches it. I get back at eleven at night. On arrival, we are told there is an alert. We have to quickly fill up and wait. I go to bed at midnight, while waiting for events.

25 June 1916

It was an undisturbed night. Departure at eight o'clock, but not for me. It is Sunday, but there is nothing to do for all that. The day drags on. Bed at ten.

26 June 1916

Up at seven. I prepare the lorry. At one, I load up at the Souilly station to go to Billemont. The road is execrable and extremely slippery. I am taking a lieutenant from the 12th Light Cavalry from Souilly to Dugny. He says he has it on good authority that the war will end in six to seven months. The road becomes even more slippery. At midnight we help eleven lorries, which are ahead of us and blocking the way, back on the road. Then, at two o'clock, it is my turn, and I slide into a deep rut about 100 metres from the unloading area. I am furious, because it is the first time it has happened to me. I work all night trying to extricate myself, a comrade pulls me out at five in the morning.

27 June 1916

At eight I return to the barracks. I am absolutely shattered, there's no other word for it. I try to get some rest and sleep from two to five o'clock, but I can feel I have caught a bit of a cold. I go back to bed at nine thirty.

28 June 1916

I'm really out of sorts. I make a trip to Billemont at twelve thirty. It will not take too long at this time of day. But at seven thirty we have to wait two hours at Dugny. There has been a fierce attack on Verdun, and we can only go one by one. It is chaos at Billemont. I unload as fast as I can and then race back to barracks, as I want to get to bed. I get back at one thirty in the morning. I drop everything and go straight to bed.

29 June 1916

I am not going out today, and so I get up at eight. I only concentrate on myself and having a wash and cleaning up. I read and write all afternoon. Bed at nine thirty.

30 June 1916

Departure at six thirty, but I have a temperature and I don't go. Someone else has taken my place. I have a complete day of rest. I go to bed at ten.

1 July 1916

I get up at five thirty. Departure at six thirty. I go to Carrières, where I have quite an accident. While loading up some empty crates, one falls directly onto my temple. Bleeding profusely, I get it patched up by a nurse and then leave again for Fleury. Bed at ten.

2 July 1916

It is Sunday, and I am not going out today. It is a beautiful day; it is really upsetting to still be here at this time. I get through the day as best I can. Bed at ten.

3 July 1916

Departure at six thirty. At the last minute, I can't leave because my lorry is out of action. It needs quite a bit of seeing to. The weather has changed. It hasn't stopped raining since this morning. I work all day on my lorry. In the evening, bed at ten.

4 July 1916

I am not going out today, because a comrade has asked if he can take my place, so that he can be with one of his mates. I make the most of it to rest up a little more. The rain has hardly let up. My colleague gets back at seven. After supper, I busy myself with my lorry, and then go to bed at ten.

5 July 1916

I get up at six, as we leave at six thirty. Then suddenly, there is a counter-order. We wait for the order to leave. At twelve thirty, we leave for the station at Fleury. I am to go to Frama. On the way, I help a comrade whose vehicle has broken down, which makes me lose a bit of time. It is raining so hard at Frama, that I have to stop unloading for half an hour. I return at eleven at night and go to bed at eleven thirty.

6 July 1916

Up at seven thirty. It is my day off. It is a beautiful day and the sun is shining, which is some compensation and lifts one's spirits. It's a good day on the whole. I go to bed at ten.

7 July 1916

An entire day of rain. I make a trip to Maison-Rouge and return utterly fed up.

8 July 1916

There is a lorry review at eleven o'clock. This irritates me to such an extent, that I go to the mess to avoid it. It is so pointless having reviews at this time. Rest in the afternoon.

9 July 1916

It is Sunday and I have a day off. My comrades and I put a good lunch together – rabbit – and invite our sergeant. We go for a walk in the woods in the afternoon. Bed at ten.

10 July 1916 no entry for this date

11 July 1916

Departure at eleven thirty. I load up at the station at Souilly to go to Maison-Rouge. My corporal comes with me. He drives, which relieves me a bit. Just beyond Ippécourt, we swerve sharply into a field; the steering column has completely snapped. I phone through to Ippécourt to send someone to help us out. In the meantime, we work on the lorry and with a little makeshift repair, manage so well that we get back under our own steam at nine in the evening. I go to bed at ten thirty.

12 July 1916

Up at seven thirty. I go to the workshops to lend a hand in the mending of my lorry. And in the afternoon, it is ready. I try it out and it seems to be running perfectly well. The afternoon is passable. I go to bed at ten.

13 July 1916

Up at seven thirty. Departure at eleven for Fleury station and from there to Maison-Rouge, where we are bombarded. One hundred and fifty metres away from us we see five horses and two artillerymen fall, and then many wounded. Fortunately, none of us are hurt. I return at seven thirty. At nine thirty, to the sound of a drum, there is a beating retreat ceremony lit by torches and a couple of lamps. I go to bed at ten thirty.

14 July 1916

I have a day off. It is National Day today. We have a good lunch and in the evening, a particularly good dinner of rabbit and two chickens which we had bought very cheaply. I had an idea to add a little fun to the evening. We put a magneto under the table with the current running along the top; every time someone came over to see us we invited them to drink a glass with us, but they couldn't as they would receive an electric shock. I was asked to decorate the room. I made a beautiful bouquet for our CO who is, of course, presiding. I make a canopy out of tent canvas and decorated it with flowers. I am complimented by everyone. A lot of people are drunk before nine o'clock. We stop at midnight, as we have had enough. I go to bed at twelve thirty.

15 July 1916

I get up at five thirty, to leave at six. I feel terrible. I have a dreadful headache and a really upset stomach. The morning after the night before. I go to the kitchen and drink a quart of coffee, and then vomit up about a quarter of it. I climb into my lorry. But everything is spinning to such an extent that I leave everything and go back to bed until nine thirty and then feel much better. The day goes by passably well. I go to bed at ten in the evening.

16 July 1916

Departure at six thirty. I go to Fleury station and then to Maison-Rouge. Everything is rapidly achieved and I am back by five past twelve. As it is Sunday and I don't like being on duty on this day, it is all or nothing. So in a rage, I polish my lorry from top to bottom. the rest of the day is tolerable. I go to bed at ten.

17 July 1916

I get up at seven thirty. The section is having a day of rest, so there is nothing to do.

A comrade returns from Paris and says he knows for a fact, that the war will be over by October. If only that were true.

The day drags by. I go to bed at ten.

18 July 1916

I am not going out today. I spend my time writing and reading. I am really depressed and very bored. I go to bed at ten.

19 July 1916

Up at five thirty. Departure at six thirty. I am to go to Frama. My magneto breaks down at Fleury, which I quickly fix. I get back at three and go to bed at ten.

20 July 1916

Up at six. I am on petrol fatigue. I don't go out today. Nobody seems to be doing anything. I spend the day as I can – in boredom mostly. It is Saint Marguerite's day, my wife's feast day. She would so like me to be there to celebrate it with her. Instead, I am here like an idiot, fighting for a problematical independence, when I should be peacefully at home enjoying a healthy and honest feast day with my family. Anyway, we have to put up with what the powers-that-be have ruled. In the evening, I am irritable and go to bed at ten.

21 July 1916

Up at seven thirty. The section is still not going out today. We are certainly not doing very much at the moment. It's a slow, aimless day. I go to bed at ten thirty.

22 July 1916

Up at seven thirty. Another day off and it is very quiet. I am bored to tears with nothing to do. I am utterly fed up. In the evening we stay outside and drink white wine with our NCO until ten thirty, when I go to bed.

23 July 1916

It is Sunday. A day of rest for everyone. We get through the day as best we can. There are new orders. There is roll call at nine and lights out at ten. Everyone is furious because the less we are given to do, the more irritable we become. For what it's worth, I go to bed at eleven.

24 July 1916

Departure at six from the Souilly station to transport grenades to Lemmes, four kilometres away. An extremely dangerous load. I get back at eleven thirty. A really health-giving outing. The orders are strict – bed at ten.

25 July 1916

We are still at rest today. We don't know what to do with ourselves. We wear ourselves out playing Thirty-one until ten o'clock, when I go to bed.

26 July 1916

It isn't my turn to go out. I am getting more and more restless. I spend the day rolling cigarettes and playing cards. Bed at ten.

27 July 1916

At rest again today. We are as brassed off as ever. The days drag out. Bed at ten.

28 July 1916

Departure at six in the morning for the station at Souilly, where we wait four hours for the munitions train. While we are waiting we see one of our planes bring a Boche plane down. I return at three o'clock. After supper, a game of cards and then, bed at ten.

29 July 1916

We are not going out today. As from tomorrow, there will be two to a lorry, because a single driver with the TM 83 was killed in an accident. At seven thirty, Sub-lieutenant Daran asks me if I would come to a rehearsal for a concert, which should take place on 15 August. There is a piano, a violin, a flute and an oboe. He has invited me to bring my clarinet and join in. I am going to do it. In the evening I am on guard duty and I go to bed at eleven.

30 July 1916

It is Sunday. We leave at seven fifteen and make a trip to Frama. We return at five minutes past midday. It is very hot. I have a few personal ailments that are getting me down. I wander about in the evening and go to bed at ten.

31 July 1916

Up at six thirty. We are not going out, but we work on our lorries. In the afternoon, I snooze under an apple tree in a meadow. Bed at ten.

1 August 1916

Up at six thirty. Departure for Souilly station and then to Maison-Rouge. I return at two, and the lieutenant immediately informs me that we leave tomorrow, or the day after, for Ligny-en-Barrois. It certainly doesn't bother me to be leaving the area as I am really bored here. We drink white wine all evening, and play cards. Bed at ten.

2 August 1916

Up at five. We leave at twelve thirty in sweltering heat. It is a long, dusty journey. We arrive at Ligny-en-Barrois at four. At last a town complete with houses and neatly dressed, even elegant, women.

The town's barracks are not at all comfortable. I will try and find a room. Our lorries are in a large auto park. There is beer to drink, and while we eat, I put back two litres to myself. We are here for a rest and eventually to transport troops. However, I don't think we will be too overworked. I wander round the town, which is pleasant. Everyone, a sociable world, is sitting outside their front doors to get a little fresh air. I feel as if I exist here.

3 August 1916

In the morning, we are busy cleaning the lorries, then in the afternoon, we are left in peace, and we make the most of it by relaxing in the fresh air. In the evening, after supper, I explore the town and drink a litre of beer in the Café des Oiseaux before turning in. Roll call is at nine here, but at ten, everyone is still in the streets.

4 August 1916

Up at two in the morning. Departure at three. We have to pick up riflemen from Villers-le-Sec and take them to Moulin-Brûlé. From there we transport the engineers to the entrance of Bar-le-Duc. We finally get back to Ligny-en-Barrois at nine thirty at night. I have a quick bite to eat, and then exhausted from the heat and the dust from the journey, I go to bed at eleven.

5 August 1916

Because of the tiring journey yesterday, they don't wake us until seven thirty. We thoroughly wash down the lorries and lubricate them. In the afternoon, we work a bit more on the lorries. Then I read and write to pass the time. In the evening, I walk round the town. Bed at ten.

6 August 1916

Up at six. At seven, we are at work on the lorries, but there is not much to do. Rest in the afternoon. We go fishing in the canal and return with a catch of 65 fish. In the evening we have a good fry-up. After dinner, a little wander around town, and then bed at ten thirty.

7 August 1916

Up at six. At seven, we are with the lorries. At eight, we have rifle practice. Everyone grumbles at this, although what we are asked to do is not very significant. Nevertheless, it is the principle – lorries and rifles are incompatible. I give my lorry a lick of paint in the afternoon. In the evening, we go into town and then bed at ten.

8 August 1916

Up at six thirty. At eight, the lieutenant orders further rifle practice. It is outrageous, as this fine fellow has never served in the infantry. (I'm not sure if he has even done his military service), and he has the nerve to order around people who know a great deal more than him. Ah well – poor anarchy! For the past two days, I have been learning English from a friend who speaks it fluently. It provides a little distraction. In the afternoon, we work as well as we can on the lorries. We have been put on alert for troop transportation. In spite of this, I go fishing with some comrades. We have another good catch and a good fry-up. I turn in at ten.

9 August 1916

We were disturbed twice during the night to transport troops, but the order was cancelled. I get up at six thirty, and go over to the lorries – where I study English. I have received my clarinet and hope to spend some pleasurable moments. In the evening after five, we go fishing. Bed at ten.

10 August 1916

Up at eight. The section left at five to transport troops; but together with a comrade, our lieutenant, and our sergeant, I am on guard duty at ten thirty with the Barthez group. It is a boring service, but we pass the time by teasing the women as they go by. In the evening, to amuse ourselves, the sergeant and I do the rounds and the patrols of the town. We stay out until twelve forty-five. I go to bed at one, and then have to get up at three to take up post. I am at rest in the afternoon. After supper I go fishing and become quite expert. Bed at ten.

11 August 1916

12 August 1916

Up at seven. At eight thirty, rifle practice (this stupid business has started up again). In the afternoon, I am bored and since I have nothing to do, I go fishing, where we are quite content. We have a delicious fry-up for dinner. Bed at ten.

13 August 1916

It is Sunday. At nine thirty, I hear part of mass. At ten thirty there is a review in service dress (how idiotic can one get). It rains a bit in the afternoon. I go fishing, and then wander around town. In the evening, after supper, we go fishing again. Bed at ten thirty.

14 August 1916

Up at seven. At nine, a little unimportant theory, then I do some writing. We are told that tomorrow, there is to be a sung mass followed by a concert at two o'clock, in which I have to play the clarinet without practice. I go fishing in the evening. Bed at ten o'clock

15 August 1916

Both mass and the concert go by the board. Departure at five thirty in the morning, We transport troops from Pretz to Nixéville. From there we go to Blercourt for more troops and take them to Fains. We get back exhausted, at eight thirty in the evening. Bed at ten.

16 August 1916

Up at seven. The whole day is spent cleaning the lorries. We go fishing again in the evening. When we return, we are told that we leave tomorrow at six in the morning to transport troops. It is all or nothing in this place. Either we don't do a thing, or we are worn out by working for days on end. Bed at ten.

17 August 1916

Up at four thirty. At six we fetch an artillery regiment and divisional stretcher-bearers from Nançois-le-Petit and take them to Nixéville, where we arrive at eleven thirty. We leave again at one thirty. It is a long way and I sleep for half the journey. We get back at six thirty, tired out. I turn in at ten.

18 August 1916

Up at six forty-five. We polish the lorries, and are pleased to do so, even though we are so tired. This takes up the morning. In the afternoon, I work a bit on my English. In the evening after supper, we go for a long walk in the woods. Bed at ten.

19 August 1916

Up at seven. There is no work order given today, so I make the most of it by writing. We potter around all day. Bed at ten.

20 August 1916

Up at seven. We're having a thrash today. Three months ago, the section bought a little pig for 20 francs. We called him Auguste. We fattened him up and took him with us wherever we went. We have just sold him to the pork butcher for 184 francs, and so from the proceeds, the lieutenant is treating us to a feast. As he is soon to be married, he is turning this into an occasion, and at his expense, he has added champagne and cigars. We set up a table in the auto park which we lay for 50 places, and decorate with flags and flowers. The lieutenant wants to preside and will eat with us.

On the menu: herring, butter, boudin, roast beef, fried potatoes, gooseberry rice pudding, wine, champagne, coffee, and cigars. When champagne is served, we each have to sing a song. I sing the 'Sixty-nine' song, which always goes down a treat. Everyone, officers and men alike, are in stitches. The lieutenant leaves at three, but the party continues.

In the evening, I go for a long walk in the woods with a few comrades. When we get back, I can only eat a little gooseberry rice pudding, as I ate far too much at lunchtime. Bed at ten.

21 August 1916

Up at seven. There are no orders to go out. The lorries are inspected. I write and study a bit of English. Bed at ten.

22 August 1916

Up at seven, and we are still not going out. I read and write, and go to bed at ten.

23 August 1916

Up at seven. Work on the lorries. At two o'clock, there is a big fuss. There is to be a review by Captain Barthez of the whole group kitted out in blue fatigues, cartridge belts, helmets and rifles. There are more than 1500 of us looking completely ridiculous, particularly as we all are of the opinion that this should not part of the automobile service. On the road to Saint-Dizier, the captain makes us present arms. We get back at last, disgusted by the whole thing. Bed at ten.

24 August 1916

Up at seven. I tinker on the lorries a bit. There is nothing to do in the afternoon and I am bored. Without telling anyone, I go fishing until five. At five thirty, just as I have finished dinner, my friend Schumpff, comes to see me. He has been able to get his wife up to join him, and he invites me to dinner with three other friends at seven o'clock at the Hotel du Cheval Blanc. Well, even though I have just eaten, I accept and we have a delightful evening that continues until nine thirty. I go to bed at ten.

25 August 1916

Up at seven. I go off to the lorries where I write all morning. There is still nothing to do and we are not going out. For the want of anything better to do, there is a tool inspection in the afternoon. After supper, we go into town, but a storm breaks and we have to take shelter in the café. Bed at ten, as usual.

26 August 1916

Up at seven. There are still no orders to go out and there is still nothing to do. A very quiet day. We are thoroughly bored. One of our good mates leaves for Paris on furlough – lucky devil. Apparently, it will be my turn in three weeks time. I can hardly wait. Bed at ten.

27 August 1916

Up at seven. It is Sunday. It is raining spasmodically. At the briefing, they ask for musicians to form an orchestra under the lieutenant's baton. I sign up, of course. Whether this project will take off or not remains to be seen, but I hope it does because we would have fun together. We go out for about two hours in the afternoon to visit my English-speaking comrade who is ill in the infirmary. After supper we have a short walk in the countryside. I go to bed at ten.

28 August 1916

Up at seven. Off to the lorries, but there is nothing to do.

At five o'clock, we hear a rumour that Italy has declared war on Germany. At six, this is confirmed in the Paris newspapers. A little later, at the group's office, we are told that Romania has mobilized and has declared war on Austria. Although this news comes from a seemingly reliable source, we remain sceptical and will wait until tomorrow for this to be confirmed in the papers. Bed at ten.

29 August 1916

We are hardly out of bed at seven, when we race to see the papers. It is true. Romania has mobilized. We are all delighted. We get a supplement of a quarter of a litre of wine to celebrate.

The day is spent pottering around as usual. Bed at ten.

30 August 1916

Up at seven. Exercises for ten minutes. The rest of the time we are free. It rains constantly in the afternoon. We are cooped up in the café in the evening. Bed at ten.

31 August 1916

Up at seven. There is still nothing to do. A quieter than quiet day. Nothing to report. Bed at ten, as usual.

1 September 1916

Still no marching orders. Nothing to do. Up at seven. Bed at ten.

2 September 1916

Up at seven. I have changed two tyres on my lorry. I also need to give it a coat of paint. I work on it all day. In the evening after supper, we go fishing. Bed at ten.

3 September 1916

Up at seven. I go off to finish painting my lorry. At midday, we receive orders to quit our barracks to give room to an entire division which is coming for a few days before returning to the firing line. We will be sleeping in our lorries. The 222nd Infantry is included among the regiments that arrive, and I am delighted to reunite with some old comrades from the 37th. We get together for a drink at the café. Bed at ten.

4 September 1916

It has rained all night. Fortunately, the work I have done on my lorry is good and has held fast. I continue with my painting and I replace a tyre. It is raining more and more. We can't go out in the evening. Bed at ten.

5 September 1916

At midnight, we receive orders for a departure at three in the morning. I argue that I can't go because the paint on my lorry is still wet. This isn't accepted and I have to go too. I am furious. At three o'clock, with the rain bucketing down we dump our things in the lorries that are not going. At three thirty, we leave, lit by headlights but in torrential rain, which doesn't let up until eleven. We go to Seigneulles to collect the 122nd infantry division, which we take to Clermont-en-Argens via Les Islettes – a village of which nothing remains. We are obliged to don helmets because of the persistent shelling in the area. What is more, we are in full view. We return at five thirty, exhausted, and I have a splitting headache. I go to bed at nine thirty.

6 September 1916

Up at seven thirty. At three in the morning, I had such a bad headache, I had to take an aspirin. At eight o'clock, I take another and then set about lubricating my lorry. In the afternoon, we are at rest because the troops passing through are giving a vocal and instrumental concert. We go along at two. It is very good. In the evening after supper a grand tattoo is played by the bandsmen of the three regiments. It is wonderful. I go to bed at ten.

7 September 1916

Up at seven. We are busy with our lorries. I have slightly injured my right hand, so I can't do much. I make the most of it and write and study a bit of English. I turn in at ten.

8 September 1916

Up at seven. My hand is still hurting and I don't do anything. On top of which, I have toothache; I shall have to have the tooth pulled out. Little by little, the troops in transit are leaving the area, and I think we will soon return to the barracks. In the evening after supper, we go for an hour's walk in the moonlight, which is superb.

9 September 1916

Up at seven. We don't do much. It is fine weather and we go fishing. In the evening, seven of us have a fry-up of 92 fish. Bed at ten.

10 September 1916

We are woken at three. Departure at four. This time fortunately, the weather is fine. We have to collect some troops from Dugny sur Meuse and take them to Trémont sur Saulx. It is very hot and dusty. We get back at six thirty in the evening. I walk round town, and then turn in at ten.

11 September 1916

Up at seven. A full polish for the lorries. We tinker in the afternoon. After supper, we move back into our quarters. We go to the café and then bed at ten.

12 September 1916

Up at seven. We are kept busy with our lorries all day. At nine in the evening, we are given warning that six lorries will leave at two in the morning. Bed at ten.

13 September 1916

Up at one in the morning. Departure at two. I lead the convoy so everything runs smoothly and everyone is happy. We are to collect some Trésor et Postes troops at Dugny sur Meuse and take them to Remicourt. As we are not pressed for time, we have lunch in a café at Remicourt and stay for two hours. We take to the road again at top speed and we get back at three fifteen. The lieutenant is amazed; he was not expecting our return before six or seven. I turn in at ten.

14 September 1916

Up at seven. We polish our lorries and then we are free. The day goes by passably well. Bed at ten.

15 September 1916

Up at seven. As I have nothing to do, I concentrate on my own affairs as I am on furlough as from tomorrow. Bed at ten.

16 September 1916

Up at seven. I get my things to together. At two eighteen, I leave with two comrades. It is a good trip and we get to Paris at one in the morning.

17 September 1916

I'm not going to be too long-winded about my leave. First because it's not about the war and secondly, such a short leave is going to be too good to find words for.

I get home at two in the morning, and find my wife and Vonvon. Lunch at midday at Joinville. In the afternoon, Vonvon introduces me to a young English soldier, who apparently, is almost her fiancé, but I don't very much like these people. I have seen too many of them in operation at close quarters. He has dinner with us at Joinville. We return at eleven.

18 September 1916

Up at eight. Lunch at home. Pay a visit to the Delapraz, Le Bazar, the Louvre, Galeries Lafayette, Madame Bakx, my sister Marie, and then dinner with my mother. Back at the house at eleven thirty.

19 September 1916

Up at six thirty. I go to Saint-Cloud to visit the my laundrywoman's fiancé at Ligny-en- Barrois. He has been wounded and is in hospital. Lunch with my sister Marie. Pay a visit to the sister of a comrade. Dinner with Madame Bakx. Back home at eleven thirty.

20 September 1916

Up at eight. I stay at home and potter around all day. In the evening we have invited the Delapraz for dinner. We have a good time. Aymée Aguellet also comes round, but later. A riotous time after dinner. Everyone leaves at eleven. Bed at midnight.

21 September 1916

My wife left this morning for Argenton to fetch our daughter. I get up at seven. At midday, I have lunch at the Galeries Lafayette. In the afternoon, I visit the Morret-Jordan, who are not there. I go and see my mother again. At six fifty-four, I go to the Gare des Invalides to fetch my wife and daughter. We get home at eight. After dinner, I have an English lesson with Vonvon.

22 September 1916

Up at eight thirty. I stay at home today to do some gardening. This evening a little English with Vonvon.

23 September 1916

Up at eight thirty. Lunch with the Delapraz. Everyone is very pleasant. In the afternoon, I stroll along the boulevards with my wife and daughter. Dinner at home. A little English in the evening.

24 September 1916

All day with my mother. We get home late.

25 September 1916

Up at eight. Lunch, and then I leave as my furlough is over. The train at three twenty-four. I am sad. I travel alone. I get to Ligny-en-Barrois at three in the morning.

26 September 1916

A hello to all my mates at three in the morning. Lunch with friends. In the afternoon, the lieutenant test drives the lorries on the road. After supper, a visit from my friend Achard, who is much better. I'm dead tired tonight. Bed at ten.

27 September 1916

Departure at five forty-five. We are going to collect the black troops at Savonnières and take them to Nixeville. we return at six in the evening having done 170 kilometres. Bed at ten.

28 September 1916

Up at seven. I clean my lorry. In the afternoon, anti typhoid vaccinations. I am forced to have it in spite of my protests that I already had one two years ago and that it made me extremely ill. And it has the same effect this time. At six I am nauseous and I throw up over and over again. I confront the doctor in front of the captain. I go to bed with a high temperature. I take it during the night and it is over forty. It is ridiculous to make people sick when they are perfectly healthy. I don't get out of bed.

29 September 1916

I get up at ten. My temperature has gone down, but it is still at 38°. Impossible to stay up all day. After a meal, I lie down on my bed again. I feel a bit better in the evening. I am caught by the Lieutenant, because he doesn't want me to eat ham. I'm forced to give in and I go back to bed at eight.

30 September 1916

I get up at eight, and I feel much better. I only feel a little pain in my shoulder. I rest all day. In the evening, after supper, we go out a bit. I go to bed at ten.

1 October 1916

The officers have organized a big boar hunt today. Some comrades and I have arranged not to go, which means we can get up at eight. After lunch I write for quite a while, and then we go for a long walk in the countryside. After supper we play Manille. I go to bed at nine.

2 October 1916

Up at seven. Not much to do. It is a long, drawn-out day. Bed at ten.

3 October 1916

Up at four thirty. Departure at five forty-five. We have to collect troops at Nançois-le-Petit and take them to Ancerville. We get back at eleven thirty. In the afternoon we work on our lorries. In the evening, bed at ten.

4 October 1916

Rest all day. I busy myself with tidying my own affairs. In the evening, bed at ten.

5 October 1916

Up at four thirty. Departure at five thirty. We are to load up a regiment's equipment at Haudainville and then take it to Naives-devant-Bar. I have two burnt-out valves and the lorry limps all the way back, and I don't arrive until eight. I go to bed at ten.

6 October 1916

Up at seven. I have to change the two valves. In the afternoon, I go off to the workshops to have the lorry's floor replaced. I turn in at ten.

7 October 1916

Up at seven. At eight I fetch my lorry from the workshops. I spend the afternoon retuning the engine. And so the day goes. Bed at ten.

8 October 1916

Up at seven. A morning spent with the lorries. A comrade and I go to high mass at nine thirty. In the afternoon, we move out of our quarters. Eight of us have rented spacious lodgings where we will be very comfortable. Another day goes by, and the rain is tipping down. By evening, we are exhausted; nevertheless, I don't get to bed until ten thirty.

9 October 1916

Up at seven. Nothing of particular importance. I'm still working on my lorry. In the evening, bed at ten.

10 October 1916

Up at six thirty. I go off to look for stone to construct a parking place for my lorry, which takes me the whole day. Bed at ten.

11 October 1916

Up at three thirty in the morning. Departure at four forty. We are going to fetch troops from Chaumont-sur-Aire and take them to Blercourt. From here, we take up others and take them back to Chaumont-sur-Aire. We return at five thirty. I have a short English lesson and then turn in at nine thirty.

12 October 1916

Up at six thirty. We clean the lorries in the morning and in the evening. In the evening, we learn that our lieutenant is leaving us for a month to act as coordinating officer at Moulin-Brûlé. We are all sorry to see him go. At nine, there is an announcement that we leave at three forty-five in the morning for personnel transport service. So – bed at nine thirty.

13 October 1916

Up at two thirty in the morning. Departure at three forty. We load up troops at Blercourt and take them to Pretz. On the way, I have two magneto failures. We get back at five thirty, exhausted. Supper and then bed at nine.

14 October 1916

Up at six thirty. I take care of my lorry, which needs a lot doing to it. I have to advance the magneto, which is a precision job that takes up most of the day. At two, there is another anti typhoid vaccination session. I tell the doctor that if he touches me, I'll shoot him. I'm left in peace, for which I am extremely grateful. In the evening after supper, I read a little then go to bed at ten.

15 October 1916

It is Sunday. I get up at seven and go to high mass. It rains torrentially all day, so we go back to our lodgings and play cards. Bed at ten.

16 October 1916

Up at six thirty. The entire day is spent working on the lorries, and the rain has not stopped. Nothing in particular. Bed at ten.

17 October 1916

Up at six thirty. At seven thirty, the lorries are partially washed. It is raining and it is very cold. In the afternoon, I am the driver for fatigue duty – wood for the kitchen. Our new lieutenant, who is very pleasant, offers us a packet of cigarettes. In the evening, after supper, we make a good fire and have a game of Manille. Then I turn in at ten.

18 October 1916

Up at six. The rain buckets down all day. All the same, we work on the lorries. In the evening a game of Manille and bed at ten.

19 October 1916

Up at six. Work of the lorries. Tool inspection in the afternoon. It is still pouring with rain. In the evening, a game of Manille. Bed at ten.

20 October 1916

Up at six thirty. Back to the lorries, but there is nothing to do on them. It is very cold. We tinker all day. Bed at ten.

21 October 1916

Up at six. We have received orders to leave at seven thirty. We are to take a mixed regiment from Tronville-en-Barrois to Nixéville. There is a dreadful accident on the way. Just before Issancourt, one of our lorries pitched into a ravine. Three zouaves are injured and our poor driver is killed. We are all deeply upset and return at eight. Bed at ten.

22 October 1916

Up at six. Departure at six forty-five. We are fetching troops from Géry and taking them to Dugny. The day goes by without any incidents. I was very cold. Bed at ten.

23 October 1916

Up at six thirty. I work on my lorry until three thirty in the afternoon. Bed at ten.

24 October 1916

Up at six thirty. We are at our lorries, but with nothing to do. My friend Achard, who has been teaching me English, is leaving us tomorrow to go to another section. I am on lorry guard duty this evening from nine until midnight. I stay until eleven fifteen, as I have had enough. Bed at eleven thirty.

25 October 1916

Up at six thirty. At our lorries at seven thirty, where there is still nothing for us to do. In the afternoon, we are accompanied by the lieutenant to a field to do some running and limbering-up exercises. It is quite pleasant, but very tiring. On top of which, it is raining, and we return at ten to five soaked to the skin. I study a bit of English with Achard in the evening and go to bed at ten.

26 October 1916

Up at six thirty. At seven thirty we are at the lorries. We fiddle around all morning. We are made to clean out a new barracks in the afternoon. After dinner, I work a bit on my English alone, so that I don't lose what I've learned. Bed at ten.

27 October 1916

Up at six thirty. At seven thirty, we are at our lorries where there is nothing to do. In the afternoon, there is a third vaccination session, and I don't even bother with it. We stay in our room for the rest of the day because of the rain. In the evening after supper, I work on my English for two hours. Bed at ten.

28 October 1916

Up at six thirty. The lorries in the morning. At one fifteen in the afternoon, there is wood fatigue duty from which we return at four thirty. It has been raining almost the whole day. After supper, I work a bit on my English. Bed at ten.

29 October 1916

Up at seven. It is Sunday. I have a wash. We give the lorries a quick once over at nine o'clock. At nine thirty, we go to high mass. It pours with rain all afternoon. I stay in our room and write. In the evening, bed at ten.

30 October 1916

Up at four o'clock. Departure at five fifteen. We are taking troops from Chamouilley to Érize-la-Brûlée. It is still raining. I am lucky as I get the job done quickly, and we get back at three fifteen. I fill up and have supper. Bed at ten.

31 October 1916

Up at three o'clock. Departure at four. We are taking men from Salonnes to Nixéville. I break down on the way and return at eleven at night. I have something to eat and then turn in immediately.

1 November 1916

Up at three. Departure at four. We are to go to Aulnois-en-Perthois to collect some troops and take them to Dugny. We get back at nine in the evening. Dinner, and then bed immediately afterwards.

2 November 1916

A comrade and I leave together on a special mission. We are going to Rupt-devant-Saint-Mihiel, and then to Gironville. A very bad road. We are within two kilometres of the Boches. Not a single shell or even a cannon shot. We return at top speed and without headlights, but on an excellent road.

3 November 1916

I get up at eight. I had a good night and I am well rested. I work on my lorry all day. In the evening, I am keen to get to bed and turn in at nine.

4 November 1916

Up at seven. Work all day on the lorries. We are told at nine thirty in the evening that we leave tomorrow morning at five. I go to be immediately.

5 November 1916

Up at four o'clock. Departure at five. The weather is fearsomely stormy – rain and wind. We are going to load up equipment at Rupt-aux-Nonains and take it to Haudainville. On the way the lorry's universal joint snaps. It is a serious breakdown, which will stop me from going out for some time. I have to wait until someone comes to rescue me, which fortunately, is not too long. I am towed for 38 kilometres and get back at ten. I have dinner and go to bed immediately afterwards.

6 November 1916

Up at seven. At eight, I go to the workshops. The work on my lorry is going to take several days. I also have to lend a hand to the mechanics. I work there all day. In the evening after supper, I learn a bit of English and then go to bed at ten.

7 November 1916

Up at seven. At eight I go off to the workshops and stay there for the rest of the day. There is a lot to do on my lorry and I work on it without stopping. In the evening, a little English and bed at ten.

8 November 1916

Up at seven. I am in the workshops by eight. There are two wheels to take off – quite hard work. I am still there working in the afternoon. In the evening I am on guard duty from six to nine. I return. I read a little and go to bed at ten.

9 November 1916

Up at seven. I'm in the workshops at eight, where I am still working on my lorry. It is still a long way from being repaired. I am there for the day. In the evening, after supper, a little English and bed at ten.

10 November 1916

Up at seven thirty. The comrades left in convoy at three forty-five. I am going back to work at the workshops. A Boche plane flies over the town in the afternoon, but without doing any damage. I read and write in the evening. Bed at ten.

11 November 1916

Up at seven. At eight, I tinker about in the workshops, but I don't achieve very much. And it continues like this for the rest of the day. In the meantime, I am still not back on the road. In the evening after supper, a little English and bed at ten.

12 November 1916

It is my feast day today – Saint René, and it's not going to be much fun this year; once again, I shall be spending it away from my family. It is Sunday. I get up at seven thirty. At nine we are to be reviewed in uniform by the lieutenant. At nine thirty, I go to high mass.

I write in the afternoon, and then four of us go for a long walk in the countryside above the town. It makes a nice change. We only return at suppertime and I go to bed at ten.

13 November 1916

Up at seven. At eight, I'm at the workshops where I work all day. In the evening, a little English. Bed at ten.

14 November 1916

The comrades leave at six in the morning for troop transportation. I get up at seven thirty. I go to the workshops for a bit, but there is nothing to do there. I rest in the afternoon. In the evening I am on guard duty from nine to midnight. I go to bed as soon as I return.

15 November 1916

Up at seven. At eight I am at the workshops. At ten I go to the dentist, but he can't see me because I first have to get approval from the doctor. God, what a ridiculous formality! I stay in the workshops all day, but I have nothing to do and as I have been standing around in a cold draught, I have caught a thundering cold. A little English in the evening, and bed at ten.

16 November 1916

The comrades left at five in the morning. I get up at eight, and I have a streaming cold. I find the doctor on his rounds and ask for permission to see the dentist. I have lunch on my own. At two, I go to the dentist. He is happy to see to my tooth, but he is booked up at the moment and makes another appointment for me – in two months time. He could not have been more pleasantly dismissive. Who knows where we'll be in two months. I do the rounds of the workshops. I have supper alone, and then go on guard duty from six to nine o'clock. I return shivering with fever. I make myself a vin chaud, and go to bed at eleven.

17 November 1916

I get up at seven thirty. I am not going to the workshops. I feel lousy and I take it easy. However, someone comes to tell me my lorry's universal joint has arrived, and in the afternoon, I help to fix it in place, but it is still not finished by the end of the day. In the evening, I go to bed at ten.

18 November 1916

I get up at seven thirty. At eleven, I am on 24-hour guard duty at the Barthez section. I will be taking the one to three o'clock shift, and then the nine to eleven o'clock shift in the evening.

There is an incident at ten at night. Someone comes for me to help control some poor man from the services who has gone mad and who is threatening to kill everyone in the section's office. He is quickly subdued. By eleven, everything is restored to order, and I go to bed until five in the morning.

19 November 1916

My shift is from five until seven in the morning. I don't go back to bed. At eleven, I step down from guard duty. In the afternoon, I am told my lorry is out of the workshops. I am still not quite happy with it, but despite this, I have been given orders to take it out on the road again tomorrow morning. I am on lorry guard duty from six until nine in the evening, and then I go straight to bed.

20 November 1916

Up at three in the morning. Departure at three thirty. As I suspected, my lorry is not performing very well. At nine thirty, I ask to return, as it has stopped working completely. I get back at midday, and immediately take the lorry to the workshops. After that, I am left in peace. I write a bit in the evening, and then go to bed at ten.

21 November 1916

Up at seven. In the workshops at eight. My vehicle is ready in the afternoon. I take it on a test run, and it is perfectly tuned. I do a little English in the evening. Bed at ten.

22 November 1916

Up at seven. I am with the lorries at eight and stay all day. A little English in the evening and bed at ten.

23 November 1916

Up at seven. With the lorries at eight. We put them into good working order. Nothing else to do for the rest of the day. Bed at ten.

24 November 1916

Up at seven. With the lorries at eight, but there is nothing to do on them. Some pointless exercises in the afternoon. English in the evening. Bed at ten.

25 November 1916

Up at seven. Over to the lorries at eight. We tune them all day. In the evening I am assigned to guard duty for tomorrow. At nine thirty, orders to leave tomorrow at three thirty in the morning. I go to bed at ten.

26 November 1916

My comrades are up at two thirty in the morning. I get up at eight. I am on guard duty all day. Nothing of any interest to report. I go to bed at nine, and get up again at eleven to go to my post until one in the morning. At one, I go back to bed.

27 November 1916

Up at seven. I am with the lorries all day, where we are kept more or less busy. A little English in the evening, and bed at ten.

28 November 1916

Up at three thirty. Departure at four thirty. We are to collect troops from Montplonne and take them to Nixéville. We are back at four thirty. No sooner are we back, than I hear our lieutenant is leaving us for Salonika. So much the better. A little English in the evening, bed at ten.

29 November 1916

Up at seven. With the lorries at eight. At two o'clock, the lieutenant comes over to say goodbye as he leaves at three thirty. The afternoon is unremarkable. I am on guard duty in the evening from eight to ten. I return at ten and go to bed.

30 November 1916

Up at seven. At eight I am with the lorries, but don't do very much. We are free in the afternoon and go off to pick lamb salad which we eat in the evening. After supper a little English and then bed at ten.

1 December 1916

Up at seven. Over to the lorries at eight, where there is nothing to do. In the afternoon, as an exercise, we are made to walk along the canal, and then we are free. A little English in the evening and bed at ten.

2 December 1916

Up at four o'clock. Departure at five thirty. We are to collect troops from Pont-sur-Meuse and take them to Charmontois-le-Roi. It is very cold. We return at five thirty. Bed at ten.

3 December 1916

Up at six thirty. At seven thirty, we work on the lorries and give them a thorough polish. We are free in the afternoon and make the most of it by resting. In the evening, bed at ten.

4 December 1916

Up at seven thirty. At eight, we're with the lorries. I go to Nançois-le-petit to get straw, and in the afternoon, we weave the strands into protective covers for the radiators. A little reading and writing in the evening and bed at ten.

5 December 1916

Up at seven thirty. At eight with the lorries, where there is nothing to do. We weave more covers in the afternoon. A little writing in the evening and then bed at ten.

6 December 1916

Up at seven thirty. At nine, we are with the lorries. At ten, we return. We are free in the afternoon. Bed at ten.

7 December 1916

Up at seven o'clock. At nine we go over to the lorries, stay for half an hour and then go back to our billet. There is nothing to do in the afternoon. We take a shower at three forty- five. In the evening, I am on guard duty from ten until midnight. Bed at half past midnight.

8 December 1916

Up at seven thirty. Over to the lorries at nine. In the afternoon we make straw covers again. And another day goes by. Bed at ten.

9 December 1916

Up at seven thirty. Same programme as yesterday, which has nothing of any interest.

10 December 1916

Up at seven. A quick wash because it is Sunday. At nine, we take the lorries out for a run. At nine thirty, high mass. In the afternoon, we go into the fields to pick lamb's lettuce, which we eat in the evening. Bed at ten.

11 December 1916

Up at one in the morning. Departure at two o'clock. We are to collect riflemen from Velaines and take them to Regret, which is just a stone's throw from Verdun. It is alternately extremely cold or extremely wet. We return at three thirty in the afternoon. I fill my lorry up, and then I have supper. Afterwards, I write, but I have such a bad headache, that I go to bed at eight thirty.

12 December 1916

Up at five. I have been ordered to leave at six fifteen with a lorry other than mine. As I don't want to do this, but neither can I refuse, I find it simplest to say I am sick. This puts the service out, I know, but I don't care. When the convoy has left, I go to the infirmary to complain about my head. But I am immediately spotted, and the staff sergeant Lemaire, a very pleasant man who is in charge of the section, is so taken aback by my effrontery that at one, he calls me into his office. We have an almost friendly discussion while I give him my side of things, at the end of which, he completely agrees with me.

At nine thirty, the convoy of which I should have been part, returns and in terrible shape. They were caught in heavy shelling at Verdun. No one is hurt, but four lorries are badly banged up and had to be towed back. I must say, I had a lucky escape there. Bed at ten.

13 December 1916

Up at two in the morning. Departure at three. We are to load up war material at Magneux and take it to Ménil-sur-Saulx. It is a very pleasant journey and not too tiring. We return at three in the afternoon. After supper, I write and do a bit of English. Bed at ten.

14 December 1916

Up at seven. With the lorries all day. In the evening after supper, we are given orders to leave tomorrow morning for two days. There has been a big attack on the Poivres side and we have to transport reinforcements. I immediately go to bed, at nine thirty.

15 December 1916

Up at five. Departure at six thirty. We are to collect troops from Behone and take them to Heippes. From there, we go to Neuville-en-Verdunois, where we are to wait. At three, we are told that our troops have taken the Poivres side. It has all gone well, and perhaps we will not have to take up more reinforcements. At five we eat at a bistro, and at eight, I go to sleep in a barn.

16 December 1916

Up at six fifteen. I am woken by the cold. Coffee is being served in the square. I drink a quarter litre, while waiting for orders. At seven, a tourist automobile arrives and orders are given to return to Ligny at eight. Everyone is pleased as it means that things must be going better at Verdun.

We get back at midday. We fill up the lorries, and get a bite to eat. Then we go back to prepare our vehicles, as we are told we leave tomorrow. I am on guard duty tonight from eight to ten. It is pouring with rain and I am not sleepy. I heat up some water, and give myself a thorough, much-needed wash. I go to bed at eleven.

17 December 1916

Up at seven, and with the lorries at nine, where there is not much to do. We are free in the afternoon. In the evening, bed at ten.

18 December 1916

Up at seven. We work all day on the lorries. Bed at ten.

19 December 1916

Up at five. Departure at six. We are going to Regret to collect the 8th Mixed Regiment, or what is left of it, as these were the troops who carried out the last attacks. The men are in terrible shape. We take them to Demange-aux-Forges. We return at nine o'clock. Dinner, then bed at eleven.

20 December 1916

Up at seven. Over to the lorries at eight thirty, where we prepare the vehicles all day in readiness for our departure ordered for tomorrow. Bed at ten.

21 December 1916

Up at four. Departure at five. We collect some troops at Rumont, and take them to Glorieux. We leave in freezing weather and return at seven thirty, in torrential rain. We have a quick dinner, and go to bed at nine thirty.

22 December 1916

Up at seven. With the lorries at eight thirty. While I am getting my lorry ready, I am told that I leave today on furlough, and will take the train at two eighteen. I immediately get ready, and at two, I am at the station. The train is late. Everything is more or less all right until we get to Épernay, where we change trains – four hours delay. We leave again at half past midnight, and the train is packed.

23 December 1916

I get to Paris at six thirty, and I am exhausted. I am soon in the metro and at home at seven twenty. My wife is about to go off to work at Nestlé. I get myself cleaned up and go to her office at midday. We have lunch at Chez Biffinger. I visit my mother and the Galeries Lafayette in the afternoon. Dinner at home. Bed at eleven.

24 December 1916

I go to the gendarmerie at Gare Saint-Mandé to have my furlough extended. And I now have two extra days. All day spent at Joinville. Bed at eleven.

25 December 1916

Christmas Day. Lunch with my sister Marie. Champigny in the afternoon to visit a factory. Dinner with my mother. Bed at eleven thirty.

26 December 1916

Up at nine. My wife and I lunch at the Trianon. In the afternoon we go to the Galeries. Dinner at home. Bed at eleven.

27 December 1916

Up at eight thirty. At eleven, I go to my cousins at Puteaux for lunch. They have been lucky enough to be mobilized on home territory, and are wonderfully set up, and safe in their own factory. I must admit, I wish the same thing could have happened to me. I return to the house at five. Bed at eleven.

28 December 1916

Up at eight thirty. Dinner in Paris. A trip to Faubourg. Dinner at home. Bed at eleven.

29 December 1916

Up at nine. A superb lunch with the Delapraz at the Savoia. Visit to the Bakx. Dinner at home. Bed at ten thirty.

30 December 1916

Up at eight thirty. Lunch at home. Visit to Marguerite Spichiger. A walk through the boulevards in the afternoon. Dinner with the Duval in the evening. Then to the La Scala theatre to see 'La Dame de Chez Maxim's'. Back home at midnight. Bed at half past midnight.

31 December 1916

Up at eight thirty. Lunch at home. Visit to the Bakx, where we have dinner. Return home at ten thirty. Bed at eleven.

1 January 1917

The start of yet another new year. Let's hope that this one will see the end of this diabolical war, and everyone's worst nightmare. My wife and I wish each other the best for the New Year at midnight. Then we get up at eight. I go with Vonvon to visit the Aguellet. Then we go to Joinville for lunch and dinner with my mother. Back at eleven and bed at eleven thirty.

2 January 1917

Up at eight. I get ready to leave. Lunch with my wife and then the train at three thirty. A long and tedious journey. My heart is aching from having to leave my family. When will I return to them for good?

3 January 1917

Arrive at Ligny at three thirty in the morning. Say hello to my mates. Bed, and then up at seven thirty. I see the staff sergeant who accepts my explanation for my extended leave, which he considers to have been a little too long. A less than adequate lunch.

God, I am unimaginably depressed! I write in the afternoon. In the evening, my comrades who really seem to like me want to celebrate my return in style. We eat the sausage and ham that I brought with me, and they contribute two bottles of good wine. Marguerite and her sister Laure pay us a little visit. A female presence in our midst, makes me feel a bit more cheerful. We have quite a party until eleven o'clock, and then I go to bed.

4 January 1917

Up at seven thirty. I work on my lorry all morning. While I am washing it, I meet an Englishman and we chat for quite a bit. He says he will meet me later at four, to go for a beer. I work some more on my lorry in the afternoon. In the evening Laure and Marguerite come to see us and we have a bit of a sing-song. Then I am on guard duty from midnight until two. I go to bed at two thirty.

5 January 1917

Up at seven thirty. Work on the lorries at nine, but I have nothing to do. My Englishman didn't turn up yesterday as promised. In the afternoon there's a rehearsal for a military parade in honour of our fine leader Captain Barthez, who tomorrow, will receive the Légion d'Honneur medal. It is ridiculous. The town doesn't give a damn about us. At three, we all return to our rooms. In the evening after supper, I do a bit of English and go to bed at ten.

6 January 1917

Captain Barthez is decorated this morning. It is a disgrace. It's vile weather and is snowing incessantly. We are free at eight thirty. I look for my Englishman and find him. I invite him to join us this evening, with Laure and Marguerite, to eat and find the three kings in an epiphany galette. We make the most of the occasion. Marguerite and Laure arrive immediately after dinner and then my new English friend. We speak English to each other all the time. We eat our galette and drink several litres of wine. I chat to my Englishman until he leaves, at ten thirty. My head is crammed. I ask him his name. It is Mr Whitton. I go to bed at eleven.

7 January 1917

Up at eight and I have a wicked headache. I take some aspirin and then go off to the lorries. Rest in the afternoon, which I make the most of by writing. My English friend will come round again this evening. He arrives with two bottles of champagne. Laure and Marguerite are there too, and we have a real party – wine, little cakes, champagne, and a few songs of all kinds. This doesn't stop me from speaking English; in fact, the opposite as I have to act as interpreter for everybody. The party breaks up at eleven, and everyone promises to be back tomorrow. Bed at eleven.

8 January 1917

Up at seven forty-five. We get to the lorries at nine. There is nothing to do. It is raining torrentially and incessantly. I go back to my room at ten. A little theory in the afternoon and then we're free, which gives a chance to write. In the evening, Mr Whitton can't come because he has lumbago. I work on my English on my own and go to bed at ten thirty.

9 January 1917

Up at seven. Over at the lorries at nine. At nine thirty, I visit Mr Whitton, who is a bit better. I stay an hour chatting with him and then go back to my room. Nothing to do in the afternoon. Bed at ten.

10 January 1917

Up at eight. Over to the lorries at nine. Mr Whitton is a little better and thinks he will come round tomorrow evening. Nothing to do this afternoon. I write. In the evening, bed at ten.

11 January 1917

Up at six thirty. At seven thirty, I'm with the lorry to take off the wheels. Mr Whitton should have come round this evening, but sends a message that he can't make it and will come over tomorrow. So in the evening, I study English on my own. Bed at ten.

12 January 1917

Up at six thirty. At seven thirty, everyone is working on the lorries, and then again at half past twelve, because there's a review by the captain at three o'clock. We are washing the vehicles in the falling snow, which is not great fun. In the evening we chat with Mr Whitton until ten thirty. Bed at eleven.

13 January 1917

Up at six thirty. At seven thirty, we are reviewed by a new captain. The snow is falling incessantly. The review goes well. Rest in the afternoon, and I write. I work alone on my English in the evening. Bed at eleven.

14 January 1917

Up at four. Departure at five. We are taking material from Érize-la-Grande to Sommedieue. There is over half a metre of snow on the roads, and the going is difficult. We return at eight thirty in the evening. We dine at nine. I go to bed at ten thirty.

15 January 1917

Up at eight. With the lorries at nine. We are told that the day after tomorrow, we are leaving for Longeville. In the evening, Mr Whitton comes round to say goodbye, because he is also leaving tomorrow, but he doesn't know where they are going. I go to bed at eleven.

16 January 1917

Up at eight. It has been snowing since last night. By the afternoon it is 15 centimetres deep. We are getting ready to leave tomorrow. In the evening at eight, there is a counter-order to our departure tomorrow, as apparently the way is blocked by snow.

17 January 1917

Up at eight. The snow is getting even deeper. There is now about 25 to 30 centimetres. Our departure is on hold and we are awaiting further orders. At eight in the evening, we are told we leave tomorrow at eleven thirty. Mr Whitton is still here and comes over for a cup of tea. He leaves at ten thirty. Bed at eleven.

18 January 1917

Up at six thirty. Everyone is packing up for the departure. At eleven thirty, we leave. We get to Longeville at one thirty. Two hours to do ten kilometres. We have found a wonderful room which is big enough to take six beds. It costs us each five sous per day. I can't enjoy it tonight, because a comrade and I have been ordered to go to the regulator at Bar-le-Duc at five forty-five. From here, we are to take four officers who are going back to the front, to Ancemont, by an extremely circuitous route. It is outrageous that so much money should be wasted on people who already earn so much. On the way, my headlamp stops working, and makes life very difficult. It is very slow going without light. We are out all night in icy conditions. At five thirty, we take two more officers, who are on furlough, to the station at Bar-le-Duc. It is doubly disgraceful this sort of carry-on.

19 January 1917

I get back at nine thirty in the morning. A quarter litre of hot coffee, then I go to wash my face. I had no sleep last night and I am exhausted. At one, I fill my vehicle up, and at three, I return to write. I am so tired in the evening that I go to bed at eight thirty.

20 January 1917

Up at four in the morning. Departure at five to transport troops a great distance away. We are to collect them from Lavaincourt. I'm in luck; I have to return, as my back door is broken and I can't carry any passengers. I get back to Longeville at one in the afternoon. I have lunch, clean up and write. Then I start working on my lorry. In the evening, I have dinner and then go to bed at nine.

21 January 1917

Up at eight. I have slept well and I feel rested. A wash and then work on the lorries. Free in the afternoon and I make the most of it by writing. In the evening we drink tea with friends. Bed at ten.

22 January 1917

We have orders to leave at four thirty, but the door to my lorry still has to be mended (I'm in no great hurry to get it done), so I stay where I am. I get up at eight. At nine I'm at the workshops, where I stay all day. In the evening, I am on guard duty from eight to ten. I go to bed at eleven.

23 January 1917

Up at eight thirty. I go to the workshops and finish repairing my lorry. I tinker all afternoon. In the evening, a little English and then bed at ten.

24 January 1917

Up at five. Departure at six fifteen. We are taking two lorries to fetch men at Landroff and take them to Autrécourt-sur-Aire. It is a good day, because we finish the work rapidly and are back by three thirty. In the evening, a little English and bed at ten.

25 January 1917

Up at six. Departure at seven. We are to load up material at Velaines and take it to Ambly-sur-Meuse. From there to Troyons-sur-Meuse to load up more material and take it to Longchamps. It is hard going and extremely cold. We get back at nine thirty at night, and have had no dinner. I have something to eat and then go to bed.

26 January 1917

Up at eight. We are not going out today. We are having a much deserved rest. At two o'clock, there is a big military parade, to honour our sergeant Clémençon, who is being awarded the Croix de Guerre, for having done what? – For having endured a shelling at Verdun. It is a disgrace, and what is even more disgraceful, there is not even one congratulatory word said in favour of the seven drivers who were with him, and who were the ones who did what was necessary. Absolutely typical of the army. We are at rest in the afternoon. I do a bit of English in the evening. Bed at ten.

27 January 1917

Up at seven thirty. I am not going out because my petrol tank has a hole in it. I have to mend it and I work on my lorry the whole day. How cold it is. It is fifteen degrees below zero. Added to which the wind bites into our faces. At four I go back to warm up a bit. Bed at ten thirty.

28 January 1917

Up at five. Departure at six. We are to load up material at Condé-en-Barrois and take it to Ménaucourt. Just before we get to Génicourt-en-Barrois, the left drive axle snaps, and I lose control of the steering, and even though I applied both the brakes, we slam head on into a tree. My comrade next to me hits his head on the reservoir tank. I hit my leg on the steering shaft and get the steering wheel full in my stomach. It is a severe shock. I get out and see that my vehicle is smashed. The crank, the radiator, ventilator, and the engine are compressed into each other like an accordion. A little further on and we would have been killed, for the tree we hit stopped us from going down a three-metre ravine. Very fortunately, a comrade is at hand to pull us out and tow us. I get back at two thirty. The lieutenant immediately calls me in to ask for an explanation for the accident. He practically bows before my driving licence, which I have had for nearly fifteen years, and recognizes that I was not to blame. We make too many outings at once with very little time to verify our vehicles' mechanics. It is so stupid, when one thinks that the accident was due to the snapping of a simple connector pin. I am really worn out this evening and I haven't the heart to do anything. I go to bed at nine thirty.

29 January 1917

Up at seven thirty. I go off to see my lorry as I have to dismantle it. It will no doubt be taken to the auto park, where I will be issued with a new one. Poor lorry and I took such care of it. It is stupid, but I feel quite cut up about seeing it go off like that. It really is a war of attrition. I work all day at the workshops. In the evening, I write a little and then go to bed at ten.

30 January 1917

Up at seven thirty. At nine thirty, as a temporary measure, I am assigned lorry No.6 to take to Verdun. On the way at Queue de Mala, the back right wheel's stub axle snapped in two. We certainly seem to be having a run of bad luck, and here I am in the middle of the road, with a serious breakdown. I phone to ask someone to come and fetch me. Fortunately, I have broken down in front of the RVF (Ravitaillement de Viande Fraîche) barracks, who give me something to eat. I spend the night in my lorry where I can't sleep as I am frozen. The thermometer reading here is 27° below zero.

31 January 1917

By ten in the morning, no one has come to fetch me. I am exhausted by the cold and lack of sleep. My legs are so numb, I can't walk. I stick a pin into my calf; I don't feel a thing and there is not a drop of blood. I'm not sure what will happen to me. I eat some frozen bread and rillettes with great difficulty. I get a sip of wine which is frozen and that's my meal. The sun comes out a bit. I stretch out on the lorry's bench and half doze off. At two, someone comes to help me get started. We have to work to get the lorry up-ended, which takes an hour. Then we have to drive backwards to Longeville. We arrive at eight thirty. I have to pay the mechanic who rescued me with white wine. I have something to eat and go to bed at ten thirty.

1 February 1917

Up at eight. I slept well and I certainly needed it. I ask to have a rest for the day, but I am immediately consigned another lorry, which I have to look after, and which takes me all afternoon. Bed at ten.

2 February 1917

Up at five thirty. Departure at six thirty. I am going to the auto park at Bar-le-Duc to tow a tourist automobile to Saint-Dizier. I make the most of it by having lunch at a small restaurant, which sets me up a bit. I get back at three. On my way, I see one of my comrades has broken down. I take pity on him and help him back on the road, so that he doesn't have to spend the sort of night that I've just been through. It takes us two and half hours, and we don't get back until five thirty. In the evening, I warm myself up a bit before quickly going to bed at nine.

3 February 1917

Up at seven. I am not going out today-, but I have a lot to do on my new lorry. I have to solder the radiator, which is leaking. This takes the whole day and I don't finish until six. I work a bit more in the evening and go to bed at ten thirty.

4 February 1917

Up at five forty-five. I have to leave at six forty-five, but it is so cold that my engine simply will not start and I don't get going until nine forty. In the company of a guard, I am to go to Érize-Saint-Dizier and pick up some old material. However, at Rozières, there is so much snow and it is so slippery, it is impossible to go up the hill. We are obliged to put on chains and cables round the wheels. In the afternoon, just as we are leaving, I drive straight into a ditch, which I hadn't seen because of the snow. It takes me an hour and a half to get out. I get back exhausted – more dead than alive. I go to bed at nine thirty.

5 February 1917

Up at eight. I don't do any work at all on my lorry in the morning. I am so stiff I haven't the heart to do anything at all. Nevertheless, in the afternoon, I do some work from one to three and then go back and try to get warm. We have a little feast in the evening with a piece of veal and garden peas. It makes a nice change for us. This is followed with tea laced with rum. I go to bed at ten.

6 February 1917

Up at eight thirty. I am not going out today, so I can look after myself a bit, as I have caught a feverish cold. I go over to the lorries at ten, but I don't work on them. In the afternoon, I stay in the warmth of my room and write, and I go to bed at nine.

7 February 1917

Up at five thirty. Departure at six thirty. We are to fetch materials at Fains and take it to the Bévaux barracks at Verdun.

On the way, the lieutenant tells me something quite incredible. Apparently, a complaint has been laid against me and sent to General Dubail at the Court Martial. One Marius Rebatel, owner of Chez Nicolas at Joinville, claims that I made seditious remarks in his hearing, which is utterly untrue, and I don't even know the bastard. The lieutenant, who is fortunately, a very nice man, says that he will look into to it for me and keep me informed. Apparently, I called the men in the trenches:

'those stupid dupes at the front'. I have to say that I am absolutely dumbfounded by this news, and I am so disheartened, I don't want to do anything. I have something to eat and go to bed at nine thirty.

8 February 1917

I have been ordered to go out this morning, but I am too downheartened to comply. I have cried off sick. I get up at eight. At nine thirty, I go to the infirmary, and there is no problem with an excuse. I have a touch of diarrhoea, and a nasty sting on my left hand is threatening to turn into an abscess. I make the most of it and stay indoors in the warmth.

9 February 1917

We had a disturbed night as the comrades were continually coming and going between midnight and five in the morning. I get up at eight thirty. At nine, I go to the doctor, who lances my finger, which is a bit painful. I rest and write in the afternoon. In the evening, I do a little English. Bed at ten.

10 February 1917

Up at eight. At eight thirty, I go to the infirmary to have my finger dressed, although I didn't see the doctor. I go to work on my lorry in the afternoon, as there is a lot to be done. It takes me four and a half hours. In the evening, we chat by the fire. Bed at ten.

11 February 1917

I wanted to call in sick for another day, but they beg me not to as the service is so stretched. Up at five fifteen. Departure at six fifteen. I am going to Bar-le-Duc to distribute spare parts in the town. A small, agreeable duty, as I get back by midday. I am free in the afternoon and I write. In the evening, a little English and bed at ten.

12 February 1917

Up at six thirty. Departure at seven thirty to take staff to Génicourt-sur-Meuse. All goes without a hitch and we get back at four forty-five. I fill the lorry up in case of an early start tomorrow. I write a little in the evening, after supper, and then as I am tired, go to bed at nine.

13 February 1917

Up at seven thirty. I work on my lorry all morning as there is a lot to be done. After lunch, I go back and work on it some more until five thirty. In the evening, we sit round the fire. I go to bed at ten.

14 February 1917

Up at five fifteen. Departure at six fifteen. I make two trips from the lorry depot at Bar-le-Duc, to the petrol depot. It is an extremely bad road and while coming down a hill at speed, I skid and drive straight into a hedge. A slight accident and I come out of it unhurt.

I get back at three. I have a wash and I write. In the evening, after supper, we sit round the fire and talk a bit. I go to bed at nine thirty.

15 February 1917

Up at eight. I am not going out today. I work all day on my lorry until four o'clock. I do a bit of English in the evening, and then go to bed at ten.

16 February 1917

Up at four. Departure at five. I load up equipment and supplies at Triaucourt to take to Frama. It is a good trip because there is a thaw and it is not cold. It is even sunny. I return at four. I write and go to bed at ten.

17 February 1917

Up at seven. Over to the lorries at eight. We are not going out because of the thaw. Work all day on the lorries. In the evening, a little English. Bed at ten.

18 February 1917

Up at five fifteen. Departure at six. I am going to the lorry park at Bar-le-Duc on wood fatigue. This doesn't take place and I am sent back at eleven. I write all afternoon. Bed at ten thirty.

19 February 1917

We are not going out today. We spend all morning working on the lorries. At two in the afternoon, I am asked, as a favour, to go to Ancemont in the evening. I accept. I leave for Bar-le-Duc at four forty-five. But they don't need me, and I am quite happy to return at seven thirty. I have dinner when I get back. Then I read and go to bed at ten thirty.

20 February 1917

Up at seven. I am not going out today. Over to the lorries at eight, where I tinker all morning. For dessert, Madame Blanche, our landlady, has made us beignets. She really is kind. It rains in the afternoon. As there is nothing to do, we go for a walk by the canal. In the evening, a little English and then bed at ten.

21 February 1917

Up at five thirty. Departure at six thirty. I go to the abattoirs at Bar-le-Duc, and then to la Queue de Mala to load up with cows' feet and rumen. I am accompanied by a butcher who pays me in Sauternes and makes me drink until I am well away. I return at top speed and am surprised I can drive so straight. I get back at seven thirty, have dinner, and then go to bed at nine thirty.

22 February 1917

Up at seven. At six I had such a bad headache I had to take an aspirin, no doubt due to yesterday's session. I work steadily all morning on the lorries. Nothing to do in the afternoon, and I make the most of it and rest. We have a game of Manille in the evening. Bed at ten.

23 February 1917

Up at seven. Work on the lorries from eight until ten. In the afternoon, I visit the lieutenant who is leaving tomorrow. I say my goodbyes and he reads me the counter-report he has made in my favour and sent to General Dubail. He is sure that it will extricate me from this affair. Then a comrade and I make a dandelion salad, which we will eat tonight. After supper, a bit of English. Bed at ten.

24 February 1917

Up at seven. I am not going out today. At eight, I go over to the lorries. At eleven, the lieutenant says his goodbyes. We will all miss him. At work on the lorries in the afternoon until four thirty. A little reading in the evening. Bed at ten thirty.

25 February 1917

Up at five thirty. Departure at six thirty. I go to Bar-le-Duc where I spend the whole day delivering wine to the quartermaster stores. I get back at five. In the evening, I am tired and go to bed at nine thirty.

26 February 1917

Up at seven. At eight, I am at work on my lorry as it needs a little overhaul, and there are at least two-days' worth of repairs to be done. I am there all day. Bed at ten.

27 February 1917

Up at seven. At eight I am at the workshops. At about three, my lorry is ready and we take it on a test run. I have finished tuning it by four. In the evening after supper, I read a little and then go to bed at ten.

28 February 1917

Up at seven. At eight I am at the lorries where I tinker all morning. In the afternoon there is nothing to do. I pass the time by writing. Bed at nine thirty.

1 March 1917

Up at seven. I am not going out this morning as they forgot it was my turn. At eight I am at the lorries. I have nothing to do there, so I return and shave. It is raining. In the afternoon, I read and write. In the evening, we sit by the fire. Bed at ten.

2 March 1917

Up at seven. With the lorries at eight. I spend the day tinkering as there is nothing to do. We chat a bit in the evening; then I go to bed at nine thirty.

3 March 1917

Up at five fifteen. Departure at six fifteen. I am taking automobile spare parts from the auto park to the station at Bar-le-Duc. I return at five thirty. I write and go to bed at ten.

4 March 1917

Up at eight. With the lorries at eight, where I put mine back into good working order. We are free in the afternoon. Two comrades and I make the most of it and go for a long walk in a very attractive spot above Tannois. We get back at four thirty. In the evening after supper, I read a bit and go to bed at nine thirty.

5 March 1917

Up at five fifteen. Departure at six fifteen. The whole day consists of a boring service between the auto park and the Bar-le-Duc station. I return at five. In the evening, I read and go to bed at ten.

6 March 1917

Up at seven. I tinker with the lorries all day. And so my day goes. I go back to barracks in the afternoon to write. Bed at ten.

7 March 1917

Up at six thirty. Departure at seven thirty. I take materials to Guerpont and to Nançois. I return at six thirty. Time for supper, and then I write. Bed at nine thirty.

8 March 1917

Up at seven. It snowed all night without stopping and there is now about 20 centimetres. I go over to the lorries at eight, but I don't stay long. I go back and have a wash while waiting for lunch. In the afternoon, it is snowing so heavily, I hardly go out. In the evening, I do a little English. Bed at ten.

9 March 1917

Up at seven. With the lorries at eight. At ten thirty we make the acquaintance of a new lieutenant (Pelletier), who welcomes us. He seems all right. In the afternoon, I tinker a bit on the lorries and then return at four. In the evening after supper, I read a little and then go to bed at nine thirty.

10 March 1917

Up at five fifteen. Departure at six fifteen. I go to the Bar-le-Duc station, but I don't start work until two in the afternoon. I get back at five fifteen. After supper I read and write. Bed at nine thirty.

11 March 1917

Up at seven. At eight I am with the lorries, where I tinker all morning. In the afternoon, we pick a good salad of dandelion leaves, which we separate and wash when we return. We chat a bit in the evening. Bed at ten.

12 March 1917

Up at four fifteen. Departure at five fifteen. I go unaccompanied to load up the baggage and equipment of a brigade at Houdelaincourt and take it to the station at Vaucouleurs. It is a beautiful drive, but tough going because of the mud and ruts. My engine overheats to such an extent that I have to stop several times on the way. I make the return journey without stopping and I do 53 kilometres in two and half hours. I get back at three thirty. I fill up and then eat. After supper, I write and then go to bed at nine thirty.

13 March 1917

Up at seven. With the lorries at eight, where I work all morning. In the afternoon, I tinker a bit. In the evening, a little reading and bed at ten.

14 March 1917

Up at six thirty. Over to the lorries at eight, where there is nothing to do. At ten, something a little out of the ordinary. From the daily report and conveyed by our section's lieutenant, I have been singled out for special congratulations from the group's chief lieutenant for keeping my lorry on the road for forty five days without the least mishap, thanks to my good maintenance and my good driving. It is not of great importance, but I am pleased all the same. I have nothing to do in the afternoon and I rest. Later, my sergeant takes me fishing, and we net about a pound of minnows. In the evening, I read. Bed at ten.

15 March 1917

Up at seven. At eight I go over to the lorries, where there is nothing to do. It is snowing hard, and I go back to my room. In the afternoon, I tinker a bit. In the evening, we sit around and chat. Bed at nine thirty.

16 March 1917

Up at five thirty. Departure at six thirty. I am on supplies duty at Bar-le-Duc. I stay there all day and don't get back until seven at night. I eat; then I write and then go to bed at ten.

17 March 1917

Up at six thirty. I go over to the lorries at seven fifteen, and I work on my lorry all morning. We are told that our lieutenant leaves tomorrow, and we are happy to hear it, as he wasn't at all to our liking and was a little too strict. I tinker all afternoon. In the evening, a little reading, and then bed at ten.

18 March 1917

Up at seven. I spend the whole morning getting washed and cleaned up. In the afternoon, I stay in my room and read and write. After supper, the weather is so fine, we go into the garden for a bit, and then we go in for a game of Manille. Bed at ten.

19 March 1917

Up at seven. I go to the lorries, but there is nothing to do. I potter around all morning. At ten there is a telephone announcement from Bar-le-Duc that gladdens our hearts – we have advanced twenty kilometres on the Somme front. We rest in the afternoon. Bed at ten.

20 March 1917

Up at five thirty. Departure at six thirty. I load up equipment at Tronville and take it to Sommedieue. Horrible weather, as it is snowing heavily. I get back at eight thirty at night. I eat and go to bed at ten.

21 March 1917

Up at seven. With the lorries at eight. We work on them all morning. We are told that we will leave Longeville the day after tomorrow for the Somme. This puts us all on end. At two we are introduced to the new lieutenant, who seems to be very nice. We all set about packing up our personal affairs. At five in the evening, we are told that we will not be leaving before Saturday night or Sunday morning. We sit about and chat in the evening. Bed at ten.

22 March 1917

Up at six thirty. We work all afternoon getting ready and then rest up. I read in the evening. Bed at nine thirty.

23 March 1917

Up at seven. There is nothing to do. I go to Bar-le-Duc in the afternoon and load planks into my lorry. I get back. I write. I read a bit in the evening. Bed at ten.

24 March 1917

We are woken at two thirty by new orders. Some of our comrades are to leave at three to collect some Boche prisoners from Fleury-sur-Aire and take them to Arcis-sur-Aube, and then they are to go to Chervey. We will leave tomorrow at eight and will join them. Our landlady, Madame Blanche, comes up to see us at four o'clock, and we horse around with Clémençon. At five, I go and get some coffee, which we then drink with milk. At eleven thirty we lunch on a chicken, which a comrade who had been on leave, brought back with him. Madame Blanche cooked it for us. She joined us for dessert, and Clémençon offered us champagne. It was one joke after another, and the meal didn't end until three thirty. Clémençon and I take it upon ourselves to do the washing up. Then I go back to write for a bit. Later on, Madame Blanche makes us a tart, and then after dinner, joins us for the rest of the evening. We lark around and have a sing-song. I go to bed at midnight.

25 March 1917

Up at five. Departure at seven. It is beautiful weather and the road is good. We say our goodbyes to Madame Blanche and kiss her three times. What a good soul. She is so kind. We get to Cheppy at three thirty. As far as the Somme is concerned, we are in fact in the Marne. There is nothing available in the way of lodgings. Four of us find a place in a pigsty – something to look forward to. Fortunately, we find some kind people who will feed us. We turn in at nine.

26 March 1917

Up at seven. At eight I go over to the lorries and work on them all day. It is still snowing endlessly, and it is extremely cold. I can't think what the hell we are here for. In the evening, I turn in at eight thirty.

27 March 1917

Up at seven. At eight, we go to the lorries and tinker with them until eleven. Our new lieutenant who seemed so pleasant, is in fact, a beast. He has just made us a speech that he wants to see us occupied all the time, even if there is nothing to do. After supper, three of us go to a café. Bed at nine.

28 March 1917

Up at seven thirty. At eight we go to the lorries and tinker. At eleven I have orders to have eaten and be ready in quarter of an hour to load up troops at Marson and take them to Mourmelon-le-Petit. But when I get to Marson, they discover they don't need me and send me back to Cheppy. When I return, I write. In the evening after supper, I read a little and then turn in at nine.

29 March 1917

Up at seven. It is still snowing heavily. We don't do anything all day. In the evening, in the space of an hour, there are three storms. Our pigsty is flooded and we have to bail water out. After supper we have a game of Manille. Bed at ten thirty.

30 March 1917

Up at seven thirty. The others left at seven in convoy. I have nothing to do. Yesterday, we found a big house to rent for eight people (20 francs a month all found). It is inhabited by an old man, and I help him move his belongings. In the afternoon, I clean the house, and then someone asks me to help start the engine of a threshing machine, which keeps me busy until five. Bed at ten.

31 March 1917

Up at seven thirty. A few comrades have gone out, but I am not included. I potter about my lorry a bit. Later, we are given the keys to the house which we have rented, and we spend all afternoon, moving ourselves in. In the evening, we can sleep at last, sheltered from the wind and the damp, and we are very comfortable. I am tired and go to bed at ten.

1 April 1917

Up at seven. I have nothing to do, but it is also Palm Sunday and I go to mass at nine thirty. After lunch, our lieutenant, who really is a nutter, makes us go to the canal to wash our clothes. We go, but nobody washes their clothes; we pick salad leaves instead. The lieutenant shows up at four forty-five, and is furious and threatens to punish us. Our reaction is a visible show of passive force – so characteristic of our section. After dinner, we write a bit. I go to bed at ten.

2 April 1917

Up at seven. As we have nothing to do, we finish settling into the house. After supper, I write and go to bed at nine thirty.

3 April 1917

Up at seven thirty. We're with the lorries at eight, but there is nothing to do. The same applies in the afternoon. I tinker a bit with my lorry. After supper, we pick more dandelion leaves for a salad. We return and I write. Bed at ten.

4 April 1917

Up at seven thirty. Several comrades left at five. I potter around all day, as I don't have anything specific to do. I read a bit in the evening. Bed at ten.

5 April 1917

Up at four. Departure at five. We load up munitions at Louvercy station and take them to Mont de Billy-de-Grand, where a new munitions depot was set up this morning. Clearly, there is a big attack planned in the area. We make two trips and then return at five forty-five in the evening. A bit of a wash, and then dinner. After the meal I write. Bed at nine thirty.

6 April 1917

Up at seven thirty. Over to the lorries at eight, where we work all day. It is beautiful weather, which cheers everyone up. In the evening after supper, I write. Bed at nine thirty.

7 April 1917

Up at three. Departure at four. We go to the farm at Mont Frenet, three kilometres from Suippes, to load up with shells. It is a wonderful depot that has been set up in a little wood, I have never seen one so well thought out. We have to take the shells to Mont de Billy. It is filthy weather and it rains all day. On top of that, I have a raging toothache and find it difficult to stay in my seat. We return at four o'clock. As soon as we arrive, we quickly check our vehicles over, and then fry up some fish, which we bought en route, and we have a salad, which we picked. We eat at seven. After supper, I write a little, and then go to bed at ten.

8 April 1917

Up at seven. We are not going out today. I have had a good w ash as it is Easter. At nine I go to high mass with a few comrades. After lunch we are free. We make the most of it and visit a chalk quarry, which is very interesting. In the evening, for supper, we make a mouth-watering potato omelette. Afterwards, I write and then go to bed at ten.

9 April 1917

Departure at eight. We are going to load up shells at the farm at Piémont and take them to Mont de Billy. It is intensely cold. It is raining, and hailing and snowing. It takes a very long time to unload and we only get back at seven. I have terrible toothache. I go to bed immediately after dinner at nine thirty.

10 April 1917

Up at seven thirty. I had a bad night because I had such bad toothache. I pluck up my courage and go off to see the doctor. He gives me a pass to go and see the military dentist at Larry, a little village about five kilometres away. I am driven there through flurries of snow. The dentist is a very nice man, who tells me my tooth is finished and that he is going to pull it out. He numbs me with cocaine, but in spite of that, and at the risk of breaking his instruments, it takes him four goes. I practically go through the roof, but afterwards, it is a great relief. At three in the afternoon, I walk back in warm sunshine. After supper, I read and write, but I am irritable. Bed at ten.

11 April 1917

Up at eight. I had a good night because I was out of pain. I work a bit on my lorry in the morning. In the afternoon, I have nothing to do, and a comrade and I pick dandelion leaves for a salad. After supper, I write, and then go to bed at nine.

12 April 1917

Up at seven. We are not going out today. I spend the day until five o'clock, digging the garden. I read after supper. Bed at ten.

13 April 1917

Up at five. Departure at six. After a kilometre I break down. I wanted to economize on petrol by inserting a smaller carburettor jet, but it hasn't worked. I left as soon as I had refitted the old one. We have to load shells from the farm at Piémont and take them to Mont de Billy. The attack must be taking place from this side as the cannons haven't stopped and the ridges are black with smoke. It is odd though, that the Boches are not responding. Perhaps they have run away. That would be really wonderful. The weather is fairly good. We return at six. I fill up as soon as I get back, and then after supper, I write. Bed at ten.

14 April 1917

Up at seven thirty. We are not going out today. At eight, we go over to the lorries where we work solidly. We have heard that yesterday at Mourmelon, a group of six automobile drivers from our section, were bombarded and killed. We are waiting confirmation of this news. In the afternoon, I do a bit of English. In the evening after supper, a comrade asks if I would swap furlough with him. I could take his place on Saturday, and he would take mine on the first of May. That suits both of us very well. Bed at ten.

15 April 1917

We are woken at five to leave at six. I'm not part of the group, as it is not my turn to go out. I get up at seven thirty. I have a quick wash and at eleven, I take my lorry to the workshops because I need to give the magneto a little advance. At one I go over to lend a hand, and remain until four thirty. After supper, I write for a long time. Bed at eleven.

16 April 1917

Up at seven thirty. I have nothing to do all day. A year ago today, I left Nancy for Lunéville to join my section. To pass the time, we work in the garden all day long. In the distance, the cannons are thundering furiously. The attack must have started. We stay in the garden until five. After supper, a little reading. Bed at ten.

17 April 1917

Up at seven. We have nothing to do today. It is vile weather. Fortunately, I have managed to borrow a violin, which helps to pass the time. After lunch, I set about tuning it; but at one thirty, we are put on alert. We leave at two forty for St Etienne-au-Temple where we load up with munitions – crates of 75s – to take to a place between Sept-Saulx and Mourmelon-le-Petit, about four kilometres from the front. We have to make our way in a very dark night, without headlights. We encounter artillery convoys, at every second and they are loading up continuously, so there are quite a few collisions.

The attack starts just as we get a there. It is appalling. The cannons are thundering, and the firing from our heavy artillery is like a fireworks display. We hurry to get out of there, as we could be hit at any time. Our return is slow as we are still driving in the dark and are still encountering other vehicles. At last, we reach the main road, which is free of traffic, and we can light our headlights. It is beginning to get light, and we arrive back at five thirty.

18 April 1917

I go to bed at seven until eleven. We only eat at midday. It is pouring with rain. We do a little work on the lorries in the afternoon and then go back to barracks to rest. In the evening, bed at nine.

19 April 1917

Up at eight. I have had a good rest. There are no orders to leave, and we spend the day tinkering. In the evening, I am introduced to a lad who plays the flute extremely well, so after supper, we have a real concert that goes on until eleven. Bed at eleven thirty.

20 April 1917

It is my thirty-ninth birthday. We leave at four to load up with shells at Nantinet to take to Mont de Billy. Then we have orders to fetch troops from Trépail and to take them above Baconnes, four kilometres from the front. We return at eleven at night after a very full day. We have something to eat. I go to bed at midnight.

21 April 1917

Up at seven. I pack my things as I am leaving on furlough along with two comrades. We leave at one o'clock, in a lorry, which takes us to Châlons-sur-Marne and we arrive at one thirty. We wander round the town, which is quite badly damaged. At six fifty-three we jump on a train which takes us to Épernay, and from there we take a goods train to Paris, where we arrive at three forty-five in the morning. I quickly find a taxi and I am at home at four thirty. I go to bed at five and I do not forget that it is my wedding anniversary.

22 April 1917

Up at eight thirty. A quick wash and brush up. Pay a visit to the Delapraz. Lunch at home. A visit to mother, my sisters and brothers-in-law, an aperitif with Georges and Jeanne, then dinner at home. Bed at ten thirty.

23 April 1917

Up at eight. Lunch at a restaurant with Marguerite and Vonvon. A walk in the afternoon. Dinner at home.

24 April 1917

Up at seven thirty. Shopping in Paris. Lunch with Marguerite and Vonvon. A walk. Dinner at home.

25 April 1917

Up at eight. Lunch in Paris with Marguerite and Vonvon. Shopping. Dinner with the Jourdan.

26 April 1917

Up at eight. Lunch at Puteaux with Marg. I meet up with Alex on our return. Dinner with my mother.

27 April 1917

Up at eight. Lunch with Marg. and Vonvon. Meet with Debout at the café. Dinner at a restaurant before going to La Scala. In the middle of the show, I feel the beginning of food poisoning from the mussels. I am so ill that we have to leave the theatre after the second act and get home fast. I am sick all night.

28 April 1917

Up at ten thirty. I feel a bit better. I have lunch at home, alone. At five thirty, I meet my sister Jeanne at CAMA (Centre d'approvisionnement du matériel automobile). Dinner at home.

29 April 1917

Up at eight thirty. I have a thorough wash and brush up. Lunch with my sister Marie. In the evening, dinner with my mother.

30 April 1917

Up at eight. Lunch at a restaurant with Marguerite and Vonvon. In the evening, dinner at a restaurant with Marguerite, and then once again to La Scala.

1 May 1917

Up at eight thirty. A thorough wash. Off to the Gare St Mandé to get my furlough papers endorsed. Back to Paris. Lunch Chez Bofinger with the Delapraz, Jeanne, Marguerite, Vonvon, and me. In the evening, dinner at home.

2 May 1917

Up at eight. I get ready to leave. I have lunch at home with Marguerite. I leave the house at one for the Gare de L'Est. We leave at three twenty-five. I feel miserable, particularly as the weather is so good. We get to Châlons-sur-Marne at nine thirty. I walk nine kilometres alone, at night, but in the moonlight and I get back at eleven thirty. I have a wash, and go to bed at midnight.

3 May 1917

Up at seven thirty. A good welcome from all the comrades, who have missed me it seems. We do not go out. I spend the day organizing my belongings. In the evening we get together with a few comrades and eat an excellent omelette with a knuckle of ham, which I brought back with me. It helps to lift the black mood that threatens to overwhelm me. We chat until ten. Bed at ten thirty.

4 May 1917

Up at seven thirty. We are not going out, so there is nothing to do all day. I sew a bit and then write. I am trying to shift my black depression. In the evening after supper, we go out to enjoy a bit of fresh air. It has been extremely hot. Bed at eleven thirty.

5 May 1917

Up at seven thirty. We still have had no orders to leave. The morning goes by passably well. In the afternoon, we have a little music with a good violinist, and have a pleasant time. We are told that an infantry division will be passing through, so we hole up in the house, so as not to be disturbed. I go to bed at ten.

6 May 1917

Up at seven thirty. The infantry division did not pass through, and we were not disturbed. There are still no orders to leave, and we are getting bored with not having anything to do. In the evening after supper, we have a walk around town, then I come back to write. Bed at ten thirty.

7 May 1917

Up at seven forty-five. We still don't go out. It is quite incomprehensible. We wonder why we are having such a prolonged rest. In the afternoon, a comrade and I go off to the fields to pick some salad leaves. In the evening, a little writing, and then I go to bed at ten thirty.

8 May 1917

Up at seven thirty. We have no orders to go anywhere today, which is really odd. We spend the day pottering around aimlessly. The weather is not good as it s raining and cold. It is still raining in the evening, and I don't go out. Bed at ten thirty.

9 May 1917

Up at eight. I have a bit of a wash. Still no orders to leave. After a meal, I am called to the office and asked if I would like to replace the mess orderly who is on furlough. I am so bored, I accept. The job will be for about twenty days. At one o'clock, I take a small truck to Châlons. The job entails, buying food for the section as well as private purchases for the comrades. It is not very complicated. We have a little free time to wander around the town. We return at five. In the evening, I write. Bed at eleven.

10 May 1917

Up at eight. A wash, and then I go to the office to get the mess lists. I leave for Châlons at one. Everything goes as it should. We wander round town. Two Taubes fly over, but fortunately don't drop any bombs. Return at five. At six I am invited to have dinner with my predecessor. In the evening, I write and then at ten I go to bed.

11 May 1917

Up at eight. I organize my trip for the afternoon. At one, departure for Châlons, but this time in a lorry as there is a lot to bring back. It takes us the rest of the day as we also have to get clothing. We get back at six thirty. I eat, and then go to the office to make my report. Afterwards, I go out for a walk; then I write and go to bed at eleven.

12 May 1917

Up at six thirty. I go to Châlons at seven because we have permission to do some shopping at the market. I buy cauliflowers for the section and asparagus for me. I get back at ten. I reorganize everything and then go back to Châlons at one o'clock. We do the mess list and get back at five. In the evening, a little writing, and bed at eleven.

13 May 1917

Up at seven thirty. A big spruce up as it's Sunday. At one o'clock we leave to do the mess duties. It is dead in Châlons as everything is closed. I am dispirited because last evening I received a letter from Vonvon telling me that Marg has appendicitis. I am going mad with worry and can't think straight. Do I have to get old before getting more news? This bloody war and how I hate those people who make other people suffer for things they haven't done. Still, I have always had faith in God, who has always upheld me. We get back at five. Bed at eleven.

14 May 1917

Up at eight. Mess duties in the afternoon. I have slightly better news of Marg, but she's still not right. Following discussions between our landlord and Group Captain Legras, we have been temporarily dislodged, and I have to sleep in my lorry. I haven't been feeling very well for the last few days, and this morning, I notice that I have brought back a good dose of gonorrhoea from my last furlough. Dirty cow, I would like to pay you back for that. In the meantime I am shivering with fever. I write a little. Bed at ten.

15 May 1917

Up at eight. I am not well and my illness seems significantly worse. I have to stop my mess duties and go and see the doctor. He would like to send me to hospital. I ask if it wouldn't be possible to treat me here. He is quite happy to try, but as far as everyone else is concerned, I have put my back out. I have to take baths and take sandalwood. I begin the treatment at once. Bed at ten.

16 May 1917

Up at eight. At nine I go to the doctor. I have been lying down all day and I am thoroughly bored.

17 May 1917

Up at eight. Still the same treatment. Three to four litres of an infusion of couch grass to drink during the day. I am still in a lot of pain. Luke warm baths throughout the day and complete rest.

On top of this, the news I have of Marg is not wonderful. I have a feeling that she too, has caught it and may be quite bad, because no one wants to tell me exactly what she has. God, how unimaginably disgusted I am by this life, and I can even say humankind, whom I accuse of causing all my pain and worries.

In the evening, I have a slight temperature, so I write quickly and then go to bed at nine.

18 May 1917

Up at eight. I am still not very well. An event: two infantry battalions are in town – so we have to move out again. Our landlord offers us a place for three in his granary. We will not be very comfortable, but that's the way it goes. I spend the best part of the day, lying on my bed. In the evening, I write and go to bed at ten.

19 May 1917

Up at eight. I am still very weary. I spend the day quietly. There is a very violent storm at about four. The post brings me better news of Marg, but things are still not right. After supper, I write a bit. Bed at nine thirty.

20 May 1917

Up at eight. At nine I go to the doctor, who exempts me for another four days. He tells me to drink quantities of the couch grass infusion. The day drags out. In the evening, I write a bit. Bed at ten.

21 May 1917

Up at eight. I am exhausted because the couch grass has proved to be very effective. From half past twelve onwards, I have not gone longer than half an hour without having to get up to urinate, and extremely painfully at that. The doctor says that is perfectly normal and that it can only do me good. So I continue with the treatment. In the evening, bed at nine.

22 May 1917

Up at eight. I was up many times last night and this morning I am dead tired and find it difficult to move. I spend the day lying on my bed. In the evening, I have quite a high temperature. I take an aspirin and then go to bed at ten.

23 May 1917

Up at eight. I only got up twice in the night. That must have been due to the aspirin. In spite of that, I still feel lousy and I urinate all the time. Still I should be feeling a little happier, as news from home is considerably better. As well as this, Captain Legras has had his knuckles rapped and he has received orders to allow us back into our house when the troops in transit have left. We can't wait for th at moment. My temperature goes up again in the evening as it did yesterday. After supper I write a bit and then go to bed at ten.

24 May 1917

I didn't have a very good night because my temperature caused me to sweat until I was exhausted. At nine thirty, I go to the doctor. When he sees how tired I am, he tells me to stop the couch grass treatment and to start regular washing with potassium permanganate. We will see what happens. I read all day to give me something to do. In the evening, I write and go to bed at ten.

25 May 1917

Up at eight. There is roll call at ten thirty. They have played us a really dirty trick. We want to move back into our house, but the office has decided that they will move in too. As we don't want this, the quartermaster has decided that there is nothing for it but to cancel our authorisation to sleep in town, and to force us to sleep in barracks (bastard).

Our day is spent moving again. We have to sleep together in a barn and for me, as I am still feeling lousy, the outlook is not amusing. In the evening after supper, I write on my knees, and then I go to bed at nine thirty.

26 May 1917

Up at seven because it is so noisy here. I am totally put off in this setting – I have always tried to avoid living at such close quarters. I stay on my bed and read. The day is passable. I go to bed at nine thirty.

27 May 1917

Up at seven. Still very noisy and I can't get used to it. In the afternoon, the lieutenant gives a comrade permission to sleep away from barracks. I ask for the same favour, but I am refused. I am getting more and more disgruntled and that's putting it mildly. After supper, I go for a small walk in the country, but I quickly get tired, as I am still not very strong. I go back and go to bed at nine thirty.

28 May 1917

Up at seven. It's impossible to sleep later than that and no point in trying, as people are up too early for that. At nine thirty, I go to the doctor who excuses me for another four days. I don't understand why I am in even more pain than before. He tells me I have cystitis and I must resume the couch grass treatment. I stay on my bed all day. In the evening after supper, I go for a short walk to the canal. Bed at ten.

29 May 1917

Up at seven thirty. I think I am even worse today than yesterday. I can't go longer than half an hour without feeling I urgently need to urinate and it is extremely painful. The doctor has gone on furlough, so if it is no better tomorrow, I will go and see his locum. I spend the day on my bed. In the evening, I go out a little and then go to bed at ten.

30 May 1917

Up at seven. I still feel awful. I go to see the doctor, but he has already been and gone. The nurse gives me four capsules of sandalwood to take during the day, but that doesn't seem to do much good. The day drags on. In the evening a short walk. Bed at ten.

31 May 1917

Up at seven forty-five. I still feel rotten. I take the sandalwood again. Tomorrow, I will go and see the doctor. I rest all day. In the evening, I write for a long time and then go to bed at ten.

1 June 1917

Up at seven thirty. I go to the infirmary at nine thirty. There is a new doctor. He gives me a thorough examination and tells me that my main problem is a deep depression. He gives me bromide to take. I rest all afternoon. I don't feel better, but I don't feel worse either. I go out a bit in the evening, and then go to bed at ten.

2 June 1917

Up at seven thirty. I don't think I feel so bad this morning, but the improvement is so slight, I hardly dare think it. I tinker with my lorry nearly all morning, and replace a headlamp, which takes my mind off things a bit. Apparently, we will soon be leaving – no later than June 7 – to barracks in the woods next to Lemmes. A nightmare for all us to have to do that road to Verdun again. Still, nothing has been decided yet. I write for a long time in the evening and go to bed at ten.

3 June 1917

Up at seven thirty. At nine thirty, I go to the infirmary. I don't feel any worse, in fact, the contrary. The doctor gives me some more things to take and orders two more days rest. In the afternoon, I walk along the canal for a little distraction. In the evening after supper, I write then go back to the canal to find my comrades. I potter around for a bit when I get back, and then go to bed at ten thirty.

4 June 1917

Up at seven thirty. There is nothing to do. I feel a bit better this morning, and I can't really think why. The morning is so-so. We go fishing in the afternoon, for something to do. Then we are given some terrible news.

Two regiments, who had been promised 35 days rest, had to go back to the front because apparently things are not going at all well on the Mont Cornillet side. When they got to the small village of Marson, a few kilometres from here, they got down from the lorries, and refused to go further demanding the respite they had been promised. They stayed there in the custody of the cavalry.

Elsewhere, a little further away, other regiments have refused to advance. They have been locked up in a town, and they are not being fed. They are surrounded by Cannons – 75s, and only have their emergency supplies for food. This seems to be the beginning of a revolt which could spread and perhaps hasten the end of the war. In the evening I write and go to bed at nine.

5 June 1917

Up at seven. I go to the infirmary and the doctor thinks I am improving and tells me to go on with the treatment.

Some hussars tell us that some of them have been designated to go to Vallon-les-Dames, about 38 kilometres from here, where they will execute a number of men who have refused to continue fighting. Things are looking decidedly bad.

We go for a walk along the canal in the afternoon. When we get back, we hear of another incident. A general went to Marson to try to calm the troops. The soldiers, ripped his stripes and decorations from him, and then, when he tried to get back into his car, they threw a grenade. Three drivers were killed and the general was wounded. This, of course, gave us plenty of food for comments and discussion. I write a little, and then go to bed at ten thirty.

6 June 1917

Up at seven forty-five. There is still nothing to do. After a wash, I wander about aimlessly all morning. After lunch we go fishing, but it is more to cool off a bit near the water, as it is very hot and humid today. I write for a long time in the evening, and work a bit on my English, which is something I haven't done for a long while. I go to bed at ten thirty.

7 June 1917

Up at seven. I go to the infirmary at nine thirty. The doctor doesn't think I am any worse and tells me to continue with the treatment. It is so hot that I stay all afternoon on my bed and read. I go to bed at ten.

8 June 1917

Up at seven. Everyone is busy packing up as we leave tomorrow for Foucaucourt-sur-Thabas, a Meuse village in the middle of nowhere, in Argonne. Apparently we will be on munitions duty. We have to leave at three thirty in the morning. I immediately go to bed at nine thirty.

9 June 1917

Up at two. Departure at three thirty. It is very cold and foggy, and it is raining a little. A slow and tiring road. However, I don't feel too bad. We arrive at Foucaucourt at four in the afternoon. Setting up is tedious, but the barracks in a large granary is bearable. We immediately find somewhere to eat in a house with a clean table. Bone tired and with no energy to write, I go to bed at nine thirty.

10 June 1917

Up at six. I have slept well. A lot of work is needed on the lorry and there are all kinds of fatigue duties until five o'clock. After supper, for a little peace, I go to my lorry to write. Then I go to bed at ten.

11 June 1917

Up at four. Departure at five fifteen for Osches to load up a regiment of mutinous troops (the 48th) and to take them to Ancemont. From there we are to go to Sommedieue, collect the 58th and take them to Reffroy. The road is almost impossable, and we are literally finished by the time we get back at two thirty in the morning. I go to bed immediately.

12 June 1917

Up at eight. My kidneys are playing up. I work on my lorry until lunch, and then continue in the afternoon. But I have soon had enough and I come back to write and get a bit of rest. After supper, two comrades and I go for a long walk round the village. I return and go to bed at ten thirty.

13 June 1917

Up at seven thirty. I go and check my lorry, where I work a bit but not very wholeheartedly. I work a bit more in the afternoon, and then come back to write. In the evening, I go for a walk, and go to bed at ten.

14 June 1917

Up at five. Departure at six. We are going to Rupt-en-Woëvre to collect a detachment from the 7th Engineers and take them to Rozières-en-Blois. In all we do about 200 kilometres in the blazing heat. On our return, we are so overwhelmingly tired that every one of us is more or less asleep at the wheel. We get back at one thirty in the morning. I drink a quarter litre of coffee and go to bed immediately.

15 June 1917

Up at eight. We immediately set to work on the lorries until eleven. More work on them in the afternoon in readiness for our departure at two in the morning.

16 June 1917

Up at seven. Contrary to what we thought there is no departure. We spend the morning until eleven o'clock, tinkering on our lorries. It is so hot in the afternoon, that we make the most of our free time and rest. All I do is to fit my headlamp with a glass pane and then I go off to pilfer cherries. I go to bed at ten thirty.

17 June 1917

Up at seven thirty. We are still not going out today. I go to mass in the morning. It is so hot in the afternoon that we go fishing for a little relaxation. I alone catch 50 minnows. We fish until five. In the evening, we pick cherries, and then I write. Bed at ten thirty.

18 June 1917

Up at eight. At one thirty, a long convoy left. There were too many lorries. But as they know I am still quite tired at the moment, they have left me behind, and I am not complaining. I work on the lorry all day, which I enjoy and find restful. In the evening I go for a walk in the countryside, and then go to bed at nine thirty.

19 June 1917

Up at eight. My comrades returned at two thirty in the morning. They have driven three hundred kilometres. They are so exhausted that by nine o'clock, only four are up. I was really lucky. I rest all day and then in the evening, I go for a walk in the countryside. I go to bed at ten.

20 June 1917

Up at seven thirty. I tinker a little all morning. I go fishing in the afternoon until five and catch about 30 minnows. When I get back, I am suddenly hit by a raging toothache. After supper, I write a little and then go to bed at nine thirty.

21 June 1917

Up at eight. I didn't sleep a wink last night, from catching a chill to my teeth. My cheek and gums are swollen. I spend all my time gargling with warm water, which helps. At two, there is a storm and torrential rain, which clears the air, and I take advantage of it and write. In the evening after supper, we go off to pick cherries. I go to bed at ten.

22 June 1917

Up at eight. The weather has changed. It is very windy and it was very cold last night. It is raining continuously, and so we have a forced rest. I spend the afternoon reading. In the evening after supper, I pick cherries again, and then go to bed at ten.

23 June 1917

Up at three thirty. Departure at four thirty. We are to load munitions at Rarécourt and take them to Bois Lecomte in the middle of the Argonne. It is quite hard work, but doesn't take that long, and we are back by three o'clock. I immediately go to work on my lorry. Then I write. After supper, I go out for a bit, and then turn in at ten.

24 June 1917

Up at seven thirty. I go straight to work on my lorry until nine thirty. Then, because it is Sunday, I have a bit of a scrub up. We rest and potter about in the afternoon. A walk in the evening. Then bed at ten.

25 June 1917

Up at eight. A very quiet day and we are at rest. I read and write. Bed at ten.

26 June 1917

Up at seven. At eight, we are told that we are going to Germay for two days on troop service. We arrive at eleven thirty at night. Because of the dust, it was a long, tedious and tiring journey. We sleep in our lorries by the side of the road. I find some hay in a field and make a bed on the floor of my lorry. I go to sleep at midnight.

27 June 1917

We get up at four, prepare our lorries and then load up the troops (the 27th Infantry Regiment). At five twenty, we leave for Herpont. It is a hard, tiring convoy and we don't arrive until nine at night. At ten, we leave again in the dark and the dust. We get back at one in the morning. I read a few letters and then go to bed.

28 June 1917

I get up at eight; I am one of the first. I work all day on my lorry, which needs it after yesterday's trip. I'm at it until five o'clock. After dinner, I write and then walk around a bit. At nine o'clock the lieutenant calls me into his office and tells me I am on furlough from July 11 as I had requested. I am pleased. I go to bed at ten.

29 June 1917

Up at eight. I work a little on the lorries and then rest. I rest in the afternoon until five. After dinner, I pick cherries. I eat a lot and bring back quite a few too. When I get back we spend a little time chatting, and then I go to bed at ten thirty.

30 June 1917

Up at seven thirty. Work on the lorries all morning to get them ready, as we are on alert. Rest in the afternoon. The alert is lifted at three. I write until five. I pick cherries and go to bed at ten.

1 July 1917

Up at seven thirty. There is nothing to do. We potter about until lunch. At three thirty, there is an immediate departure to collect 1200 wounded men from the Hesse forest. There was a ferocious bombardment by marine cannons and there are not enough ambulances. Fifteen minutes later, we leave at top speed for Remicourt, where we wait for two hours. Then they realize they have asked for too many lorries. Ah – a wonderful French cock-up again. With empty lorries we go back to barracks and arrive at ten past ten. I am not sleepy and I write until midnight. Then I go to bed.

2 July 1917

Up at seven thirty. Work on the lorry all day. In the evening after supper, we help the people who are feeding us to bring in a cartload of hay, which is very tiring work, but at helps pass the time. I return. We chat for a while, and then I go to bed at ten thirty. Bringing in the hay earned us a glass of wine.

3 July 1917

Up at seven thirty. There is nothing to do. I wander about all morning and afternoon. In the evening after supper, we unload two cartloads of hay, which takes us until eight at night. Then, as it is very mild, I stretch out on the grass until ten forty-five. I go to bed at eleven.

4 July 1917

Up at seven thirty. We are not called out and I have nothing to do. I potter about all day, which drags. In the evening, I pick cherries and I write. Bed at ten.

5 July 1917

Up at seven thirty. We are not going out. There is no more to do than there was yesterday. I potter about all day and I am bored. I pick cherries in the evening. Bed at eleven. I have eaten so many cherries that I can't sleep. My stomach goes gloop, gloop, every time I turn in bed.

6 July 1917

Up at seven thirty. I mess about all morning. We leave at six fifteen in the evening for Brocourt, where we load up 220 mm shells which we take to the Bois de la Marre, 1500 metres from the lines. The cannons roar thunderously and the place is unsafe. We leave at dawn at top speed because we are in full view of the enemy. I get back at five twenty.

7 July 1917

I fill my lorry up and then go to bed until ten. Then lunch. Afterwards, I stretch out on my bed and sleep until four. In the evening I write and go to bed at eleven.

8 July 1917

Up at five thirty. At nine thirty, the bed installations in the lorries are reviewed by the captain – how ridiculous!! We play cards in the afternoon and evening. Bed at ten.

9 July 1917

Up at seven. At eight thirty, I leave on furlough from Èvres station. There is a stop at Revigny where I have lunch. A good journey.

10 July 1917

I arrive at the Gare de l'Est at six thirty and I am at home at seven. The door is locked as my wife is in Switzerland and I don't know where Vonvon is. A quick visit to my mother. Then into Paris to see Vonvon. Lunch at the Rue de Montmorency with the Delapraz. In the afternoon

I meet my sister Jeanne at CAMA. An aperitif and then I have dinner with the Delapraz. Bed at eleven thirty.

11 July 1917

Up at eight. I get dressed and have lunch with Vonvon at la Chaussée d'Antin. Then I wander the boulevards. I go home and then at six, an aperitif with Georges and Jeanne. Afterwards, dinner with my mother who presses me to stay the night, which I do and go to bed at eleven.

12 July 1917

Up at eight. I set about finding a bicycle. Lunch with Vonvon at Châtelet, Chez Chartier. Dinner with my mother in the evening. Bed at eleven.

13 July 1917

Up at eight. Lunch at home where I have invited Vonvon, and have made the occasion quite festive. In the evening an aperitif with César at l'Espérance, and then dinner with Roger and Marguerite Spichiger and one of her friends. Afterwards we go to the premier of Le Sursis at La Scala. Bed at one in the morning.

14 July 1917

A very quiet day for me, as I am certainly not going to the parade, which I couldn't bear. I have lunch with my mother. In the evening, I have dinner with my sister Marie, and then go home to bed at eleven.

15 July 1917

Up at five forty-five to join the others for a bicycle ride. We should have left at eight, but we are delayed by the rain until eleven. Our party consists of Marguerite Spichiger, César, two of his friends, Vonvon and me. We have lunch at Grobois. We play the fool all day. We go back to César's place for dinner. In the evening, we have music and dancing. I go home and we go to bed at midnight.

16 July 1917

Lunch at Puteaux. Back for dinner with my mother, where I stay the night.

17 July 1917

Up at eight. I get back home at nine. At midday, I collect Vonvon from the office, who comes with me to the Galeries, where I have lunch with Madame Perroud and a lot of the others in this set of women. In the afternoon, I do a little shopping in Paris. I go home for a little rest, and at seven, I go to César's for dinner. I get back and go to bed at eleven thirty.

18 July 1917

Up at eight. I fetch Vonvon from the office and we have lunch at the Chaussée d'Antin. I have a quick look round the Galeries and then do some shopping in Paris. I go back to the house, and then fetch my sister Jeanne from the CAMA. We have an aperitif and then I have dinner with my mother and stay the night.

19 July 1917

Up at eight. At eleven, I fetch my daughter, and then we have lunch with my mother. We stay there for the afternoon, and then at about six thirty, I take my daughter back to school. Vonvon comes to the house at seven thirty and we have dinner with the Delapraz. At eleven, Vonvon and I go back to the house and to bed.

20 July 1917

Up at seven thirty. Vonvon stays and comes with me to the station as my furlough is over. We have lunch together and then I look in on my daughter, and then take the train at two twenty-five.

21 July 1917

After a long journey, we get to Bar-le-Duc and we are told that the section has moved. We are taken to the new place, which is between Lemmes and Ancemont, in the middle of a field next to an airfield. Not a single tree to shelter the encampment. We spend the day settling in. I go to bed at ten.

22 July 1917

Up at seven. I work on my lorry. At two I leave for the station at Landrecourt to fetch men returning from leave and take them to the Bévaux barracks at Verdun. I return at six. I fill up. I have something to eat, and go to bed at nine thirty.

23 July 1917

Up at eight. Departure at two thirty for the station at Dugny and Fauborg Pavé at Verdun. Return at six thirty. I am exhausted, and I think my illness has started up again. I have something to eat and then go to bed at nine thirty.

24 July 1917

Up at eight. I am not going out today, so I rest. I don't feel well either, so I go and see the doctor who gives me two days sick leave, and orders a purge of castor oil for tomorrow morning. I have a gastric problem. In the evening, I walk through the fields, and then go to bed at nine thirty.

25 July 1917

Up at eight. I am still not well and I am feverish. I spend the day pottering about. In the evening, it rains and there is a storm. I go to bed at nine thirty.

26 July 1917

Up at eight. I am still not well, as I still have a temperature. I go to the doctor in the afternoon. He takes my temperature and it is 38.8°. He is surprised and says to return tomorrow, if it hasn't gone down. I am given cupping for a bit of relief. I stay lying down and then take two quinine tablets and go to bed at nine thirty.

27 July 1917

Up at eight. I am less feverish, but I still feel very weak. I spend the whole day reading and resting, as it is extremely hot. I am extremely upset because I have had news that my wife is still unwell and she is with Jeanne Delapraz in Switzerland. I am waiting impatiently for more news.

This evening at eleven, an hour after going to bed, there is a fearsome explosion. The Boches have blown up the munitions depot at Saint-Michel near Verdun. We immediately go outside and see a huge glow. We go back inside, but we hear the shells exploding all night long.

28 July 1917

Up at eight. I tinker with my lorry's silencer until midday. The heat is torrid. I rest and read in the afternoon. I go to the doctor who gives me another two days off. In the evening after supper, it is so hot that we stay outside, and lie on the grass until ten. I go to bed at ten thirty.

29 July 1917

Up at seven thirty. A quick wash and then I work on my lorry. The heat is overwhelming. I stay most of the day on my bed, flattened by the heat. At about five, there is a violent storm, which cools the air a bit. After supper, I wander around. I go to bed at nine thirty.

30 July 1917

Up at eight. I work a bit on my lorry, and then spend the rest of the day lolling on my bed. In the afternoon, I visit the doctor, who gives me two more days' sick leave. In the evening, we all chat a bit. Bed at ten.

31 July 1917

Up at seven thirty. There is nothing to do and I am bored. At eleven, it starts to rain and continues without let-up all day. I spend my time reading and writing. Bed at nine thirty.

1 August 1917

Up at eight. I go over to my lorry, which needs a lot of work. I spend the whole day tinkering. In the evening after supper, there is an artillery duel on the Côte 304 and we climb a ridge to watch. Then we come down again and I go to bed at ten.

2 August 1917

Up at seven. I wash and then eat at nine thirty. At ten fifteen, I leave for the station at Dugny. The weather is vile – very windy and rainy. I make two trips between Dugny and Houdainville fetching and carrying men going on, or coming back from furlough. I return at four forty-five. After supper we sit around and talk amongst ourselves for a bit. Bed at ten.

3 August 1917

Up at seven. I have work to do on my lorry, which takes me all day. It is raining without let-up. In the evening after supper, we have a game of Manille. I go to bed at ten.

4 August 1917

Up at seven. I am free because my lorry has gone without me. I wander about all day. A game of Manille in the evening, and bed at ten.

5 August 1917

Up at 8. I am not going out. I am thoroughly bored all day. In the evening we talk for a bit. I go to bed at ten.

6 August 1917

Up at seven. I get ready. At ten I go to Dugny and make two trips taking men on leave from Verdun to the Tour du Champ. We return at six thirty in the evening. After supper, a game of Manille and bed at ten.

7 August 1917

Up at seven. I am not going out today. I work on my lorry all morning. I do a bit of sewing in the afternoon to pass the time. In the evening, a game of Manille and bed at ten.

8 August 1917

Up at seven thirty. Again nothing to do all day. I read and write. In the evening after supper, we go for a long walk round the airfield. Then at about nine, there is a terrific storm. I go to bed at ten.

9 August 1917

Up at seven. I am not going out and there is nothing to do. I spend the day reading and writing. In the evening we have a game of Manille, and then I go to bed at ten.

10 August 1917

Up at seven. I have a minor repair to do to my lorry, which takes me all day. In the evening after supper, we pick and eat fresh fruit. We go back to have a game of Manille. Bed at ten.

11 August 1917

Up at seven. I work all day repairing my lorry, which helps pass the time. In the evening after supper, we walk round the air observation post which is next to the barracks. We have a long talk with the observers, and then we go back. Bed at ten thirty.

12 August 1917

Up at seven. It takes me the morning to finish repairing my lorry. In the afternoon, I read and write. In the evening we go out to see what is happening on the ridges, as there is a great deal of firing. We watch as a French plane brings down a Boche plane. It is quite late and we go back. I go to bed at ten thirty.

13 August 1917

Up at seven. I have a meal at nine, and then I leave at nine thirty for Landrecourt, to fetch men returning from leave and take them to Verdun.

We make two trips. The first goes without a hitch; during the second, we are caught in a fearsome storm. There are lightning bolts all about us. I have never seen – or felt – so much water. We are soaked to the skin, and as we arrive in Verdun, the shells fall around us too, and add the finishing touch to the day. I finally get back at five thirty, when I can change. The artillery is fierce and we go over to the air observation post, but we can't make out anything extraordinary. I go to bed at nine thirty.

14 August 1917

Up at seven. It starts to rain again. I work on my lorry all morning. At midday the quartermaster asks me if I have enough English to act as interpreter for an American infantry battalion. What a pity that my knowledge of that language is not enough for me to go. That would have been a dream position. In the afternoon, I read and write. I go to bed at ten.

15 August 1917

It was difficult to sleep last night for the thundering of cannons coming from the direction of Côte du Poivre. Then at eleven, a storm breaks out again and the rain pours down on us. This morning I get up at seven. I work on my lorry until lunch. It is a miserable afternoon for a feast day, as it has been raining almost without a break.

16 August 1917

There is a change of service. Things are hotting up to such an extent on our side, that furlough service has been suspended in favour of munitions transport. Up at six. Departure at seven. We are to load up at Lempire and go up above Belrupt.

We make four trips during the day. It rains incessantly and the road is extremely slippery; it is all too easy to go into a skid. I return at eight in the evening. After eating, we talk for a long time. Then I go to bed at ten thirty.

17 August 1917

Up at seven. I work all morning repairing the floor of my lorry. In the afternoon, I pass the time by reading and writing. We have a game of Manille in the evening, and I go to bed at ten thirty.

18 August 1917

Up at seven. I am with the lorries all morning. I spend the afternoon reading and writing as there is nothing else to do. In the evening a game of Manille. Bed at ten.

19 August 1917

Up at seven forty-five. I spend the morning until lunchtime, giving myself a thorough wash and general clean up. Departure at four in the afternoon for Côte 304 to take shells to the Bourrus Wood. I have never experienced anything like what I lived through today. How I came out of it alive, I will never know. We were riddled with shells and poison gas shells that were raining down on us. My friend Corporal Malfroy and I were in the last lorry in the convoy and we were to watch the backs of those ahead. In short, we were to do what we had to do to the very end, whatever the cost, and not leave until everyone had got out safely. But as the battle unleashed its full fury all around us, it certainly seemed as if we would be staying for good.

All the same, everything was going as well as it could, and we were hoping to get out of there soon, when I hear, 'Besnard, help me – *over here quickly, or I won't make it.*' It was my friend Sergeant Clémençon, who had been hit by a poison gas shell, and he was in an extremely bad way. He knew my reputation as a stretcher-bearer and was appealing to my duties as such. He is awkwardly placed and not easy to get to; but I manage to leap over to him, and see that he is not physically wounded but is suffering badly from gas poisoning. He is not easy to carry, as he weighs 103 kilos. I drag him as best I can into a ditch behind a sort of platform of earth, which gives some protection from the shells that are hailing down around us.

We stay like this for seven hours, while I make him suck mentholated alcohol from my finger, to stop him from suffocating. While this is going on, I am called again by Desbordes, one of my comrades and a very nice fellow, who asks me to come and get him as he is badly wounded. Once again, I have to jump to reach him and I drag him over to my other patient. He has been hit by a shell in his right arm and he is bleeding profusely. His face and hands have also been burnt by gas. By the light of the exploding shells, I manage to give him some very rudimentary bandages.

After a long time, the fury subsides a bit, and leaving my two patients in the ditch, Malfroy and I go off to see if we can find a way out. There is nobody around, not an officer – or man in sight. We hoist our two wounded men into the lorry. I take the wheel and Malfroy walks in front to direct me. I am sure I am driving over the bodies of horses, and perhaps men as well.

Finally, after toiling for two hours, we get to the bottom end of the village of Bétzenville, where I find my lieutenant, who, not a hair out of place, demands to see the wounded men. I see red and tell him roughly that the place is dangerous, and that he'd be better off at least five kilometres away, and I add that if he had deigned to accompany us up to where we have just been, he wouldn't be quite so calm now. He does not come back at me, but does what I suggest. Malfroy tells me I am a complete imbecile, and that I've taken a short cut to prison. But

I don't care. I'm beside myself with anger. I have also been affected by the gas, and my stomach feels as if it is on fire.

We set off again. A few kilometres further along, I see the lieutenant at the side of the road. He asks again to see the wounded men. I tell him he can see them at close quarters, because they are going in his tourer and he is going to take them immediately to the hospital in Bar-le-Duc. He carries out my orders there and then, without saying a word. Malfroy tells me I'm going to bring the sky down on my head. My stomach is burning up and I don't answer him. I light a cigarette and we set off again.

We get back at three thirty in the morning. I drink more than a litre of coffee, and then numbed with fatigue, I go to bed.

20 August 1917

I get up at eight. The pain in my stomach was so bad I couldn't sleep. I go over to my poor lorry, which is badly damaged. The headlamp is in smithereens; the canvas sides are in tatters, and the bodywork is badly dented.

At nine o'clock, I am called to the office by Group Captain Truc. Here we go; as my friend Malfroy predicted, I'm for the chop for having spoken to the lieutenant the way I did last night. Now that the incident is over, I feel a little shamefaced, but I'm not ready to apologize. But there is a dramatic turn of events. I go into the shed, which serves as the office. Captain Truc leaps to his feet and in front of my lieutenant, heartily congratulates me. The lieutenant comes over to me, shakes me by the hand three times and apologizes for not being at his post at the critical moment. Captain Truc promises that he will make this affair his business, which sets me wondering.

In the afternoon, I learn that I have been cited for the **Croix de Guerre**, but I am not setting great store by this. The fact that I had an officer with me means that he is the one likely to get the decoration. There is no justice within the military, and once again, I am not surprised. I am still feeling very uncomfortable from the effects of the gas, and I go and see the doctor, and if he doesn't say I should go to hospital – I think he must be a bit mad. I ask if we can defer it for a few days, promising myself that I would not go back to him and that I would treat myself. I am tired and I go to bed at nine thirty.

21 August 1917

Up at seven. I am still in pain, however, I think it is a bit better. At ten we leave for the station at Èvres from where we make two munitions trips to Rarécourt. This takes the whole day and I return at eleven at night. I go to bed as soon as I get back.

22 August 1917

Up at eight. I still have pains in my stomach, and I am exhausted. I learn that my nomination for the Croix de Guerre has caused much jealousy and even some loud objections, but I couldn't care less; the whole business disgusts me. I work on my lorry until lunch.

At one, we are told that we leave in five hours. We are to load up at Maison-Rouges and take supplies to the batteries above Gemainville. Happily, this all goes without a hitch and we return at three in the morning. I am so hungry, I eat until four. Then I go to bed.

23 August 1917

I get up at seven thirty. I organize my lorry, and then as I am not going out, I rest until the afternoon. At seven in the evening, I am astonished to get a visit from my friend Xavier who is with the artillery and is in barracks near us. We haven't seen each other for three years, and we are delighted. We have some champagne and I go off to ask for the day off tomorrow, so I can spend the day with him. I go to bed at ten.

24 August 1917

There is a departure at midday, but I have nothing to do as I have asked for the day off so that I can meet up with Xavier. I wait for him all afternoon, but he had to go out on service. We catch up with each other at six. Bed at nine thirty.

25 August 1917

We are woken at four thirty. Departure at five thirty. We load up at the munitions depot at Lemmes and make two trips to the depot at the Champ de la Gaille. We return at four. In the evening after supper, I drink champagne with my friend Lefèvre. Then I go to bed at nine thirty.

26 August 1917

Up at eight. I get dressed up to go to the nine o'clock mass at Lenoncourt, but there is no service, so we return. We have orders for the evening. We leave for Frama at five, to load up with 220 mm shells to take to the batteries a kilometre or so north of Montzéville, and about three kilometres from the Boches.

Because of the events of eight days ago, the group today designates me Convoy Nurse and gives me the Red Cross armband to wear. So, if we have any wounded, I am to treat them. (Now, isn't that good substitute for the Croix de Guerre?) Our service goes well and in spite of encountering a little shelling further on, we come out of it and return at eleven. I have a bite to eat and go to bed immediately.

27 August 1917

Up at eight. I fill up my lorry, but I don't do any more work on it as I have to take it to the workshops for a complete overhaul. I read and write in the afternoon, and then in the evening, Lefèvre comes over to visit. We drink a good bottle of Graves, and then play Manille. I go to bed at nine thirty.

28 August 1917

Up at seven. At eight, I take my lorry to the workshops and set to work immediately with one of the mechanics. There is a filthy, very cold wind. I work all day. In the evening after supper, I visit Lefèvre and spend a little time with him. I go to bed at nine thirty.

29 August 1917

Up at six forty-five. I go to the workshops and work all day on my lorry. My comrades have gone off on troop transport service and do not return until one thirty in the morning. In the evening after supper, I go and see Lefèvre and we spend the evening drinking champagne, then I return and go to bed at ten.

30 August 1917

Up at seven. I go to the workshops to finish work on my lorry. I work until three o'clock, and then take it out for a test run. It drives well. I return and rest a bit. In the evening after supper, I visit Lefèvre, and then go to bed at ten when I get back.

31 August 1917

Up at seven. There is no departure today. I pack up my things because we are moving tomorrow and going to Saint-André. In the evening, Lefèvre comes over. We drink a few good bottles of wine. Then I go to bed at ten.

1 September 1917

Up at one thirty in the morning. I collect men back from furlough at Rupt-en-Woëvre. I get back at six in the morning. I have coffee and then get my belongings together for the move. At midday, Lefèvre comes over to say goodbye. At half past twelve, we leave. We get to Saint-André at one thirty. We are not in the village itself, or even near it, but on a ridge in the middle of fields and in wooden barracks very much like the ones we have just left. We settle in again. In the evening, although extremely tired, we have a game of Manille. I go to bed at ten.

2 September 1917

Up at eight. We are not going out. I work a bit on my lorry, and then in the afternoon, I read and write. In the evening we walk round the village and then return for a game of cards. But at that moment, we are alerted that there are Taubes flying over; so it is instant lights out and bed.

3 September 1917

Up at seven. A bit of work on the lorries. In the evening, bed at nine. We have hardly turned in when we have to leave the barracks and sleep in the woods, as the Boche planes keep flying over trying to find us. We go back at midnight and are told that there is a departure at four thirty for troop transport.

4 September 1917

We leave at four thirty. Just before Bar, we load up marine staff equipment and transport it to Glorieux. It is a disgrace. I have twelve old bicycles in my lorry. We make good time and return at two thirty. I rest. In the evening we go for a walk, and then I go to bed at nine thirty.

5 September 1917

Up at seven. We slept in the woods until one in the morning because the Boche planes flew over again. I work on my lorry all morning. Then I spend the afternoon, reading and writing. At eight thirty, I take all my bedding into the woods and sleep at nine.

6 September 1917

I return to barracks at three and go back to sleep. Up at six thirty. We go to Heippes to load up munitions to take to Carrières. The trip goes well. We return at one thirty. I wash my face, and then I write. A storm is predicted, which is good, as it means we'll not be visited by the Taubes tonight. I go to bed at eight thirty.

7 September 1917

Up at seven thirty. We had a peaceful night, undisturbed by the Taubes. I write and read all morning. The weather clears in the evening, but I decide not to sleep in the woods, because it will be too damp. Bed at eight thirty.

8 September 1917

We are woken at four thirty. Departure at five thirty for Heippes and Champs de la Gaille. I have a second driver who asks if he can go in my place and I let him go. He gets back at eleven. I work on my lorry in the afternoon. The weather is overcast again, so the Taubes will no doubt leave us in peace tonight. After supper, the weather is so heavy that for a while we stay outside sprawled on the grass. I go to bed at nine thirty.

9 September 1917

Up at seven. It is Sunday and we are resting. At eight thirty we go to mass. In the afternoon we go into the woods to pick hazelnuts. In the evening, bed at nine.

10 September 1917

Up at four thirty. Departure at Five thirty. We are going to Lemmes to load up crates of 75s and we make two trips to Carrières. We are shelled a bit on the way. We return at four and I receive the news that I have been awarded the Croix de Guerre, with the following citation:

> 'Is awarded to Driver, René Besnard TM 77 on the recommendation of the DSA (Direction de Service Automobile). During the night of 19 August to 20 August, 1917, René Besnard showed great devotion to duty during a violent bombardment of Poison gas shells. In particularly perilous conditions, he went in search of, and pulled to safety, his sergeant and a wounded driver.'

I am very pleased, as my actions have been recognized and rewarded. We talk about it for a long time, and then I go to bed at nine.

11 September 1917

Up at seven. My second takes care of the lorry, as I have many letters to write on the subject of my Croix de Guerre. I am at it pretty well all day. In the evening, a select group of us drink a bottle of bubbly, and then I go to bed at nine.

12 September 1917

Up at seven. My second has gone on convoy with the lorry. I am at rest and I make the most of it by writing more letters, and the same thing in the afternoon. Bed at eight thirty.

13 September 1917

Up at seven. Last night, The Taubes visited us again. and they did some damage in the surrounding areas, but missed us. I work on my lorry in the morning, and rest in the afternoon. It starts to rain in the evening. I go to bed at nine.

14 September 1917

Up at four thirty. Departure at five thirty. We go to Bois des Huit Chevaux to load up the equipment of a territorial regiment. Everything goes more or less smoothly, but when we get to Hans, our destination, we are then sent to Saint-Jean-sur-Tourbe and then to Laval and then finally, to a camp four kilometres from the lines. On the way back it is so intensely dark, that I can't follow the road. At Saint-Jean-sur-Tourbe, I give up and sleep in the Lorry, and I do not set off again until six thirty in the morning.

15 September 1917

We leave again at six thirty, still soaking wet from the day before. It is still raining. After Clermont we stop for something to eat in the middle of the road, and then arrive back at ten. I get something to eat. In the afternoon, I work a bit on the lorry. I am worn out and go to bed at eight thirty.

16 September 1917

Up at seven. It is Sunday and we are not going out. I have a bit of a scrub up. It is beautiful weather and I spend the day resting. We are worried that the Taubes might visit us again tonight, and I go to bed at eight thirty.

17 September 1917

Up at seven. We are not going out today. I take the lorry out for a run. I read and write in the afternoon. We chat a bit in the evening, and then I go to bed at eight thirty.

18 September 1917

Up at eight. We are still not going out today. There are strong rumours that we will be leaving the area, but nothing is certain. I spend the day reading and writing. It is a clear day and we worry about the Taubes. Bed at eight thirty, as there is a blackout.

19 September 1917

Up at eight. We are not going out and there is nothing to do. Last night, the Taubes flew over and again dropped bombs in the Ippécourt area, but we were untouched. We spend the day reading and writing. In the evening, bed at eight thirty.

20 September 1917

Up at four. Departure at five. We are going to Lemmes to load up crates of 75s to take to Carrières. We have two trips to do, but I pay a colleague (two francs) to do the second in my place, because my friend Lefèvre is back in the area and I want to have lunch with him. We get back in the evening at five thirty. Bed at eight thirty.

21 September 1917

Up at seven thirty. I spend all morning and part of the afternoon working on my lorry, as apparently, we are transporting troops tomorrow morning. It is a very clear evening, and we fear the Taubes will be back. I go to bed at eight thirty.

22 September 1917

Up at seven thirty. The comrades left in convoy at two in the morning, but I am not included in the party, and I am not complaining. I spend my day tinkering. In the evening, bed at nine.

23 September 1917

Up at seven. It is Sunday and we are free. I use the time to scrub myself up a little and then in the afternoon, a few comrades and I go for a long walk in the woods. They are beautiful at the moment, but what a pity that they should have to be admired at such a time. In the evening, we are visited once again by the Taubes, and we are obliged to extinguish all the lights and go to bed at eight thirty.

24 September 1917

We are woken at one thirty in the morning. We are to fetch troops from Braux-Saint-Rémy and take them to Islettes. Then we take others from Foucaucourt to Froidos. We get back at three in the afternoon. We immediately get to work on the lorries, because apparently, we will be leaving early tomorrow morning to go to Blacy for a rest. At eight, the Taubes are there again, but I am so sleepy, I think that they could fall on the barracks and I wouldn't hear a thing. Bed at eight thirty.

25 September 1917

Up at four. We pack everything up and leave at five thirty. We don't hide the fact that we are all delighted to be leaving this inhospitable spot. Apparently, we are going to Blacy, two kilometres from Vitry-le-François for a month's respite. We get to Blacy at one thirty, and I immediately set about finding a barn to rent (on sight), which is full of agricultural equipment, but where two comrades and I settle in, with the sole object of getting a bit of peace. We get ourselves unpacked and established and then have something to eat. Then we wander around the town. I feel so relaxed that I can write with a clear head. Still, I am very tired and I go to bed at nine.

26 September 1917

Up at seven thirty. I slept like a log, and I needed it. I fill up my lorry and then have a thorough wash as there is plenty of water. In the afternoon I tinker about on my lorry, and then write until supper. Then there is an upset. We are told that we have to leave the barn and come back to barracks. I ask to see the lieutenant. It makes me furious that we are not allowed a little more freedom while we are at rest. I write a bit more, and then go to bed at nine

27 September 1917

Up at eight forty-five. Roll call at seven and the bad life begins. Lorry cleaning. I am at it all morning. I am so fed up in the afternoon, that I don't do a thing. I haven't been able to see the lieutenant, so we are not moving out tonight. I spend the afternoon mucking about until supper, and then we go for a walk round town. When I get back, I write and go to bed at nine.

28 September 1917

Up at six thirty. Roll call at seven. The lorries are washed top to bottom for an inspection due tomorrow. After lunch I go and see the lieutenant and ask him permission to stay in the barn. He agrees immediately, and then tells me he would like me to wear my Croix de Guerre ribbon pin. I promise to do so. He also asks if I would like to have a look round Vitry. I say I would, and he gives me leave to go on Sunday. In the evening, I walk round town. I write and go to bed at nine thirty.

29 September 1917

Up at six forty-five. We have nothing to do and I use the time to tidy my belongings. In the afternoon I help the peasants, whose barn we are renting, to hoist 70 kilogram sacks of oats into the loft. That passes the time until supper. In the evening, a small walk, and then I write and go to bed at ten.

30 September 1917

It is Sunday and a day of rest. Up at seven forty-five. I wash and spruce myself up and put on a three-piece suit complete with my Croix de Guerre. After a meal, four of us go into Vitry-le-François for the day, where we intend to stay for dinner. We wander around Vitry all day, which has nothing really to boast of. Then we have good meal at a restaurant and get back at eight thirty. I write a little and then go to bed at ten

1 October 1917

Up at seven forty-five. I potter about all morning. In the afternoon, I receive orders to take my lorry to the workshops. I have to take the whole lorry apart so that the engine can go to Vitry on Saturday. I work until supper and then can't do any more. A small walk in the evening and then, tired out, I go to bed at eight thirty.

2 October 1917

Up at six forty-five. At seven fifteen, I am at the workshops where I stay until eleven. At one o'clock, I go back again and stay working on my lorry until four. And then I have had enough. I leave everything and go and wash my face before supper. In the evening a short walk. I write and then go to bed at nine thirty.

3 October 1917

Up at seven. At seven thirty I go to the workshops, where we stay until eight thirty without working, as it is pouring with rain. I go back in the afternoon, but by four o'clock, I am so fed up, I ask permission to leave. It is granted. I use the time to have a bit of a scrub up. After supper, I go for a walk alone in the countryside, and then I go to bed at nine.

4 October 1917

Up at six forty-five. At the workshops at seven thirty, where I work all day until four fifteen. After supper, it's raining so hard it's impossible to go out. I write, and then go to bed at nine.

5 October 1917

Up at seven. At the workshops at seven thirty. I work as I did yesterday, until four thirty. I go back to wash. We leave this evening at eleven o'clock, for an important transportation of troops, which will last until late tomorrow evening. Fortunately, I can get out of this service as I am still working on my lorry at the workshops, otherwise I would have had to go. In the evening after supper, I write a bit, and then as it is very cold, I go to bed at nine.

6 October 1917

The comrades left last night in dreadful weather conditions – rain, wind and bitter cold. I was cold all last night and if it continues like this, we won't be able to stay in our barn because it is too windy. Up at seven thirty. I go to the workshops at eight thirty. I'm an hour late, but nobody says anything.

I go back in the afternoon at one thirty, where they are waiting for me to take engines to be repaired to Vitry. It starts to pour with rain on the way, and it doesn't stop until we get back. We unload an engine, which takes us up to supper. In the evening, I write and then go to bed at nine.

7 October 1917

Up at seven thirty. It is Sunday, and I am not going to the workshops. The comrades returned at three in the morning in vile weather. I make the most of my free morning, by washing and dressing with care. I spend the afternoon reading. And then, in the evening we arrange a small dinner with champagne, which is quite amusing. I go back to the barn at nine. It is still pouring with rain. I am so cold that I haven't the heart to write, and I go to bed at nine thirty.

8 October 1917

Up at six forty-five. At seven thirty, I go to the workshops where I work all day. It rains without let-up until supper. Bed at nine.

9 October 1917

Up at six forty-five. At seven thirty, I'm in the workshops. I tinker all day, but without much enthusiasm as I am dead tired. I leave the workshops at four fifteen, and wash my face before supper. I write for a long time in the evening. It is still pouring with rain. I am not sleepy, so I read a bit more. Bed at nine thirty.

10 October 1917

Up at seven. I go to the workshops at seven thirty. I hurt my finger yesterday, and ask for the day off, but apparently, there is too much work to be done and I am refused. I am annoyed and do not do anything all morning. Just to keep me warm, I tinker a bit in the afternoon, until supper. In the evening, I write. But I am very cold and I go to bed at eight thirty.

11 October 1917

Up at seven. At the workshops at seven thirty. Nothing new – the same as all the other days. I tinker until supper. Bed at nine thirty.

12 October 1917

Up at seven fifteen. It hasn't stopped raining since four this morning. I'm not going to the workshops because the weather is too bad. At about nine, I am ordered over to take a wheel off my lorry. I am furious because I have to lie on my back under the vehicle in five centimetres of water. The rain stops in the afternoon and I go back to the workshops, where I tinker.

At four fifteen, I leave to start another big job. To protect us a bit from the cold, the people with whom we are lodging have lent us a huge awning, which they normally use to cover their threshing machine. And so, in the middle of the barn we construct a sort of tepee which takes our three beds, a night table and a large table and benches. It provides us with some shelter and none too soon, because it is tempestuous outside – the wind is howling and the rain torrential. The installation of a generator and an acetylene lamp comfortably completes our lodging. The work takes us until supper. Then I write and go to bed at nine.

13 October 1917

Up at seven fifteen. It was a very stormy night, but under our awning, we weren't cold. I go to the workshops at eight and in spite of the rain, work there all day. I write for quite a long time in the evening, and then go to bed at nine.

14 October 1917

Up at eight. It is Sunday and a day of rest. I have a bit of a scrub-up and then at one o'clock, three of us go to a concert, from two to six, given at the convalescent depot in Vitry. We have great fun, and then we go back and have dinner with some hospitable people. Added to the mess food, there are two snared rabbits, which we bought. We have an excellent meal accompanied by a bottle of champagne. The evening goes on until nine thirty. I go to bed at ten.

15 October 1917

Up at seven. I have a bit of a headache and quite a bad stomach ache due to our feast last night. At seven thirty, I go to the workshops. My engine has been serviced and has come back from Vitry, and I work on it all day. In the evening we have more roast rabbit which we wash down with two bottles of champagne. I go back to write and go to bed at nine thirty.

16 October 1917

Up at six forty-five. At the workshops at seven fifteen. My lorry is almost ready and I think it will be out of the workshops by tomorrow. At eleven, I go and see the lieutenant to get my furlough papers endorsed so that I can leave tomorrow. (My Croix de Guerre gives me the right to two extra days leave.) At one forty-five, there is a health inspection. At three, I go back to the workshops and finish work on my lorry. At four thirty, I go back to our lodgings to clean up. During supper, the lieutenant calls me to the office and gives me back my papers. I go back to my supper. There is nothing to write tonight, as I leave tomorrow. I read a bit, and then go to bed at nine.

17 October 1917

Up at seven. At seven thirty, I go over to the workshops and put the final touches to my lorry, and get the engine going. In the afternoon, I pack up my belongings and at seven in the evening, I leave with many comrades. I am taking back two 75 artillery shell cases and a snared hare. We get to Vitry-le-François at seven forty-five, and then take the train for Paris at nine forty-one.

18 October 1917

We arrive at five thirty in the morning. Quickly into the metro, and at six thirty, I am home. My wife and Vonvon are both there and in good health, which I am delighted about. After the usual greetings, I go to the barber. Then I wash thoroughly from head to foot, get dressed, and we set off to Marguerite Spichiger's wedding. We take a taxi and get to the church at five past twelve. Everyone is pleased to see me, because they weren't sure if I would be there or not. My Croix de Guerre solicits many congratulations.

After the ceremony we go to Chez Debouse, where lunch is served – a buffet. We dance and have a great time. Then taking a taxi again, we go to Madame Spichiger's house where we have dinner. This goes on until midnight, by which time, many of the guests are well away. I am holding up well and my head is still clear.

At midnight, we go to César's place and drink white wine, and talk until three fifteen in the morning, when the party breaks up. The cold night air hits me, my head spins and it is my turn to be caught. I get back to the house completely drunk, and have the greatest trouble taking off my shoes. I finally get to bed at three thirty.

19 October 1917

Up at ten. I have such a headache even my hair hurts. My wife is not going to work, so we can relax. I go and see my mother in the afternoon and then fetch my sister Jeanne from the CAMA. We have aperitif with her friend Marcelle, and then I go back home. I am still quite woozy, and I go to bed at ten.

20 October 1917

Up at eight. I dress and at ten thirty have an aperitif with Comte, a friend of mine. I return home at midday for lunch, and at two o'clock, we are at La Scala to meet up with César and Jane. We have an amusing afternoon. We have dinner at home at seven thirty. I read a bit and then go to bed at ten thirty.

21 October 1917

Up at eight. We have lunch at midday and then visit Monsieur Morret and Madame Jourdan. We have dinner with my mother, where we eat the hare that I brought back with me. It is absolutely excellent. After a good dinner we return home and go to bed at eleven forty-five.

22 October 1917

Up at seven thirty. My wife has gone back to work. I am alone with my daughter who I will take back to school a bit later on. I do a much-needed tidy-up in the garden. At eleven, I take my daughter back and then meet my wife at her office, to go for lunch. After that, I visit Monsieur Jacquin and then go back home where I have quite a bit to do. Then we have dinner and go to bed at ten.

23October 1917

Up at seven fifteen. At seven thirty, the plumbers arrive to do some repairs and I am obliged to stay at home for lunch, as they don't leave until two. At six, I fetch my wife from the office and we come home to eat. I go to bed at nine thirty

24 October 1917

Up at seven thirty. I potter around all morning and then fetch my wife from her office, to have lunch. Afterwards we visit our friends the Jugery. Then I meet up with another friend, Nicolas, and stay an hour with him drinking coffee at the Hôtel de Ville. After that, I go and see my sister Marie and then go home. After dinner, we go to the Delapraz and spend the evening with them. We return home at eleven and go to bed at eleven thirty.

25 October 1917

Up at seven thirty. I wash and brush myself up, and at eleven, fetch my wife from her office. We have lunch at Puteaux, so that I can visit my aunts, who are always so kind to me. We leave at three thirty to visit Madame Crustini, and then we go and see my daughter at her school. From there we go to my mother's and then to my sister Marie where we have dinner, and stay until ten thirty. We are back home at eleven and go to bed at eleven thirty.

26 October 1917

Up at seven thirty. I fetch my wife from her office at midday. We have lunch and then I return home where I have a lot to do. At six, I go back to get my wife, and from there we meet up with Monsieur and Madame Bakx at the Hôtel du Palais Royal, who take us to dinner at Poccardi's. We have an excellent meal and we drink a toast to my Croix de Guerre, with champagne. The party breaks up at eleven and we go home to bed at eleven thirty.

27 October 1917

Up at eight. At eleven I meet up with my comrade Debout at the Terminus Nord for an aperitif. At half past twelve, I fetch my wife from her office, and find she is with my cousin Bourdieu from Toulouse. We have lunch together and César joins us at Chez Bofinger. After lunch, I pay a visit to Monsieur Calton, who gives me a very warm welcome. At four, I go to Galeries Lafayette to see Madame Perraud, and then rejoin my wife and Bourdieu at La Rotonde. We have an aperitif, and then take a taxi to the Louvre and the Hôtel Moderne.

We go back and have dinner at home. Vonvon comes back with toothache and a sore throat. We continue the evening with a bit of music. We go to bed at eleven thirty.

28 October 1917

Up at eight. At midday we have lunch at my mother's. Gustave my cousin is there and has made a special trip from Normandy to see me. We spend the afternoon together. At five thirty, we go to Monsieur Morret for dinner. We make the evening last, and then go home to bed at ten thirty.

29 October 1917

Up at eight thirty. I take my daughter back to school at eleven thirty, and then fetch my wife for lunch. I do a little shopping in the afternoon and then go home at four thirty. I meet my wife at six thirty at the metro and we go home for dinner. César and his wife come round later in the evening and we party until midnight.

30 October 1917

Up at nine. I fetch my wife at midday and then we have lunch at the Papillon Bleu with César and his wife. Victor Vidoz gives us a table in a private room. We stay until three thirty. Then César takes me to his office. At six, we go back to his house and have dinner there. We go home to bed at eleven.

31 October 1917

Up at nine. At twelve fifteen, I have lunch with Vonvon in the Rue St Honoré. I go with her to the end of the road and then to the Galeries Lafayette; from there to the Gare de l'Est, to check my train timetable as I have to leave quite soon. Then I visit Alex who is not at home. Back to the Place de la République where I have an aperitif on my own. Then I fetch my wife to have dinner with my sister Marie, whom we leave at eleven o'clock.

1 November 1917

Up at nine. I go to the town hall to get my sugar rations book and then on to the station to have my leave papers endorsed. I say my goodbyes to César and go home to find Edmond who has a forty-eight hour furlough. Then Vincent and Guite who have returned from their honeymoon, come round to say hello. We have lunch at midday. In the evening, we have dinner with my mother, and then go home at eleven o'clock.

2 November 1917

Up at seven. I dress quickly. At eight, I say goodbye to Vonvon and then leave with my wife and daughter. We drop Nysette off at her school and then go to the Gare de l'Est where my brother-in-law Edmond is waiting for me. At nine thirty, he leaves me.

At five past ten, we leave Paris. I have a good journey to Vitry-le-François and get there at three. At three forty-five, I am at Blacy, and my comrades give me a warm reception. I learn that there have been many medical examinations and that I have to have one too in view of our possible departure to Salonika. We will see.

I also learn that our chief, Captain de Fontenilliat, wants to make sure that every man has his due and to that end, I am to be officially decorated tomorrow, in front of 250 men. I could have done without all this formality, and I am a little dazed. I set up my bed and have supper with a comrade. I can feel an immense black mood hanging over me. I write for a long time, and then make myself go to bed at nine thirty.

3 November 1917

I get up at eight, stupefied from so much sleep. But how different it is from sleeping at home. I get dressed and get ready for the parade. We leave at one o'clock in our lorries, for Vitry-le-François.

At two o'clock in the main square, and with the infantry band playing, I am officially decorated by Captain de Fontenilliat. As he is attaching the Cross, the pin is a little blunt and won't go through the cloth, and he says. *'You have a thick skin, old boy.'* To which I reply. *'Sir, I have not always been with the automobiles.'* and he says, *'I know. It shows, and I congratulate you.'* And although I am not fond of pomp and ceremony, I have to admit, I am extremely moved.

It is all over quite quickly and we return to Blacy at two thirty. I offer champagne to all my comrades who are delighted and also much moved. And so I have won a bit more appreciation from my comrades and my chiefs. After supper, we go over to our landlady, Madame Arnoult, and I give her two bottles of champagne. Then I turn in at ten.

4 November 1917

It is Sunday and I have nothing to do. I get up at eight. Immediately after lunch, I offer champagne to eight comrades who weren't with us yesterday. We go to a concert at the convalescent depot at Vitry. It is very good. We come away at six and a lot of us have dinner together. We have an amusing evening until ten. I go back and write until eleven and then go to bed at eleven thirty.

5 November 1917

Up at eight thirty. I get dressed slowly to kill time. After lunch I make cigarettes with a little cigarette rolling device that I brought from home, and then I tinker about on my lorry. Afterwards, I visit a comrade from the section next to us. In the evening after dinner, I write a bit and then go to bed at nine.

6 November 1917

Up at eight. I get dressed and go and try out a lorry. In the afternoon, there is wood fatigue duty, which goes on until two thirty. After supper a few of us go to the café for a beer. I return at eight thirty to write. I am not sleepy and I read until nine thirty. I go to bed at ten.

7 November 1917

Up at nine. I dress and then have a meal. In the afternoon I make cigarettes to kill time. For dinner, in the evening, we have two partridges, which a comrade brought back from the Ardèche. So four of us get together for a little feast with champagne. It ends at nine thirty. I write and then go to bed at ten.

8 November 1917

Up at eight thirty. I potter around until lunch. In the afternoon, it is very cold and I work a bit on my lorry to warm up. In the evening after supper, we have a game of Manille. Bed at nine thirty.

9 November 1917

Up at eight. I work a bit on my lorry. After lunch, it pours with rain, and the afternoon is spent sitting around and talking. After supper, I write and then go to bed at nine.

10 November 1917

Up at eight. I wander about until lunch. It is still raining. More mucking about in the afternoon. One of our comrades is being sent to Salonika on the fifteenth. After supper, someone comes to tell me that I am on duty tomorrow and will leave at six o'clock. I go to bed at nine.

11 November 1917

Up at five thirty. Departure at six. We go to Vitry-en-Perthois where we load up collapsible wooden barracks, and take them to Jussecourt. We get back to Vitry-en-Perthois at eleven and then set off again for Charmont and return to Blacy at six forty-five. On the way, Captain Truc, shakes me by the hand and congratulates me on receiving the Croix de Guerre. I thank him most sincerely. At seven, I eat, then write and go to bed at nine.

12 November 1917

Up at eight. It is my feast day. Once again, I have to spend it far from my family. Ah well – I work on my lorry. At about ten, we are told to make ready as we will leave at the end of the week for Aisne or to the Meuse.

At about five in the evening, we are told that we are leaving tomorrow morning and are going in the Verdun direction. We are all upset. At six, it is official. We definitely leave tomorrow at eight – only two groups of us. One group will go to Fère-en-Tardenois, and the other to Villers-Cotterêts. Immediately after supper, I pack my belongings and go to bed at ten.

13 November 1917

Up at five thirty. I load wood for the kitchen into my lorry. We leave at top speed at eight. Just before Épernay, I break down. I check and see that the magneto's carbon brushes have completely burnt out, and it is impossible to carry on alone. Fortunately, one of my good comrades from the Ardèche tows me, but we have to go so slowly that we lose the convoy, and only get to our destination at Villers-sur-Fère when it is pitch dark.

I have something to eat, but we are very unsettled and go to a café for a glass of wine, and then return to sleep. We are lodged in wooden barracks that are extremely cold, but being so tired, we will no doubt sleep. I go to bed at nine.

14 November 1917

I get up at eight. I slept but I was cold. We set about settling in. It is so foggy we can't even see each other. There is fatigue duty all day. We look for a room to rent. Someone tells us about one, which we will probably take tomorrow. After supper, I write, but it is too cold and I go to bed at nine.

15 November 1917

Up at eight. I was not warm last night. After lunch, I am on fatigue duty in the workshops until four. We have found a room to rent for three people, and we hope to move in tomorrow. After supper, I write a bit and go to bed at nine.

16 November 1917

Up at eight. I potter all morning. In the afternoon, we move as we have rented a large room from a potty old boy who fortunately, is not there during the day. In the evening, we make a good fire, which makes us feel better. After supper, I write. Bed at ten.

17 November 1917

Up at eight. We slept well in our new lodgings. I get the coffee. At eight thirty, I'm with the lorries where I tinker a bit. At eleven thirty, the lieutenant calls us all together, and forbids us to sleep in town. I immediately take him aside and get permission for my comrades and me to stay where we are. I tinker around on my lorry in the afternoon. After supper, we make a good fire and I spend the evening writing. Then I go to bed at nine thirty.

18 November 1917

I am woken at four thirty with orders to leave at seven. I get up at five forty-five. At seven, two lorries leave for Nesles to load up baggage and equipment belonging to a divisionary group of stretcher-bearers, which we take to Le Charmel about fifteen kilometres from there. It is a short trip and goes without a hitch. We get back at three thirty in the afternoon. I scrub up a bit, which I didn't have time for this morning. We have good fire going in our room. I warm myself up and then have supper. Afterwards I write a bit and then go to bed at nine.

19 November 1917

Up at eight. I work on my lorry all morning. I rest in the afternoon. After supper at seven o'clock, someone comes to tell us that we are to assemble at eight for extra petrol and oil as we will leave in the night on a major troop transportation. There will be about four or five hundred kilometres to cover. I immediately do some writing and then go to bed at nine.

20 November 1917

We are woken at six for a departure at seven. We only leave at eight thirty for Fère-en-Tardenois, to get petrol. In the meantime, we receive another order that we are leaving the area altogether. A few of us go off to collect all our bedding and personal belongings. We load up with extra fuel, and we only leave at three in the afternoon. We have to follow the convoy of lorries carrying troops and provide a fuel service if needed. We travel through a pitch black night, bringing up to the rear of a convoy, and go first to Soissons, then back to Vic-sur-Aisne via Compiègne and Noyon, and then we stop at Esmery at three thirty in the morning.

On the way, a lorry catches fire, and the incident has created such a furore that we are forbidden to sleep in our vehicles. We look for a gîte and find an unpleasant corner in a barn whose roof is full of holes. The Boches have destroyed everything here. Fully dressed, we sleep more ore less well until seven o'clock. We set off again at eight.

21 November 1917

We stop at a little adjacent village where we supply fuel to the passing lorries. We do not yet know when we are to leave here or where we are going next. It is still pouring with rain. At three, we are ordered to take four lorries to help out four others that have broken down two kilometres beyond Vic-sur-Aisne. We leave in the pitch dark and tow the lorries back at four thirty in the morning. I stay where I am in my seat and sleep without waking until seven thirty.

22 November 1917

We spend the day settling in even though we don't know if we will be here for any length of time. We find a barracks with wireframe bunks. I move in at seven thirty and sleep.

23 November 1917

Up at seven. I was cold all night and the bunk's wire has given me backache. We work on the lorries all day in case we have to suddenly leave. We have found a shack that will do to sleep in. Seven of us move in. At four in the afternoon, we receive an order to pack up and be ready to leave in an hour. We put everything back in the lorries. By eight o'clock, there are still no further orders to leave, and we sleep in our lorries.

24 November 1917

Up at eight. I didn't sleep too badly. In spite of the hasty orders, we were not disturbed during the night. At nine, I take my lorry on water fatigue. I spend the afternoon tinkering and settling in. There are still rumours of an imminent departure. I take my bed back to the shack, but in case we are suddenly called out, we have to keep all our equipment with us. After supper, I write. There is a howling wind and it is pouring with rain. I go to bed at nine

25 November 1917

Up at seven thirty. We have had very little sleep because of the tempestuous wind and rain. But at least I wasn't cold. I spend the day tinkering. Departure is imminent – but we still don't leave. At eight o'clock, it is so cold, that I go to bed.

26 November 1917

Up at eight. I was cold last night and it is freezing outside. As soon as we are up, we hunt around in the ruins to find a woodstove, which we find without difficulty. Then I work on my lorry. In the afternoon, we set our stove up and rapidly install it with a makeshift flue. We find oak beams, and soon have a fire so hot it is unbearable. I spend the rest of the afternoon tinkering. After supper, I write and while the rain rages outside, we spend a comfortable moment next to our fire. I go to bed at nine.

27 November 1917

Up at eight fifteen. It is still pouring with rain. I rest all morning. In the afternoon we are officially notified that we leave the village tomorrow, but we don't know at what time. There are rumours going around, probably well-founded, that there is to be a troop transport and that we will leave at some point during the night. We immediately pack up all our baggage and equipment and then return to our shack to our red-hot stove. I write in haste and go to bed at nine.

28 November 1917

Up at midnight. We leave at one to collect some troops at Estrées-en-Chaussée in the English sector. My magneto causes a short breakdown on the way. I do not have any troops with me as my lorry was not needed. We take the troops to Estrées-Saint-Denis, behind Compiègne.

On our way back, just as we are leaving the small village of Champien, the tie rod on the steering column snaps, and I can no longer drive. The lieutenant wishes me a good evening and leaving me and a corporal by the side of the road, promises to have me out of there first thing in the morning. As we have all our equipment with us, we set our beds up in the lorry and go to bed at midnight.

29 November 1917

Knocked out by fatigue, we slept like logs. We get up at eight and have a breakfast of corned beef. Then, while I am waiting for the mechanic, I get everything set up for him. By half past twelve, no one has turned up. At two, someone comes to get us and at three, we set off and are back at camp by three thirty.

We have just arrived, when a young lieutenant who is in charge of the transport, warns me that he has condemned me to four days confinement at the police station, for being rude to him the night before. I am livid and argue the toss, and prove to him that it was quite the other way round and that his behaviour towards me had been unacceptable. He tore up the punishment docket there and then. At six, we receive warning to be on the alert for another departure, and we are obliged to sleep in our lorries fully dressed, which I do at nine thirty.

1 December 1917

Up at eight, and we were not called out. I spend the day tinkering. At six in the evening, we are put on alert again, which I ignore. I get undressed and go to bed.

2 December 1917

Up at eight. We were not called out in spite of the alert. Spent the day mucking about. In the evening after supper, I write and then sleep at nine thirty.

3 December 1917

Up at eight thirty. It was very cold last night and there was quite a hard freeze. Another day spent mucking about. I read and write in the evening. Bed at nine.

4 December 1917

Up at eight thirty. At midnight, some Taubes flew over the region. There were no incidents here, but six kilometres away at Ham, we learn that five men have been killed and that the railway line has been cut in many places. The day is uneventful. In the evening, it is so cold, I go to bed at nine.

5 December 1917

Up at eight fifteen. The Taubes bothered us from midnight to four in the morning. We are still not going out. We learn that the bombing of Ham last night was so severe, that staff headquarters are moving out tonight. After lunch, we have to thaw out the water pumps which are frozen. In the evening after supper, I write. Bed at nine.

6 December 1917

Up at eight. We are not going out and there is nothing to do. There is an inspection at three thirty, by a staff officer – a total idiot – who finds fault with everything. It is disgraceful. After supper, I write. Bed at nine.

7 December 1917

Up at eight fifteen. Still nothing to do. I potter around all day. We were bombarded last night. After supper, we wait around for our letters, which are late. They arrive at eight. Bed at nine.

8 December 1917

Up at eight fifteen. I find things to do all morning. At three, there is a minor alert, and every one has to go to their lorries, as there is an inspection by another officer Captain Colau. It all goes well and we are free at four. After supper, I write, and go to bed at nine.

9 December 1917

Up at eight. It rained all last night and is still raining this morning. I have a bit of a scrub up as it is Sunday. It is a boring day. After supper, one of the comrades entertains us with monologues and imitations, which whiles away part of the evening. Bed at nine thirty.

10 December 1917

Up at eight. The weather has improved. There is nothing to do all day. This is becoming really tedious. I write and then go to bed at nine.

11 December 1917

Up at seven thirty. I am on wood fatigue. We fetch it from above Libermont. It is below freezing and it is very cold. The afternoon is spent in unalleviated boredom. After supper, I write and go to bed at nine.

12 December 1917

Up at eight fifteen. We wait the whole morning for a general who is coming to review us. In the end, he doesn't come. Tonight, the cannons are firing heavily on Saint-Quentin, and we expect to be called out. A little writing and bed at nine thirty.

13 December 1917

Up at eight fifteen. The cannons were thundering loudly all night. Nevertheless, we weren't called out. A comrade and I make a rice cake in the afternoon, which we all enjoy later on at supper. Bed at nine.

14 December 1917

Up at eight fifteen. There is nothing to do. I spend my time darning my socks. After supper, I write. Bed at nine.

15 December 1917

Up at eight. There is still nothing to do as we are not going out. I spend the day sawing wood to warm up a bit. I write and go to bed at nine thirty.

16 December 1917

Up at eight fifteen. A bit of a scrub up as it's Sunday. In the afternoon, a few of us go for a walk of about eight kilometres (there and back) to a farm where they practice mechanized agriculture. But it is so cold, we don't stay and come straight back again.

When we get back we hear we may be leaving for Alsace, but nothing is official yet. It is extremely cold and our little stove barely warms us. I go to bed at nine thirty.

17 December 1917

Up at eight. There was a gale all last night and we reckon the snow to be about 30 centimetres deep. We have to shovel the roads around the lorries. There is still talk of our leaving tomorrow. But this evening we have had no official orders. I write a bit and go to bed at nine.

18 December 1917

Up at eight. There is still talk of a departure. In the afternoon, we receive an official order. We leave the day after tomorrow at midnight, and we will take the train to either Mondidier-les-Vosges, or to Italy. Whichever it is, we are definitely leaving. After supper, I write. The Taubes fly over and drop their bombs not very far from us. They bother us until eight thirty. Anyway, I go to bed at nine.

19 December 1917

Up at eight. We spend the entire day packing up. We are at it non-stop. It is official; we leave tomorrow morning at seven for Longueau, where we will board the train on Friday at ten. We have supper at four thirty. Then I write. I go to bed at nine.

20 December 1917

Up at five. Departure at eight. We drive the whole way through snow. In some places it is over a metre deep. There are Boche prisoners everywhere clearing the roads. There are two groups ahead of us who left yesterday, but who hold us up to such an extent that we don't arrive at Villers-Bretonneux until ten at night. We are told to sleep in our lorries on the side of the road.

We leave at nine tomorrow morning. I settle in, as I am extremely tired. I miss my footing and fall so hard that I hurt my wrist quite badly. I have been speaking English throughout the journey, as we are in these good fellows' sector. I go to bed at ten.

21 December 1917

Up at seven. We get ready, but do not leave until nine. We arrive at Longueau at midday. The station is so crowded that we are ordered to bypass it and go into Amiens. We park our vehicles in the Boulevard du Cange, and then at number 69, we find a kind woman who will feed us in the warmth of her kitchen. We then walk around the town. We visit the cathedral and the main streets, which are very elegant. We go back for supper at five and learn that we will not be leaving before the day after tomorrow at five o'clock in the morning. An hour later, we are told that we leave tomorrow at five o'clock in the morning. We eat and I go to bed at nine thirty.

22 December 1917

Up at three. Departure at five. We go 500 metres and are then told that we will not be leaving until ten thirty. We go to the station at Longueau and start embarking. All goes well. We leave at ten past four. There are four of us sleeping in my lorry, which is rocked by the train, and it is extremely cold. We manage to sleep in spite of it. S

uddenly, someone wakes us and tells us that our wagon is on fire caused by friction. I look outside and see that we are at Pantin, a step away from Paris. We are left on a siding and the train goes on without us. It is four in the morning and we go back to sleep.

23 December 1917

I get up at seven thirty. At eight I go to a bistro and telephone the Delapraz to tell my wife to join me here. I wait for her in vain, because by five to eleven, our wagon has been repaired and we are attached to another train. We are frozen, but the night is more or less bearable, and we manage to sleep fairly well.

24 December 1917

It is seven thirty in the morning. We have arrived at Thaon-les-Vosges, a place that I knew well at the beginning of the war when I was with the infantry. We disembark here and go to the outskirts of Igney village. Three of us immediately set off and find a small room for five sous each per day, and we move in with our beds. Then, we are allowed to eat in a large, well-heated kitchen. The Maillard are a kindly family of four – a father and a mother, whom I immediately dub Grandma. Their eldest daughter is married and pregnant. I can never remember her name, but for some reason I call her Sidonie. Their younger daughter is a beautiful girl of eighteen, who sadly, is dying of tuberculosis. We eat, but afterwards, I am so tired I can only write a few hasty words before going to bed at nine.

25 December 1917

It is Christmas day. Up at eight. I slept well and I needed it. I dress and at ten we go to mass at the military base. It is a sung mass and very well done. After the service we go for a glass of white wine with our landlord. For lunch, our landlady has made a big dish of red cabbage coleslaw, and for dessert she serves us a tart and other little delicacies. We spend the rest of the afternoon chatting sociably. For dinner, a comrade brings a chicken to which we add a tin of peas and a bottle of champagne. More chat and then we turn in at ten.

26 December 1917

Up at seven. At seven thirty, I have fuel fatigue at Épinal. It is very cold. It is snowing and freezing. We get back at midday. In the afternoon, I stay in the warmth and write. In the evening, we have hot wine with our hosts. I go to bed at ten.

27 December 1917

Up at eight. I spend the whole morning getting myself cleaned up. I write in the afternoon. In the evening, we have the contents of a food parcel, which was sent to one of the comrades – a delicious chicken stuffed with olives. After supper, I write some more and then go to bed at nine thirty.

28 December 1917

Up at eight. It is snowing in earnest. We have been ordered to attend assembly, which we are not happy about. In the afternoon, we clear the snow in the streets until two thirty. After supper, we have hot wine with our hosts, who have made baked apples to mark the departure of our friend Espie, who is going back to the interior. I write a little and then go to bed at ten.

29 December 1917

Up at six. Three of us accompany our friend Philippe. It is impossible to get my lorry started, so we have to give up and we take his belongings and go with him on foot to Thaon. We return at ten. I spend the afternoon writing in the warmth. In the evening, we make hot wine. I go to bed at ten thirty.

30 December 1917

Up at eight. A quick scrub up and then I go to mass at ten. It is a beautiful day and in the afternoon, I go for a walk in the country, even though the snow is twenty centimetres deep. I return at three, and then I write. In the evening after supper, we chat a bit. I go to bed at ten.

31 December 1917

Up at eight fifteen. The morning goes by quickly. In the afternoon, I chop up wood, and then write. After supper, the young invalid of the house comes to chat to us and stays for a long while.

1 January 1918

I wake up at seven thirty. At eight o'clock, Madame Müller (Sidonie) comes into the room to kiss me and to wish me a happy New Year. I am still in bed, and she takes advantage of me by putting a snowball in my bed. A charming joke, which isn't in the least amusing as it has forced me to get out of bed.

The good wishes go on all morning. There is nothing more trying than having to respond to whole lot of strangers, when on this of all days, one would rather be kissing one's own family. I go to high mass at the military base, and it is very well sung. After lunch we go for a walk in the countryside, but it is so cold that after an hour we return. After supper, we go to our hosts, eat cake, and go a bit mad until eleven thirty. When I go to bed at midnight, I find a handful of salt in my bed, so I have to remake it. They really do have a very strange notion of jokes in this part of the world. I get back to bed at half past twelve.

2 January 1918

Up at eight forty-five. After lunch, my comrades and I visit a textile factory, which is very interesting. When I get back, I write. After supper, we join our hosts for cake and champagne, which we had received as part of our New Year's Day rations. I go to bed at ten thirty.

3 January 1918

Up at nine. At two in the morning I had a painful attack of diarrhoea. After breakfast, we turn the engines of our lorries to warm them up a bit. In the afternoon after lunch, I write some more. Afterwards we talk for a while and then I go to bed at ten.

4 January 1918

Up at eight. It is extremely cold and is exactly 20 degrees below zero. We spend the morning chopping wood. I potter around in the afternoon. After supper, I write. We chat for a bit, and then I go to bed at ten thirty.

5 January 1918

Up at eight thirty. The morning goes by fast. I have asked permission to go to Thaon this afternoon. Alex and I buy an Epiphany cake from Mademoiselle Thérèse Montaron, with whom I have renewed my acquaintance. Then we make a few more purchases and return for supper. After supper, I write. Bed at ten.

6 January 1918

Up at eight. At ten, I go to mass. After lunch, I write a bit, and then we share our Epiphany cake with our hosts and the charming wife of one of our comrades, Lauzeral. She was able to come up here for a few days. She is very vivacious, and I behave with my usual zest; we have a lot of fun together, and there is with much laughter. I go to bed at eleven.

7 January 1918

Up at seven. I have wood fatigue at seven thirty. We have only gone half way, when we are made to turn back, as wood is not given out on a Monday. (Very professional not to have realized that.) In the afternoon we visit the textile factory again, and in more detail. I find it very interesting. After supper, I write. We talk, and then I go to bed at ten

8 January 1918

I get up at seven. An amazing sight – outside the snow is 30 centimetres deep. Nevertheless, we still have to do wood fatigue. It is really hard going as the snow is 40 centimetres deep in the forest. In the afternoon, we clear the snow from around our lorries. Then we visit Madame Lauzeral between four and five, who offers us champagne and cakes. She is the most charming person. After supper, I write and go to bed at nine thirty.

9 January 1918

Up at eight forty-five. I am very tired because I have caught a cold. It is still snowing. I don't do anything all day. After supper, I write, and we talk. I go to bed at ten.

10 January 1918

Up at eight thirty. The wind has blown the snow in drifts sometimes as deep as 80 centimetres. There is nothing to do during the day. In the evening after supper, we talk for a bit and then I go to bed at ten.

11 January 1918

Up at eight twenty. I spend the whole day replacing the canvas on my bed. After supper, I write. Bed at ten.

12 January 1918

Up at eight. We have a quick lunch because quite a few of us have planned to visit the renowned bleaching and dyeing factory at Thaon. We leave at midday and at one o'clock present ourselves to the factory porter. What a pity we had to ask a favour of this officious flunkey, one would rather have chucked a brick at a ferocious guard dog. He tells us most disagreeably that it is impossible to visit the factory. We insist on seeing the director, and he tells us to come back at two if we want to see the manager.

We walk off our annoyance round the outskirts of the factory, discussing the best way to persuade someone who would very likely be completely indifferent to our request. Finally we go back at two, and see the porter again, who now, slightly less cantankerous, takes us to see the manager. We feel the round has all but been won, as we are quite sure our eloquence will win the civilian over. Civilians yes, but we had not given a thought to military authority. We are barely half way there, when we hear someone yelling at us, and turning we see a jumping jack, truncheon in hand, and his face congested with fury. Looking more like a ruffian than an honest man, he orders us to leave without even asking us what we are doing here. We can't help smiling at his bright red face and his imbecilic behaviour. We hazard a small request, but this puts him into the devil's own rage, and he threatens to throw us out by force. Whereupon, the smiles turn to hilarity and without hurry, we leave that inhospitable place, though somewhat stunned all the same. I would not have excused a civilian for this sort of behaviour, but from an ex colonial sergeant, forced into a duty beyond his control, I can forgive anything, and I even feel sorry for him that such a duty has turned him into a complete idiot.

Oh, noble military profession how deeply I hate you for obliging me to obey orders given by people who are not worth a hangman's rope. If I had to live my life over again, I might make a good groom, but never a military man.

We leave the place and go to Mademoiselle Thérèse for a few pastries. How restful to look at that charming face after the obnoxious vision we have just been subjected to. To think that these scoundrelly officers dream of coupling with beautiful women such as these. And to think too, that there are still people who actually like wearing those outdated red culottes. Ah, how I would much rather see the beribboned and certainly pink culottes of Mademoiselle Thérèse. But why these bad thoughts when I know well that she is the consecrated bread that is eaten only in church, and that if one is blessed with this at home, one must not penetrate the sanctuary of others? We go back to warm up. After supper, I write. I go to bed at ten.

13 January 1918

Up at eight thirty. I scrub up a bit and then we go to ten o'clock mass at the military base. In the afternoon, a friend and I walk a little along the road to Thaon. At the level crossing, we encounter two charming young girls who hold the gate open to let us through. When we reach them, we risk greeting them, and they immediately reply and we start talking. They are two quite bright, well-educated girls. We ask if we may walk with them to Thaon. When we go our separate ways, they shake hands with us, thus ending an idyllic hour.

We return and start preparing dinner, as we have invited Madame Lauzerel for dinner tonight. We sit down to table at six and have a delightful evening. Of course, I do my best, as usual, to make people laugh, and I am successful for Madame Lauzeral laughs heartily. The evening goes on until ten. I go to bed at ten thirty.

14 January 1918

Up at seven thirty. We go over to a nearby factory and find coke on a slag heap. We fill up a sack and take it back with us to make a good fire. We go back for more in the afternoon and find enough to heat us for quite some time. After supper I write, and then go to bed at ten.

15 January 1918

Up at eight thirty. There is freezing rain, and it is a sheet of glass outside. I stay in all morning. In the afternoon, I go and fetch Grandma from the washhouse and come back soaked. After supper, I write. Bed at ten.

16 January 1918

Up at eight thirty. It is pouring with rain and there is a complete thaw. I spend the afternoon covering my lorry with canvas. After supper, I write and go to bed at ten.

17 January 1918

Up at eight. An uneventful morning. At one thirty, we fetch more coke. In the evening, Madame Lauzeral comes for dinner. I go to town on decorating the table, and we have an evening of laughter and gaiety. Maria Ballaut joins us for dessert, and there is even more laughter. Several bottles of wine later, the party breaks up at eleven thirty. I go to bed at midnight.

18 January 1918

Up at nine twenty. I am little worse for wear from last night. The morning goes by quickly. In the afternoon, I take my lorry out and then come back to write. I go to bed at ten.

19 January 1918

Up at eight. At the morning report, there is an announcement that there will be roll call at seven o'clock in the morning, and then the morning report at ten thirty. Roll call again at five, and then lorry guard duty at night – wonderful! To work my annoyance off, I go for a walk with two comrades to Noméxy. We go via the canal and take the road back. I write when we get back. Madame Lauzeral and Mademoiselle Ballaut pop in to say hello. We fool around for a bit and I invite them to dinner tomorrow evening. With that, I go to bed at eleven.

20 January 1918

Up at six forty-five. Roll call at seven. Morning report at ten thirty. A comrade and I go to Thaon in the afternoon and drink a bock at the Chalet Suisse. Then back to prepare dinner for our guests. They arrive at six and we live it up until midnight. I go to bed at half past twelve.

21 January 1918

Up at six forty-five. Roll call at seven. And so the morning goes. At three in the afternoon, there is an arms review. In the evening, I am on guard duty from six to eight. I go to bed at ten.

22 January 1918

Up at five. Departure at six. We go to Arches to load up dismantled barracks to deliver about a kilometre from there. We work on this all day and get back at seven in the evening. I was convoy chief.

Madame Lauzeral and Mademoiselle Ballaut are waiting for us to return because they want to see me driving my lorry. Naturally, I start showing off. Then they come over and spend part of the evening with us. I suddenly get a stitch in my side, and as soon as they leave, I go to bed at nine thirty.

23 January 1918

Up at eight thirty. I take a couple of aspirin as I have a headache and I still have a stitch in my side. I then take the lorry out for a run. I work on it some more in the afternoon, and then go back to write.

Madame Lauzeral, who is leaving soon, and Mademoiselle Ballaut are coming for dinner. We eat at six thirty and there is much laughter. We drink champagne with our meal. At eleven fifty, fooling around noisily, we take the women home. When I get back, I go to bed at one.

24 January 1918

Up at eight. I feel a bit hung over. I wash and then in the afternoon, I work on the lorries. There is health inspection at three (how stupid). At four, I go back and the two women are there. Madame Lauzeral has come over to say goodbye. We joke around a bit, but although I don't show it, I am very upset to see her go; she is a wonderful woman. I write after supper and go to bed at ten.

25 January 1918

Up at four thirty. We go to the station to wave goodbye to Madame Lauzerel. She is delighted to see us there. When I get back I tinker a bit. At six thirty, there is wood-chopping fatigue in the Thaon forest. I have brought a cold meal with me and I stay the whole day. I get back at four completely exhausted. I write a bit and then go to bed at nine thirty.

26 January 1918

Up at eight. I have slept well. I tinker all morning. In the afternoon, we are ordered to work on the lorries from one until five, even though there is nothing to be done to them. I am bored. After supper, I write. Bed at ten.

27 January 1918

Up at eight. I scrub up a bit, and then go to mass. In the afternoon, we go for a walk in a lovely spot on the banks of the Moselle. We return at four. In the evening, I read and write a bit, and then go to bed at ten.

28 January 1918

Up at eight. I sew all morning. In the afternoon, I ask the lieutenant permission for Alex and me to go fishing. We fish from two to four and catch 170 big minnows which Grandma fries up for us for our supper. After our meal, Mademoiselle Ballaut comes round – a very short visit. I write a little and go to bed at ten.

29 January 1918

Up at eight. At ten, there is an equipment review, and then at one fifteen we are taken by lorry to Thaon, and on some unknown ground, we practice manoeuvres in honour of some captain who is being decorated with the Légion d'honneur tomorrow. This is farcical as the manoeuvres are extremely badly executed.

30 January 1918

Up at eight. At ten, I get some very upsetting news. My friend Alex is going off to be a driver-gunner with the artillery – GM (Groupe d'Automitrailleuses) 561, who are part of our group. Borne is going back inland tomorrow, Lauzeral leaves on furlough tonight, and I am relieving the nurse during his furlough. Our clan is going to be much depleted and I shall be on my own for fifteen days.

We go to Thaon for the famous award ceremony. It doesn't go too badly. We return at half past twelve. I get my instructions for my new duties at the infirmary. After supper, we go to the station to see Lauzeral off at six thirty. When I get back, I write. I go to bed at ten.

31 January 1918

Up at eight. At nine I take up my new service at the infirmary. Doctors Subert and Häys are very pleasant and I get on well with them. My duties are not very difficult. At one, I say goodbye to my friend Borne who is going to the interior, but I am absolutely delighted to see him again at supper. He's not leaving until tomorrow. He will share my room. He has something to eat and after supper we go to the café. I go to bed at ten thirty.

1 February 1918

Up at eight. Borne left at seven. I'm at the infirmary at nine. The rounds at ten. Captain Truc says goodbye to us at two o'clock, for he too is going to the interior. I stay all day at the infirmary doing the dressings. After supper, I write. I read for a short time and then go to bed at ten.

2 February 1918

At twelve fifteen we are suddenly woken up. There is an alert. Everyone has to have their engines running and to be ready to leave in half an hour. We hurry but without panic, and wonder if there really is a departure.

After a moment, we are told that it was only an exercise and after being inspected by Captain Kock, we are sent back to bed at one thirty. I go back to bed but my feet are so cold that by three o'clock, I am still awake. I get up at eight. The rounds at ten thirty. The doctor is as pleasant as before.

A young girl from the factory is brought to me in the afternoon. A splinter has penetrated deep under a nail. I do a little minor surgery with a lancet. She asks me what she owes for my trouble. I claim two big kisses, which she gives me with pleasure. In the evening, I am bored on my own. After supper, I write and then read. I go to bed at nine thirty.

3 February 1918

I get up at eight fifteen. The rounds at ten thirty. At eleven, a lieutenant calls me to one of his sick men. I go immediately. He is suffering from severe cold. I cup him in the afternoon. I go back and forth all afternoon. In the evening, I write. At nine thirty, I give myself an envigorating footbath, and then go to bed at ten.

4 February 1918

Up at eight. The rounds at ten thirty. I fiddle about all afternoon and I am very bored. I read a bit. Bed at ten.

5 February 1918

At five I am woken by Grandma's cries of distress that echo throughout the house. Suzanne, the poor invalid, has died of her illness but without suffering. I am dismayed. The house is turned upside down. At eight I get up and try to help to these good people, who are grief-stricken. I pay my respects to the poor wasted body lying peacefully there.

The day gets taken up. In the afternoon, I do the rounds with the doctor, which goes well. In the evening after supper, I keep vigil with Sidonie. Then I write. We do this until one in the morning. Dead tired, I eventually get to bed at one thirty.

6 February 1918

Up at eight. I have slept little. The rounds at ten thirty. I spend the afternoon bandaging. In the evening after supper, Alex, who has returned from Luxeuil-les-Bains, comes to see me. He will share my room with me tonight. We chat a bit and then I go to bed at half past twelve.

7 February 1918

Up at seven thirty. I have to help my good people as the funeral is at nine thirty. I help to put the body in the coffin. At nine, everyone leaves, and a comrade and I lay a large table in one of the rooms for the meal afterwards. I then go to the church. The gravedigger is alone and can't do everything, so a comrade and I help lower the coffin into the ground. Then everyone goes back to the house. We eat quietly in our room, but from the room next door, the sounds of loud voices and laughter, shock me so deeply that I have to leave. I go to the infirmary and spend the afternoon there. Grandma invites us to dinner. There are ten of us at table. It is not a sad occasion but everyone is tired, and we get up at eight thirty so that they can all get some rest. I go back to my room and go to bed at nine thirty.

8 February 1918

Up at seven thirty. I help put the dishes away from the day before. The rounds at ten thirty. I spend the afternoon doing the bandages. In the evening, Alex has dinner with me. After supper, I write and then go to bed at eleven.

9 February 1918

Up at eight. The rounds at eight thirty. In the afternoon, I bike into Thaon to get medical supplies. I take the opportunity to see Alex. When I get back, I find a general carry-on, as we have to move to another barracks at the other end of the village. Now I have to leave my kind people with whom I have been for six weeks. I have found another room with a bed, where I think I shall be comfortable. In the evening, I go to the café for a bit. Then I write and go to bed at ten thirty.

10 February 1918

Up at seven. At eight, we move out and I take possession of my new room. The rounds at ten. All sorts of rumours are flying around about a possible future move. Alex comes over and we spend the afternoon together. He has dinner with me at Grandma's, because she doesn't want me to eat anywhere else. I accompany Alex part of the way back, and then I go to my new room and go to bed at nine.

11 February 1918

Up at eight. I have slept well in my new bed. I do the rounds at ten. I learn at the infirmary that our lieutenant is going to Salonika, and that we will leave on the fifteenth for Darney, but nothing has been decided yet. The afternoon is spent as usual. In the evening, I have a game of cards with some comrades at the café. I return and go to bed at nine.

12 February 1918

Up at eight. Rumours of an imminent departure abound, but no one knows anything exactly. The doctor still hasn't arrived by eleven, so I don't wait around but go for lunch. I go back to the infirmary in the afternoon, where I write. At two thirty, the lieutenant assembles the section to say goodbye. I do not go, and I am very pleased I did not, because it was a painful review. Only three men shook his hand. The others refused. He was quite tearful. Half an hour later, he comes to see me at the infirmary to say goodbye and to tell me his woes. As I don't have anything against him personally, and have no complaints about him, I shake his hand and we chat for quite a while. In the evening after supper, Alex comes over. We go to the café, and then I accompany him back. On my return, my new landlady Madame La Sauce gives me carnival doughnuts to eat, and we chat until ten. I go to bed at ten thirty

13 February 1918

Up at eight. The rounds at ten. They are saying that the group has been broken up and that our section will join Heusch's group. If so, we will be going to Chavelot, but nobody knows yet. In the afternoon, I go to the infirmary to write. After supper, a few of us go to the cafe. I return and go to bed at nine.

14 February 1918

Up at eight. The rounds at ten. They are now saying we will be with Lecomte's group and that we will stay in the village, but nothing is certain yet. In the afternoon, I go to the infirmary and write. In the evening, I play cards. Bed at nine thirty.

15 February 1918

Up at eight. I'm on duty at the infirmary. My comrade comes back from leave and takes up his duties again. I muck around all day. We have found some tobacco, so I make cigarettes. We go to the café in the evening. I go to bed at nine

16 February 1918

Up at eight. I cut up wood for something to do. My friend Lauzeral is back. We eat together, and I move him in with me. In the evening, we spend a little time at the café. I go to bed at nine.

17 February 1918

Up at eight. At ten, I go to mass. In the afternoon, Lauzeral and I go to Thaon and return via the canal. I write. In the evening, we go to the café where I amuse myself by singing in public.

18 February 1918

Up at eight. At ten, we are told we have a new lieutenant, who apparently, is not easy to get on with. In the afternoon, we are moving out again, this time to the industrial area where the factories are.

Lauzeral and I immediately find a room to rent, but we can't move in until tomorrow. In the evening, the Ballaut invite us for a game of cards. At nine, they serve us tea, little cakes and Mirabelle. They are truly delightful people. They make us promise to come back. I go to bed at ten.

19 February 1918

Up at seven. At ten, we are assembled to meet our new lieutenant, who gives us an extremely long-winded speech. He doesn't seem to be very congenial. At two, I take off to Grandma's to write. We go to the café for a bit in the evening. I go to bed at nine.

20 February 1918

Up at eight. It was extremely cold last night and there was a freeze. I have a quick wash, and then spend an uneventful morning. In the distance, the cannons are roaring. In the afternoon, I stay in my room and write.

21 February 1918

Up at eight. I spend the morning mucking about. As it was still very cold last night, we set up our stove in our room, which takes a while. Then we hunt for coke. In the evening after supper, we make a good fire. I sit near it and write. I go to bed at ten thirty.

22 February 1918

We are woken abruptly at four forty-five. At five forty-five, we leave. We have transport duty from Bulh to Col de la Chipotte. There is a surplus of eight lorries when we arrive, so I take advantage and I am back at ten o'clock. The freeze has been succeeded by the rain and it hasn't stopped all day. In the afternoon, I stoke up the fire in our room and I write. In the evening, after supper with Grandma, I am invited to eat waffles with a comrade. We fool around a bit and laugh a lot. I get back at nine and go to bed at nine thirty.

23 February 1918

Up at eight. At nine, I wash my lorry. In the afternoon, there is review by our new captain – Captain Lecomte. He asks to see my award and congratulates me on by brave conduct. At two forty five, I go back to my room to write. After supper, we go to the café for a bit, and then return to make a good fire. I read a little and then go to bed at ten.

24 February 1918

Up at eight. At ten we go to mass. We stay in our room all afternoon and I catch up with my correspondence. We go to the café in the evening. I read a bit when we get back, and then go to bed, at ten thirty.

25 February 1918

Up at eight. We spend the morning cleaning tools, which are reviewed at two o'clock. Then I go back to my room to write. In the evening, we go round to the Ballaut, but as Mademoiselle Maria is there alone, we only stay a moment. We go back. I read a little and go to bed at nine thirty.

26 February 1918

Up at eight thirty. There is nothing to do. In the afternoon, we look for coke and then I go back to our room to write. After supper, we go to the café. As I am not sleepy, I read for quite a while and then go to bed at eleven thirty.

27 February 1918

Up at eight. There was a hard freeze, but now it is raining. Nothing to do all day. I am on guard duty tonight until seven in the morning. In the afternoon, I write. I mount guard at seven. I am on duty from nine to eleven. After that I lie down on a stretcher, but the police station is so cold, I give up any idea of sleep, and pace backwards and forwards. I am back on duty between three and five in the morning. At three forty-five, I am so cold that I abandon post and go back to my room. I go to bed at four.

28 February 1918

Up at nine. I don't do anything in the morning. In the afternoon, I write and then after supper, we go to the café for a bit and then to the Ballaut at seven thirty. They very kindly serve us tea. We leave them at ten thirty. I go to bed at eleven.

1 March 1918

Up at nine. The morning goes by fast. From one o'clock to two, we have to work on the lorries. After that, I go back to write. We spend a little time with Grandma in the evening, and then return. I read a little and then go to bed at eleven.

2 March 1918

Up at eight. Nothing to do. We look for coke in the afternoon. I come back to write. In the evening, we go to the café for a bit. I go to bed at ten.

3 March 1918

Up at eight. At ten o'clock, I have a medical before going on furlough tomorrow. We have coffee with the Ballaut in the afternoon. We come back at about four. In the evening we go to the café for a bit. Then I read for a while and go to bed at ten.

4 March 1918

Up at seven thirty. I see the lieutenant in his office, who confirms that I am on leave. I tidy my belongings and get dressed. I say goodbye to Grandma and to Maria, and then return. Then there is a big upset because we have been told furlough has been suspended. But it is sorted out in the end. I have lunch quickly, and then a comrade and I take the train at eleven twenty-five. It is snowing in earnest. The journey is uneventful, but there are many delays.

5 March 1918

We get to Paris at ten o'clock. I get my furlough endorsed, and collect my ration tickets. Then I take the metro and I am home at ten thirty. A very quick scrub up. At midday, I fetch my wife from her office. She has taken the afternoon off. At four thirty, we visit my mother, and then my daughter. We have dinner at home and then visit the Delapraz for while. We return at eleven. Bed at eleven thirty.

6 March 1918

Up at nine. I stay at home all day. In the evening we visit our friends, who live opposite us. I go to bed at ten.

7 March 1918

Up at nine. We have lunch at Puteaux. We pay several visits in the afternoon, and in the evening we have dinner with my sister Marie. Bed at eleven.

8 March 1918

Up at nine. We visit various friends in the afternoon, and then have dinner in Paris and go to La Scala. At eight forty-five during the first interval, there is an air raid warning. We immediately take shelter in the Porte St Denis metro. We stay there three hours and I fall sound asleep on one of the staircase steps. The train starts running again. We take it and we get home at two in the morning. We eat and go to bed at three.

9 March 1918

I stay at home all day. In the evening at six, we fetch our daughter from school and take her home with us. I go to bed at ten.

10 March 1918

Up at nine. We get dressed and go to my mother for lunch. We spend the whole day with the family. In the evening, we have dinner with my sister Marie and we return home at ten.

11 March 1918

Up at nine. I work in the garden and then take my daughter back to school. I fetch my wife from the office, as she went back to work today. We have lunch and in the afternoon, I work in the garden. We have dinner at seven thirty.

At nine, while I am writing in my office, I hear a cannon shot and the air-raid warning siren. We go to Madame Hollunde opposite and stay until the Gothas have gone. It is dreadful, the bombs are falling everywhere. The all-clear sounds at half past twelve. I go to bed at one fifteen.

12 March 1918

I am woken at eight with the news that a bomb landed very near my daughter's school. I race over there. It fell on a house opposite the school and caused a lot of damage. I fetch my wife from the office at midday. Paris has been badly hit and the Ministry of War is on fire.

I pay a few visits in the afternoon, and then return to do more work in my garden. In the evening, we pay a short visit to Madame Lefèvre. When we get back, I read a bit and go to bed at ten thirty.

13 March 1918

Up at nine. I work in the garden. At ten thirty, I go and see my daughter, and then fetch Nénette Lacroix. At midday, we meet up with my wife and Théo in front of the Hotel Moderne. Théo invites us for lunch at Le Grüber. Afterwards, I go back to the house. At seven, I fetch my wife and we go to my mother for dinner, and stay the night. I go to bed at eleven.

14 March 1918

My wife is not very well. She decides not go to work and stays at home all day with me. I work in the garden all afternoon. In the evening, I read a little and then go to bed at eleven.

15 March 1918

Up at nine. I fetch my wife from the office at midday. We have lunch together, and then go for a walk along the boulevard while waiting for Maurice Jourdan, who we are meant to be meeting. But he doesn't turn up.

At one forty-five, there are two immense explosions, and everyone thinks it is another Gotha raid and takes shelter. My wife and I run to the cellars of No. 90 Boulevard Beaumarchais. A short while later we learn that it is a grenade factory that has exploded at Courneuve, with disastrous results. When we come out, the road is covered in debris and glass from shop windows shattered by the force of the explosion. I do a little shopping and then return to the house.

In the evening, we have dinner with the Delapraz who give us the warmest reception. We leave them at eleven. I go to bed at eleven thirty.

16 March 1918

Up at eight. At ten thirty, I go to Joinville for an interview with Maître Gosset, to apply for a job in his factory. He keeps me for lunch and I leave with him at two, for Paris. Then I meet up with Monsieur Calton, the Jourdan and the Morret. I go home at seven. After dinner, I read a bit and go to bed at eleven.

17 March 1918

Up at eight. I go to the station to have my furlough papers stamped. Then I go to the Delapraz to say goodbye, and I am regaled with champagne. We then have lunch with my mother. In the afternoon, I help Georges with the garden. At six, we visit the Longuet. At six thirty, we go home and I pack my belongings for my departure tomorrow. We have dinner and I go to bed at eleven thirty.

18 March 1918

Up at seven thirty. At eight thirty, I leave the house. We drop my daughter off at her school, and my wife comes with me to the station. At nine thirty, I meet up with my friend Malfroy, and leave my wife at nine forty-five.

We take the ten thirty-five train. It is a long, tedious journey, which lasts until six in the morning.

19 March 1918

After leaving the station, I go to my room, where nothing has changed, and then I go for a coffee and say hello to all my mates. I shave and have a thorough wash. Apparently, we still have no work. I write all afternoon. In the evening after supper, I go over to Grandma and Sidonie, who are delighted to see me again. Then Lauzeral and I spend the rest of the evening with the Ballaut. They are all pleased to see me again, especially Mademoiselle Maria, who ever the tease, steals a small silk handkerchief from me, which she refuses to return. We are given little cakes and tea laced with Mirabelle. We leave them at ten. I go to bed at ten.

20 March 1918

I slept like a log. There is nothing to do. I write all afternoon. In the evening we go to the café for a bit, and then I read and go to bed at ten.

21 March 1918

Up at six thirty. At seven thirty, I go to the Thaon forest to chop wood. I finish the work fairly quickly and return at three fifteen. I write and then have a wash. After supper, we spend the evening playing cards with the Ballaut. We have tea laced with Mirabelle and return at eleven. I go to bed at eleven thirty.

22 March 1918

Up at eight thirty. At the morning report, we are told that we leave on the 31st for Gérardner. Good. That will provide some distraction. I spend the afternoon tidying my belongings. I am on guard duty in the evening – from eight to ten and then from two to three fifteen in the morning. I go to bed at four.

23 March 1918

Up at eight thirty. There is still nothing to do. I spend the day writing. In the evening we visit the Ballaut, and return at eleven thirty. I go to bed at midnight.

24 March 1918

We are woken at one in the morning. We leave at two. We load up troops at Seichamps and take them to Azerailles. Then we return and get back at eleven in the evening. I have something to eat and go to bed at eleven thirty.

25 March 1918

Up at eight forty-five. I work on my lorry. At eleven we are ordered to leave at two o'clock for Charmes. We are ready leave at two. At two thirty, there are more orders to say we are not leaving. We all go back to work on our lorries. However, an important transport and change of barracks is envisaged for tonight, so we hold ourselves ready. We briefly visit the Maillard and the Ballaut, and then return at nine thirty. I go to bed at ten.

26 March 1918

Up at seven thirty. Nothing happened last night. At ten thirty, we are ordered to be ready to leave at eleven. We pack up everything again, and then wait. At four we set off. We have a two-hour sleep en route at Neufchâteau.

27 March 1918

We're off again at three in the morning. We are to load up at Naives-en-Blois. I am towing the mobile kitchen to Cramant which takes the rest of the night. We arrive at Gionges at five in the morning. At eleven thirty, we leave again. We load up troops at Bouy and spend three days on the road taking them to Ailly-sur-Noye. We do not stop except to fill up with petrol. We eat while we drive and we do not sleep.

28 March 1918

We are still on the road. I break down about three kilometres from Château-Thierry. I spend part of the night with a mechanic repairing the magneto.

29 March 1918

Still on the road. I have something to eat at Château-Thierry. In the evening we come to Villers-Cotterêts, where we have a short stop.

30 March 1918

We set off again and we are on the road all day and night.

31 March 1918

We reach Ailly-Sur-Noye at four in the morning. We unload the troops and leave immediately in the direction of Vauchamps. Finally, we stop at Crépy-en-Valois for the night.

1 April 1918

At three in the morning, we are off again, and are on the road for the rest of the day and night. We arrive at Vauchamps at four forty-five in the morning.

2 April 1918

At seven, we leave again for Sevran-Livry. We drive the whole day, and get there at eleven thirty at night and meet up with the rest of the section. I can at last sleep a bit in my lorry, which I certainly need, since I have been on my own from the beginning of the trip with no relief.

3 April 1918

We leave Sevran-Livry at seven in the morning. We are to go to Luzères to transport munitions. We travel all day and part of the night.

4 April 1918

We arrive at Luzères at four thirty in the morning. I am exhausted – shattered. I sleep immediately. I only have a short sleep and wake at nine. There is munitions duty from seven in the evening, but as I am the only driver in my lorry, I am not part of the service. I make the most of it by writing a little and then still in my lorry, I go to sleep at ten o'clock.

5 April 1918

We are woken at six thirty. Departure at seven thirty. We are taking shells from the station at Conty to Cottenchy. the service lasts all day and all night.

6 April 1918

I am whacked when I return. My lorry is immediately requisitioned by someone else. I take the opportunity and write. In anticipation of another departure, I go to bed at eight.

7 April 1918

I slept all night. We leave at eight. I load up long-range 155s to take to Mesnil-Saint-Firmin. It is a hard, tedious convoy that lasts all day and all night. We get lost and I end up getting back on my own at two in the morning.

8 April 1918

I go to bed at three. I am up at eight. I have to have my lorry's water pump repaired. Then I have lunch with some kind people, where I eat a good bacon omelette, which makes me feel a bit better. I go over to the workshops in the afternoon.

In the evening, I walk for a bit and then go to bed at nine.

9 April 1918

Up at eight thirty. There was no service, so I slept all night. I work on my lorry in the afternoon until three, and then I write. At five thirty, I am assigned to a service. Twenty-four lorries go to the station at Quevauvillers to load up with staff equipment and provisions. I'm fortunate enough to be redundant and I go back to barracks at midnight. I go to bed at one o'clock.

10 April 1918

Up at seven thirty. I prepare my lorry, which will be driven by someone else tomorrow. Then I have a bit of a scrub up. In the afternoon, my lorry is towed back, and needs a small repair. After supper, I write and go to bed at nine.

11 April 1918

Up at seven thirty. We leave at nine thirty, but in another lorry as mine is not ready. We load up 155s at Bacouël to take to the Bois Bernard. It is a very bad road – a long, hard and tedious journey. We get back at one thirty in the morning. I go to bed at two.

12 April 1918

Up at eight. I get my lorry ready, as it is to be driven by someone else. Then I attend to my own affairs for a bit. In the afternoon, I write. At three thirty, my lorry comes back and the water pump has been damaged. I will have to work on it tomorrow. I go for a short walk in the evening and then go to bed at ten.

13 April 1918

Up at eight. I work on the repair to my lorry. I take my time and the work lasts all day. In the evening after supper, I walk round Conty village. I go to bed at nine thirty.

14 April 1918

Up at eight. We are officially at rest, for the day. I take the opportunity, to tidy my belongings a bit. In the afternoon, I write and in the evening after supper, I go for a short walk. I go to bed at nine.

15 April 1918

Up at four. Departure at four forty-five. We are to load up at Namps-Quevauvillers station. I break down on the way, which delays me and there is nothing for me to load when I get there. I return to the barracks at three with an empty lorry. I set about repairing it. After supper, I go for a walk. Bed at nine.

16 April 1918

Up at eight. I spend the whole day at the workshops. In the evening after supper, we spend a little time at a café in Conty. I return and go to bed at nine thirty.

17 April 1918

Up at eight. Departure at midday. We go to the station at Conty, but we do not load up until four o'clock. From Conty we go to the depot at Flers-sur-Noye. I get back at seven. I eat and then go for a short walk. I have been with the section two years today. Bed at nine thirty.

18 April 1918

Up at eight. At ten, I test drive my lorry, which has just left the workshops. In the afternoon, I write. In the evening I go for a walk. I go to bed at nine.

19 April 1918

Up at five thirty. Departure at six thirty. We go to Conty station to load up and then to Flers-sur-Noye. We do this a second time and then another trip to Oresmaux. I return at eleven thirty and go to bed at midnight.

20 April 1918

Up at eight thirty. Today, is my fortieth birthday. I am working on my lorry, when I am called by the lieutenant, who asks me if I would like to be his chauffeur and drive a Delaunay-Belleville, which has just been issued to him. Our lieutenant is called Despins and he is a very decent fellow.

To drive a tourer with good wheels rather than a lorry is certainly tempting, but all the same, I know that the work involved will be hard. After thinking about it for a while, I lay down my conditions before the lieutenant. I will be his driver and mechanic to his heart's desire, but I will not be his domestic. I joke that he had better not forget his provisions, because I won't share mine; and then I tell him I don't like being criticized and that I am quite short tempered. But at this, he butters me up and tells me he likes my frankness and that he knows me to be an excellent driver and he has been given leave to have me as his personal driver, and he is quite sure that we will get on very well, and to please accept his proposition. I make up my mind there and then and accept.

I have look at the car. It is a magnificent 20-horsepower torpedo that had once belonged to a certain Barino, of the Boulevard des Invalides in Paris. It is a little slow on the uptake and does not always stop when it should. Its brakes need to be watched. Otherwise, it is a fairly fast-moving vehicle. I take the wheel and try it out and push it gently to seventy. It drives well, but I feel it can do with a little tuning, which I will work on tomorrow. In the evening after supper, I go to Conty and then go to bed at ten

21 April 1918

Up at six. We leave at six thirty to load up at Conty, and we stay the whole day. My tourer is not pulling well. I take it to the workshops to tune it and the lieutenant and I are out all afternoon with it. We get back at seven. I eat. I write and I go to bed at eleven.

22 April 1918

I have been married fifteen years. Up at five thirty. Departure at six fifteen. My lieutenant is on duty at the station at Bacouël. We arrive at seven and stay all morning. In the afternoon, I am ordered to drive a lieutenant to Saint-Sauflieu and then return to Bacouël, where I stop for a while. I discover an English cooperative and buy cigarettes – five hundred for my lieutenant and five hundred for me. We leave the station at six and go to Group 14 at Fleury, and Group 15 at Monsures, to give a report of the mission. We finally return at seven. I eat and go to bed at ten.

23 April 1918

Up at four forty-five. Departure at five thirty. Convoy munitions service between Conty and Oresmaux. We make the trip three times and one trip to Jumel. Then we have an errand at Dury. We return at seven. I eat and go to bed at nine.

24 April 1918

Up at six. Departure at seven. My lieutenant is on duty supervising a delivery at Oresmaux. We are there for the whole day. We leave at five and are back at five fifteen. I eat and to bed at nine thirty.

25 April 1918

Up at eight. I am not on duty. I take the opportunity of washing my car. At ten I drive it to Monsures. In the afternoon, the lieutenant and I leave at two to look for suitable barracks, because we are leaving Luzières tomorrow. We cover 100 kilometres, without finding what we need. We get back at five fifteen. I go for a walk. Bed at ten.

26 April 1918

Up at five. Departure at six fifteen. We are to load up at Conty station to go to Hébécourt. I make four trips in the tourer. We return to Luzières at seven to pack up. The road is blocked and we have to wait until nine before leaving. We leave at last and arrive at Taisnil at ten.

I make a bed for myself in my car, and sleep at ten thirty.

27 April 1918

Up at six. I had little sleep as I was folded in two in my car, and I wasn't warm either. I am not going out today, and I make the most of it by working hard on my car. Then a lot of us start looking for lodgings. I unearth a room, which we clean out and five of us move in.

In the evening, I write a bit. Bed at nine thirty.

28 April 1918

Up at eight. I am not going out again today. It seems as if the service is slowing down a bit. I spend the day again with the car which needs a lot of care. In the evening I go for a walk and go to bed at ten.

29 April 1918

Up at six. Departure at six forty-five. We are on unloading duty at the Saint-Sauflieu depot. I spend the whole day under a fine rain. We leave again at five thirty and are back by six. I eat. I go out for a bit and then go to bed at ten.

30 April 1918

Up at eight. I am not on duty today. I work on my car, and then in the afternoon, I write. It is pouring with rain. I eat and go to bed at nine.

1 May 1918

Up at ten past six. We should have left at six fifteen – so we're late and we have to step on it. the road is bad I go into a skid and the car swerves dreadfully, but fortunately without mishap. We are on convoy duty and make the trip between Conty and Flers-en-Noye five times.

I get back at seven thirty. I eat and go to bed at ten.

2 May 1918

Up at five thirty. Departure at six thirty. We are on loading duty at Conty and stay there for the whole day. I take the opportunity of polishing the car, and then I write. I return at three thirty. I shave. I eat at six and go for a walk. Bed at ten.

3 May 1918

I am not going out today, so I can rest. I spend the time getting my correspondence up to date. I go out a bit in the evening and then go to bed at nine thirty.

4 May 1918

Up at eight. No service today. I work on my tourer. At three, I go with the lieutenant to do some personal shopping. We go to Conty, Poix-de-Picardie, Creuse, Parménil, and back to Taisnil. After dinner, I write a bit and go to bed at ten.

5 May 1918

Up at eight. It is a day of rest for everyone. I attend to my own affairs, and have a thorough wash and grooming session. I have a break in the afternoon. After dinner we go for a long walk in the woods which are superb. I return and go to bed at ten.

6 May 1918

Up at five. I am on loading duty at the Croissy-sur-Celle station. I have a break and then I return at three. In the evening, I write a bit and go to bed at ten.

7 May 1918

Up at seven. Departure at eight. We go to Amiens to load up equipment for the Engineering corps. A whole section of the town has been destroyed. From there we go to three different depots, the furthest being Fouanceau, where there is some heavy fighting. On my return to Bacouël, I make a false move, hit the embankment and puncture the radiator. I have to get a lorry to tow me back, and I arrive at eight. I eat and then go to bed at nine thirty.

8 May 1918

Up at seven thirty. I dismantle the radiator and take it to the workshops, and someone repairs it for me immediately. I fix it back in place, which takes up the afternoon. In the evening, I go for a walk and then go to bed at ten.

9 May 1918

Up at seven. Departure at eight fifteen. We load up at Bacouël and make two trips to Saint-Sauflieu. Today, I am going with the group's staff sergeant, as my lieutenant has a day of rest – but not me – we get delayed on route, to the extent that I don't get back until seven thirty. I eat, chat a bit, and then go to bed at ten thirty.

10 May 1918

Up at seven. We wait for the order to leave, which doesn't come until two o'clock. We leave for Bacouël to load up and make two trips to Saint-Sauflieu. The train doesn't get in until four o'clock, which means we have to drive most of the night. I get back at one thirty and go to bed at two.

11 May 1918

Up at seven. We wait again for the order to leave, but it doesn't come. At two, I go with the lieutenant to the group at Namps-Aumont. I get back at three. Then I go with Lieutenant Jobert to Bacouël to see if the train we are waiting for has arrived. We are told that it will not be coming today. So we return at six. I eat, go for a walk and go to bed at ten.

12 May 1918

Up at five. Departure at five thirty. I am driving the staff sergeant again. We load up provisions at Namps-Quevauvillers to take to Bacouël. I get back at eleven forty-five. In the afternoon, I write, and then at four, I drive the lieutenant to Saleux. I return, eat, and go to bed at ten.

13 May 1918

Up at six. Departure at six thirty. We are on unloading duty at Oresmaux where I spend the day in unremitting rain. In the afternoon, we return via Dury and Saleux. I return at six. I eat and go to bed at ten.

14 May 1918

Up at eight. It is a day of rest. I work a bit on my tourer, and then I go for a walk. In the evening, I drink a good bottle of wine with a comrade who is going on leave. I go to bed at ten.

15 May 1918

Up at seven thirty. I have to go to Poix-de-Picardie at one fifteen. The lieutenant then tells me that I will not be going and that I am free. I spend the day writing. In the evening, I go for a walk and then to bed at ten.

16 May 1918

Up at seven. It's a nice day, which gives me the chance to wash the car. Then I see that the ball bearing on the front right wheel is broken. That means I shall be unavailable for a good while. In the afternoon, I write and then I rest as it is very hot. We go out for a bit in the evening. Bed at ten.

17 May 1918

Up at eight. I make the most of the good weather by working on the car. It is very hot in the afternoon, so I have a siesta, and then read and write until supper. Afterwards, we go for a walk in the woods to get some cooler air. I go to bed at ten.

18 May 1918

Up at eight. As the car is still out of service, I am at rest, but I work on it all morning. In the afternoon, I read and write. In the evening I go for a short walk and then go to bed at ten.

19 May 1918

Up at eight. I change a tyre on the tourer in the morning. The lieutenant tells me he will get someone else to repair it, so that if we have to leave, I can go under my own steam. That would not displease me. I tinker all afternoon. In the evening, I have a game of football with some Americans who are in the area, but they play like thugs. I go to bed at eleven.

20 May 1918

Up at eight. There is still nothing to do. I work a bit on my car. The sections are not going out, but are preparing for another departure. In the afternoon, I read and write. A walk in the afternoon and bed at eleven.

21 May 1918

Up at seven. My car is at the workshops. they are going to fit a makeshift roller while waiting for a ball bearing to be sent. This takes the whole day. At seven in the evening, we take the car out for a test run. I have the quartermaster and his secretary with me, and we go first to Bacouël to buy English cigarettes, and then to Namps-Quevauvillers for a mint liqueur and water. When I get back, I take the wheel off. It has overheated a little and there is a little adjustment to be made, which I will do tomorrow. I go for a walk and then go to bed at ten.

22 May 1918

Up at eight. I go to the workshops, where they are fixing my car. In the afternoon, I test drive it by going to Hébécourt to fetch my lieutenant. It is still overheating a bit, but less than yesterday. In the evening after supper, we stretch out in the grass to get a bit cooler. I go to bed at eleven.

23 May 1918

Up at eight. I work on my car. In the afternoon, the lieutenant and I go to Conty to do some shopping. The weather has suddenly changed and it is cold. After supper, we go for a walk in the woods. Bed at ten thirty.

24 May 1918

Up at seven thirty. At eight the lieutenant tells me to be ready in quarter of an hour to go to Conty. We are going to buy provisions for his mess. So the two of go to the market, which is quite amusing. Then I take him to Luzières to the Josse's farm, to buy two chickens. Marie-Thérèse who greets me, asks me to help her catch the chickens – and the lieutenant joins us in a stampede across the farmyard. We return at ten thirty. In the afternoon, I am free and I take the chance to write. In the evening after supper, although it is raining, we go for a walk. I go to bed at ten.

25 May 1918

Up at seven. I am not going out today. I use the time to fine-tune my car. At two in the afternoon, just as I am settling down to write, I am called away by the lieutenant. At two fifteen, we take another lieutenant to the Forêt d'Eu, where he will spend 48 hours with his wife. We drive along some very pretty roads and it is an agreeable outing. I get back at five thirty. I eat. I write and then go to bed at ten.

26 May 1918

Up at five. Departure at six. We go to Croissy-sur-Celle to load up engineering equipment to take to Sains-Morainvillers. We get back at three. After supper, I go for a walk in the woods. I go to bed at ten thirty.

27 May 1918

Up at seven thirty. I am not on duty today, so I work all morning on the car. It is my daughter's tenth birthday – how time flies. In the afternoon, I hold myself in readiness to leave, but in the end I remain. I read a bit and go to bed at eleven.

28 May 1918

Up at five. Departure at six. We load up at Bacouël to go to Hébécourt, Saint-Sauflieu, and Saint-Fuscien. We unload at the three depots and then return at four. After supper, I write and then go to bed at ten thirty.

29 May 1918

Up at eight. I work on the car in the morning. In the afternoon, I take the lieutenant to do some shopping in Poix. I get back at five thirty. We immediately set off again for the station at Croissy-sur-Celle, where we collect a lieutenant whose tourer has broken down. We return at six thirty. I eat, write and go to bed at ten.

30 May 1918

Up at eight. I work on the car. Tomorrow, we are going to Francastel. At one o'clock, we go to the station at Bacouël. We unload at two depots, Saint-Sauflieu and Saint-Fuscien. This takes us most of the night. I get back at one fifteen in the morning. I go to bed immediately.

31 May 1918

Up at four thirty. We leave at five with our baggage on board, as we are staying overnight at Francastel. There is a munitions convoy, which will be loaded at the Crèvecoeur-le-Grand station and taken in two trips to the depot at Beauvoir. I do a lot of driving and in all, cover over 300 kilometres in one day. I get back at eight thirty in the evening. I find a corner of a barn to sleep in. I have something to eat, and then tired out I go to bed at ten.

1 June 1918

Up at four forty-five. Departure at five thirty. I am accompanied by the staff sergeant. We go to the station at Croissy-sur-Celle, to load up engineering equipment. I notice that my wheel is about to fall off. Instead of going to Sains-Morainvillers, I stay behind at the station.

At seven I set off again and we get back at eight. I sign my car in and they will repair it. I eat and chat a bit. I go to bed at eleven.

2 June 1918

Up at eight. I slept well in spite of the aeroplanes flying overhead on reconnaissance, which I barely heard. It is Sunday, and I have a thorough wash. In the afternoon, I write and rest. In the evening, I lie on the grass in the fresh air. Bed at eleven.

3 June 1918

Up at eight. I tinker all day on my car. In the evening, I walk around for a bit. At ten we are told that we leave tomorrow for Belleuse. We immediately pack up in readiness. I go to bed at ten thirty.

4 June 1918

Up at eight. Nobody is going anywhere today. I work as usual on my car. We are ready and waiting for orders to leave the village. I walk for a bit in the evening, and then I go to bed at ten thirty.

5 June 1918

Up at eight. I have nothing to do. I spend the time making a box that the lieutenant needs. In the afternoon, we are meant to be leaving the village for Lavaquerie, but then there is a counter-order for us to stay where we are. In the evening I go for a walk and then go to bed at eleven.

6 June 1918

Up at eight. Still nothing to do. I tinker on my car. In the afternoon, I write and in the evening, I read. I go to bed at ten thirty.

7 June 1918

Up at eight. Still nothing to do. I spend the day tinkering. I go out a bit in the evening and then go to bed at ten.

8 June 1918

Up at eight. Nothing has changed. I work a bit. I read and then go to bed at eleven.

9 June 1918

At midnight, the lieutenant comes over to tell me to be ready to leave at any minute for troop transport, which will last several days. They work all night to get another car fixed up, but it will not be ready in time, and we will have to do part of the journey in mine. I get up at three; at four I am all set to leave, when I am told the car in question is not ready, and that my own car will not hold the road. At four thirty, the comrades leave, but I stay behind. I spend the day reading and writing. It starts to rain in the evening. Bed at ten thirty.

10 June 1918

Up at nine. I have caught up from the night before. The men return from their convoy at ten. We learn that we will leave tomorrow morning for Lavaquerie. Bed at eleven.

11 June 1918

Up at seven. We are actually leaving. We pack up our belongings and wait all day, and eventually, we leave at nine thirty in the evening. We get to Lavaquerie at eleven thirty. I immediately find a nice barn belonging to a retired policeman. It is attached to the same house, where my lieutenant is billeted. Several comrades and I move in. I go to bed at midnight.

12 June 1918

Up at eight thirty. I have slept well. I work for a bit on my car and then in the afternoon, we get properly settled in. I go for a walk in the countryside in the evening. Bed at ten.

13 June 1918

Up at eight. At ten I take two comrades to the dentist in the small village next to ours. I am back by eleven. In the afternoon, I tinker. In the evening, we spend a little time in the café. I go to bed at eleven.

14 June 1918

Up at eight. I tinker a bit. In the afternoon, I take the car out to try out the brakes which I have tightened. In the evening, I go for a walk in the countryside. I go to bed at eleven.

15 June 1918

Up at eight. A very quiet day for there is nothing to do. I spend the day reading and writing. In the evening after supper, Lauzeral and I pick a beautiful bunch of cornflowers which I give to my lieutenant. I go to bed at ten thirty.

16 June 1918

Up at eight. It is Sunday. I give myself the usual thorough scrub up. In the afternoon, I take the lieutenant to Poix, where we stay for a while. In the evening after supper, I try out a Ford. I talk for a while. Bed at ten.

17 June 1918

At three in the morning the lieutenant wakes me and asks me if I will go with him, in spite of the extremely unreliable wheel. I agree. At four, we leave for the station at Bacouël and get there at five thirty. There is a white frost and it is very cold. We help to unload shells and then return at ten thirty.

In the afternoon, we leave again at two o'clock, to go to Grandvilliers and the market to do some shopping for the lieutenant's mess. We return at three fifteen. We leave again immediately for Bacouël, then to Saint-Fuscien, and then back to Bacouël. We run into quite a storm on the way.

We finally arrive back at Lavaquerie at six thirty. I am quite tired, as we have driven 200 kilometres. In the evening, I go for a walk to unwind. I return to write and go to bed at ten thirty.

18 June 1918

Up at eight. I have had a good, much-needed rest. Since I am in the mood, I take the car over to the pond to wash it. Then I work on it for the rest of the day. After supper, I go for a walk in the countryside, but the rain forces me to go back inside. I go to bed at ten.

19 June 1918

Up at eight. There is nothing to do. I work at patching up the paintwork on my car, which takes up part of the day. In the evening, a short walk and bed at eleven.

20 June 1918

Up at eight. There is still nothing to do and I continue painting my car. In the evening, I read and write, and then we chat for a while. I go to bed at eleven.

21 June 1918

Up at eight. I tinker all day, as there is nothing else to do. In the evening, I read and write. Bed at ten thirty.

22 June 1918

Up at eight. I busy myself making a wire carrier for my car, which takes up the day. I go for a walk in the evening and bed at ten thirty.

23 June 1918

Up at eight. The usual thorough scrub up as it is Sunday. At eleven we go to mass. I spend the afternoon reading. In the evening after supper, some comrades and I go to Beaudéduit to drink cider. I write for a bit and then go to bed at eleven.

24 June 1918

Up at eight. The service has really slowed down and nobody is going out. For something to do I make a magneto key. In the evening, we go for a walk. I read a bit and then go to bed at eleven.

25 June 1918

Up at eight. there is still nothing to do, and I am getting thoroughly fed up. In the evening after dinner, we go back to Beaudéduit to drink cider. I return. I read. Bed at eleven thirty.

26 June 1918

Up at eight. There is still nothing to do. I spend the day reading and writing. In the evening, I read some more and then go to bed at eleven.

27 June 1918

Up at eight. It's the same old story – nothing to do. I sew a bit in the afternoon. I read a bit in the evening and go to bed at eleven.

28 June 1918

Up at eight. No change to the story. However, there are rumours in the air of an imminent departure. I tinker all day. In the evening, I read and write. Bed at eleven.

29 June 1918

Up at eight. We pack up, for tomorrow we leave for Champagne. At four, I learn how to drive a Ford because tomorrow, I have to make the journey in one. The car is a nasty cuckoo. At nine thirty in the evening, there is a counter order and I am allowed keep my own car. I repack everything into it, and then go to bed at eleven

30 June 1918

Up at four. We leave at six. It is a long, tedious drive. We get to Rozières at five in the evening. We find an omelette to eat, but nowhere to sleep. At ten, I roll up in my blankets and sleep in a ditch at the side of the road.

1 July 1918

We are woken at four. At five, we fetch troops from the village itself, and taking a long and difficult road into the Champagne region, we drop them off in the Massy Forest. It is now eleven at night. From here we transport our barracks to Villers-au Bois.

I sleep in my car, and although uncomfortable, I sleep like a log. It is two in the morning

2 July 1918

Up at eight. A quick wash and then five of us construct a tarpaulin tent as we are billeted in the middle of a forest. It takes us the entire day. By evening, I'm knocked out with fatigue and go to bed at ten.

3 July 1918

Up at eight. I slept well in our tent and wasn't cold in spite of a quite strong wind. I work on my car in the morning, and then at three o'clock, I take over to the workshops where they will make another makeshift ball bearing.

In the evening after supper, we go for a walk. I go to bed at ten.

4 July 1918

Up at six. At six thirty, I am at the workshops where they are repairing my car. At three thirty, it is ready. We take it out for a test run to a pretty village called Le Mesnil, and then return. In the evening after supper, we go for a good long walk in the woods. I go to bed at ten thirty.

5 July 1918

Up at eight. At ten, I drive a comrade to the infirmary in Fulaine-St-Quentin, a little village close by. I tinker in the afternoon, and in the evening, I write. I go to bed at ten.

6 July 1918

Up at eight. At ten, I drive another comrade to the infirmary, and then leave on service at three. We load up provisions at Connantray and Étoges. We work all night and only get back at two in the morning. I go to bed at three.

7 July 1918

Up at eight. I work on my car and then rest a bit in the afternoon. At eight in the evening we leave to fetch colonial troops from the Marchand division in Étoges, and take them to Moslins. It takes all night and we return at four in the morning.

8 July 1918

Fifteen minutes after we return, we are off again for to transport another lot of troops, which lasts until eleven. When we get back, I have a bite to eat and then collapse onto my bed and sleep until three. Then I work on the car. After supper, I write a little and go to bed at ten.

9 July 1918

Up at eight. At nine, the lieutenant and I drive to Vertus and return at eleven. I rest in the afternoon as I have a bad pain in my ribs. I think it is a nervous pain. After supper, I write. Bed at ten.

10 July 1918

Up at eight. I slept badly because of the pain in my sides, so I potter about all day. I go to bed at nine thirty in the evening.

11 July 1918

Up at eight. I am not going out today. My ribs are a bit better. Our day is taken up making the tent fast as it has been affected by the bad weather. I write in the evening and go to bed at ten.

12 July 1918

Up at eight. As we have nothing to do, we make a wall of packed earth around the tent, which takes us the whole day, and I am exhausted. I write and go to bed at ten.

13 July 1918

We are woken at five, and told that we will leave in two hours for another village. We are up in an instant, pack everything up and in an hour we are ready. But we are delayed and don't leave until twelve forty-five. We have a trip of forty kilometres and arrive at Saint-Gibrien, about five-and-a-half kilometres from Châlons-sur-Marne. Our barracks are Adrian Huts. I have a bite to eat and go to bed at eleven.

14 July 1918

Up at five. I have rested a bit. I scrub up because it France's national day. We all have lunch together. When we get to the champagne, the lieutenant has a glass with us. In the afternoon, I wander along the banks of the Marne. We leave at nine in the evening (Long live France!) to load up troops at Cudery and take them to Saint-Hilaire-au-Temple.

As we drive through Châlons, both on our way there and on our way back, we are bombarded by long-range shells. We have to unload the troops at Dampierre-au-Temple because the neighbouring villages have been bombed and we can't drive any further. Our side are attacking and the cannons are firing furiously.

Taking a very rough road, we return at four thirty in the morning. I drink a little coffee and go to bed at five.

15 July 1918

Not being able to sleep any longer, I get up at nine. I work on my car and then the rest of the day is more or less spent writing. At nine as I am getting ready to go to bed, the lieutenant tells me to get ready to help a convoy out of an area that is being bombarded by shells and poison gas shells. We leave at nine thirty for Meulette and then Bussy-le-Château, where we meet the convoy in question on the road. On our way, as we went through Châlons, we were bombarded twice. On our way back, the town is being bombed by the planes overhead. We bypass it and get back to barracks at one. Bed at one thirty.

16 July 1918

Up at eight. Impossible to sleep from the noise of everyone coming and going. I ask the lieutenant permission to sleep away from the barracks and along with a few comrades, take my bed into a barn. I work on the car and in the afternoon, I take it to the workshops to be fitted with the ball bearing, which has at last arrived. There is a departure tonight, but thankfully, I am not included in the convoy.

Just as I am about to turn in, some planes fly over, and the ferocious dogfight that follows, keeps us watching until midnight, when I go to bed.

17 July 1918

Up at eight. I work on my car as I am not going out. I rest in the afternoon and write. There is a storm in the evening, which will keep the planes away. I go to bed at ten thirty.

18 July 1918

Up at eight. I slept well because it rained most of the night and kept the planes away. I tinker a bit. At four thirty, I am told that we leave at five. I quickly have something to eat, because I am sure I will be included. But no, I am to stay. After supper, I potter around until eight when I am given notice to be ready for another departure. I am about to go to bed when the planes return. They set fire to three different places in Châlons. Tired of waiting, I go to bed at eleven thirty.

19 July 1918

Up at two in the morning. We leave at two thirty to load up munitions at Meulette and take them to the Enghien Forest. As we drive through Châlons we can see seven houses on fire. When we get to Meulette, we learn that my lieutenant is not the convoy leader. So after I have replaced a punctured tyre, we return to Saint-Gibrien and get there at six. I don't go back to bed but work on my car. In spite of the planes overhead, I am tired and go to bed at ten.

20 July 1918

Up at nine. In spite of the cannonade, I slept well. At one thirty, we receive orders to leave the village, and we're not sorry to go. We are packed up and ready in an hour. We retrace our steps a bit and at seven, we arrive at Écury-le-Repos. I have to wait for our baggage as it is coming by heavy rail.

With leave from Lieutenant Férrié, I have found a place to sleep in a small stables attached to the house where my lieutenant is billeted. I go to bed at midnight.

21 July 1918

Up at eight. It rained for part of the night and at five this morning, we had to move our beds as the water was coming in on us. No one has told me I am on duty this morning, and since it is Sunday, I rest. In the evening after supper, we go for a walk in countryside, which is magnificent. I go to bed at ten.

22 July 1918

Up at eight. I work on my car all day, as I have to tighten the brakes and then test them. In the evening after supper, I sit on the grass and read. Then I chat a bit with my lieutenant. Bed at ten thirty.

23 July 1918

Up at eight. As it is raining, I can't do very much work on the car. In the afternoon, I go out with my lieutenant on a personal errand. We drive to Fère-Champenoise and Connantray. We get back at five thirty. In the evening, I write and then go to bed at ten.

24 July 1918

Up at five thirty. We leave at six thirty. We load up equipment from an air base at Couraujean and take it to Baye. It is an eventful trip and as it is a fine day, it has seemed more like an outing. I get back at five thirty. I eat. I write and go to bed at ten.

25 July 1918

Up at eight. I work on my car. At eleven, my lieutenant and I go to Bergères-les-Vertus. I return at half past twelve. I have lunch and have a rest. At four, I go out again to Aulnizeux, and get back at five thirty.

In the evening, we go fishing for crayfish which are to be found in the area, and we catch thirty-four. I return and go to bed at eleven.

26 July 1918

Up at two in the morning. We leave in convoy at three. We load up Italian equipment at Esternay. In the car I am carrying a lieutenant and a wounded captain. Equipment and passengers are unloaded at the Sainte Touche camp. Five kilometres away from barracks, A tyre bursts. I change it in the pouring rain. No sooner back than we have to go out again to the Brigade Group at Bergères-les-Vertus. I get back at one thirty in the morning and go to bed at two.

27 July 1918

Up at nine. I had a good night's rest. I work on the car until eleven and again in the afternoon, until three thirty. In the evening, I write and go to bed at ten.

28 July 1918

Up at five. Departure at six. We load up munitions at Avize and take them to the de Laborde farm. We go through Epernay, which has been devastated by bombardments from the air. The Moët et Chandon buildings have been burning for two days. We return at five in the evening. I write a little and then go to bed at ten thirty.

29 July 1918

Up at eight. One of the car's tyres burst of its own accord last night. I change it and in the afternoon, give the car a bit of a clean. In the evening, many of us go to a film being shown in a barn. We get back at ten. I go to bed at eleven.

30 July 1918

Up at eight. We are not going out today and I use the time rubbing the hood down with linseed oil, which takes up a good part of the day. We go fishing again for crayfish in the evening, but by nine, we have only caught three. Bored, I return, chat for a bit and then go to bed at ten.

31 July 1918

Up at eight. I work a bit on the car and in the afternoon drive my lieutenant to Bergères-les-Vertus. In the evening, I stay up quite late talking. Then I read a bit and go to bed at eleven.

1 August 1918

Up at eight. I have to fix a rim tyre to the back of my car and then I give it a bit of a clean. It is so hot in the afternoon that I lie on my bed and read. I go for a walk in the evening and turn in at ten.

2 August 1918

Up at eight. I tinker a bit in the morning, and in the afternoon, drive my lieutenant to Trécon. After supper, I write and then go to bed at ten.

3 August 1918

Up at eight. An uneventful morning. I run my captain and lieutenant to Aubaizeux. We return at four. After supper, I write and go to bed at ten.

4 August 1918

Four years ago today, I left my family to go to war. It is infamous when I think how I have had to put up with four years of this undignified existence to say nothing of the pain of separation.

Up at six. Departure at seven. We are going to Bergères-les-Vertus to collect some Italian workers and take them to Herbisse.

We return at two thirty, but then I return to the Brigade Group at Bergères-les-Vertus. I eat at five thirty and then go to Sommesous. I get back at six thirty. I turn in at nine, as I have bad toothache.

5 August 1918

Up at eight. I work on my car, and then in the afternoon go to the Brigade Group at Bergères-les-Vertus. I am told we will be moving on probably tomorrow morning. In the evening, I write. Bed at ten.

6 August 1918

Up at three. Departure at four. We pack everything up, as we are not coming back here. We go to Montmirail and load up with provisions and take them to the station at Épernay-Cumières. We are going to Mareuil-le-Port, which just fifteen days earlier, was occupied by the Boches. We arrive in torrential rain. There is nothing sadder than the village which is completely destroyed. A château – belonging to one Maître Robert, a solicitor at Épernay – riddled with shells serves as the barracks. The officers find rooms in the upstairs apartments. The rest of us make our quarters in the cellars. There are beds and besteads everywhere. I take a bedstead, roll out my mattress and numbed with fatigue, go to bed at eleven.

7 August 1918

Up at six. Departure at seven. We load up with provisions at Oeilly to take to the 10th division who are in the fighting lines. We go across a pontoon bridge opposite Jonchery and go through Châtillon-sur-Seine, Ville-en-Tardenais, Olizy, and many other villages, where there is nothing left – instead of houses, just piles of rubble.

There are so many dead horses and dead Germans at Ville-en-Tardenais that the place is a health hazard.

We return at two. I get properly settled in. I write and then go to bed at ten.

8 August 1918

Up at five. I leave in the place of a comrade who has to replace a broken coil spring in his lorry. He catches up with me on the way and I return at nine. At two forty-five, the lieutenant and I drive to Fère-Champenoise to fetch Lieutenant Péquignot, who is back from leave. He is two hours late. Then it's a race to Sommesous, so that my own lieutenant, who is going on furlough, can catch his train. But in spite of my speed, he misses it and has to wait until tomorrow. I go back to barracks with Lieutenant Péquignot and even though we are going in the direction of the firing lines, I turn my headlights on.

We arrive back at ten thirty. The lieutenant does not want me to eat alone at this time of night and invites me for a meal at his mess. So we eat together and I leave at eleven thirty. I go to bed at midnight.

9 August 1918

Up at eight. As my lieutenant is not here, I imagine I will have a bit less work. I spend the day working on the car. After supper, a mechanic and I are called out at five forty-five to Olizy, to help someone who has broken down. I get back at seven thirty. I write and read. I go to bed at ten.

10 August 1918

Up at eight. I work on the car and notice that the distributor cogwheel is damaged, which means I can't drive. I report it and wait for someone to get on to it – nobody does and I don't say anything. After supper, I go for a walk across the fields to take a look at the devastated countryside. I go to bed at ten.

11 August 1918

Up at seven. I am called out on convoy, but as my car is not fit to be driven, I can't go. I spend the day reading and writing. I go out for a bit in the evening. Bed at eleven.

12 August 1918

Up at seven thirty. My car is being repaired. All they have done is to take the clutch out to fix the throttle valve. I take it out for a test drive at four and everything seems in perfect order. I go for a walk in the evening and then go to bed at ten.

13 August 1918

Up at eight. I am not going out, so I tinker on the car all day. After supper we walk to a small neighbouring village. It has been destroyed like all the others around. I go to bed at ten.

14 August 1918

Up at eight. I tinker a bit. I rest in the afternoon and write. I go for a walk in the evening, Bed at ten.

15 August 1918

Up at six. We load up with wine at Oeuilly station and take it to Bouy. I get back at four. It is so hot in the evening that we go into the countryside to cool off. I go to bed at ten.

16 August 1918

Up at eight. I give the car a bit of a polish. At two, Lieutenant Péquignot asks me to take him and a very young sub-lieutenant (22 years old – four medals) from the 103rd to Orlais. When we arrive, the sub-lieutenant gives me a five-franc tip, which was very nice of him. I get back at four. I write for a bit. Bed at ten.

17 August 1918

Up at eight. I spend the day tinkering. In the evening we sit about talking until eleven thirty. I go to bed at midnight.

18 August 1918

Up at five. Departure at six. We are taking the 103rd from Mareuil-le-Port to Dampierre-au-Temple. Then we come back to Port-à-Binson where at five forty-five we collect stretcher-bearers from the seventh division and take them to Saint-Hilaire-au-Temple. we are greeted by two shells as we arrive. On the way back, I am driving at seventy when a tyre bursts, and I go into a skid. My lieutenant and I might well have been killed had it not been for a pile of stones that stopped us from turning over. I arrive back at two thirty in the morning and go to bed at three.

19 August 1918

Up at six. I slept little but well. I am not going out and I spend the day working on my car. We talk in the evening. Bed at eleven.

20 August 1918

Up at eight. I had a good night's rest. I tinker all morning. In the evening, we go for a walk to Sarsénil. Bed at ten.

21 August 1918

Up at five. Departure at six. We take provisions to Faverolles and return at five in the evening. After supper, a small walk. Bed at ten.

22 August 1918

Up at eight. We are not going out today. I spend the day tinkering. In the evening we go for a walk in the countryside. At six a Boche plane, drops six bombs in the area. I go to bed at eleven.

23 August 1918

Up at seven. My lieutenant returned from furlough at eleven last night. At seven thirty he called me to his room, and after greeting each other, I went to fetch his luggage from Port-à-Binson. At nine, we both went to the Brigade Group at Mardeuil, and returned at eleven thirty. I spend the afternoon tinkering. In the evening, we talk for a bit. I go to bed at ten.

24 August 1918

Up at eight. I am not going out today, and I spend my time making a trunk for my car. In the evening, I write for a bit and then go to bed at ten.

25 August 1918

Up at five forty-five. Departure at six. We load up provisions at Dormans to take to Aougny. We return at four thirty. At five thirty, we leave again for the Brigade Group at Mardeuil. I get back at six thirty. I have something to eat, go for a walk and then go to bed at ten.

26 August 1918

Up at eight. I give the car a thorough going over. In the evening, a short walk. I go to bed at ten.

27 August 1918

Up at eight. I am not going out and spend the day tinkering. In the evening we go for a long walk. I go to bed at ten thirty.

28 August 1918

Up at eight. I thought I would be going out, but it seems not. At two, the lieutenant and I drive to Port-à-Binson to have our photographs taken by an events photographer. We bring him fuel and also a candle for him to develop the pictures. When I get back, I write. In the evening, we go for a walk. I go to bed at ten.

29 August 1918

Up at five thirty. Departure at six fifteen. We load up provisions at Dormans to take to Aougny. We return at five. I have supper and I write. At nine, we are told to be ready either later tonight or tomorrow morning to transport troops over 1200 kilometres, which will take four days. We await further orders. I go to bed at nine thirty.

30 August 1918

Up at eight. The troop transport hasn't happened. However, it has only been suspended and I get my car ready. I tinker all afternoon. In the evening, I go out for a bit and then go to bed at ten.

31 August 1918

Up at eight. Still no orders to leave. I tinker all day. In the evening, I go out and then go to bed at ten.

1 September 1918

Up at eight. It is Sunday and very strangely, I am not going out. I spend the day writing. At four, I go to Mardeuil. After supper, I write. I go to bed at ten.

2 September 1918

Up at five. Departure at six. We load up with provisions at the station at Bertheney. We get back at five in the evening. At six, I return to Mardeuil and then back to barracks at seven. I write for a bit. Bed at ten.

3 September 1918

Up at three. The transport order has arrived. We leave at four, load up munitions at Crezancy and take them to the Americans in the woods of Meunière. From there we go to Chierry and have to spend the night on the road. At eleven, I sleep on the floor of a lorry.

4 September 1918

Up at four thirty. Departure at five thirty. We load up with dismantled barracks and take them to villages that have been demolished. At eight, we have orders to return to Mareuil-le-Port. We hit a storm on the way back and it is pitch dark, which makes driving very difficult for me. Eventually, we get back at ten. My lieutenant invites me to eat with him at his mess. Here's a little glimpse of what these gentlemen eat. I have soup, two baked eggs in sorrel, steak with peas and macaroni, cheese, and apple tart. On which I sleep at eleven.

5 September 1918

Up at eight thirty. I spend the day working on the car which needs some attention. In the evening, I write for a bit and talk. I go to bed at ten.

6 September 1918

Up at five. Departure at five forty-five. We load up provisions at the station at Dormans to take to the farm at Bertheney. We return for lunch at eleven thirty. We leave again at one thirty and return at three thirty. At five we go to Mardeuil and then on to Ay, Dizy and Magenta.

We return via Épernay, where my lieutenant makes a purchase. At that moment the DSA (Direction de Service Automobile) commander, comes over and sentences me to fifteen days in prison and my lieutenant to eight days, because I left the engine running when I stopped. What a bastard. I have never been punished for anything, and this seems particularly harsh. I am outraged and my lieutenant even more so. I am so angry, that I drive badly and at top speed. We go straight to the Brigade Group and tell the story to Captain Heuch, who has taken over while Captain Fontenilliat is on furlough. He tells me not to worry about it as he thinks the punishment is absolutely ridiculous and that he will tear it up when he receives it. Still, it really rankles. I get back at seven. I eat and go to bed at ten thirty.

7 September 1918

Up at eight. I work on my car. In the afternoon, I rest. In the evening, I go for a walk and then go to bed at ten.

8 September 1918

Up at eight. I am not going out. There is nothing to do all day. It is raining. I spend the day reading and writing. Bed at ten.

9 September 1918

Up at eight. Again, I am not going out today. I spend the day writing. Bed at ten.

10 September 1918

Up at eight. Still not going out. The rain is torrential and is coming in everywhere in the château, except perhaps, in our cellar. I read and write. Bed at ten.

11 September 1918

Up at three thirty. Departure at four thirty. We are going to the station at Épernay to load up provisions to take to Sarcy. Then the lorries are to take equipment to eleven different places. I spend the day driving backwards and forwards and have a puncture en route. I get back at six in the evening. I'm meant to be going out again at eight, but there is a counter-order at nine, which is fine by me. Bed at ten thirty.

12 September 1918

Up at eight. I work on the car. In the afternoon, I spend the afternoon at the Brigade Group and get back at six. In the evening, I write and go to bed at ten.

13 September 1918

Up at five thirty. At six, we go to the Brigade Group where I stay for the entire day, and have my car fitted with new canvas. I return at six thirty, but go out again at eight thirty to drive two officers to Crézancy. They tip me two francs (not very generous).

On the way back I have a puncture and have to change the tyre in torrential rain. I get back to Port-à-Binson – to where we moved in the afternoon – at eleven. My lieutenant has found me a spot to myself in a stable, where I shall be very comfortable. I go to bed at midnight.

14 September 1918

Up at eight. I work on my car. At four in the afternoon, I go to the Brigade Group and get back at six. I have something to eat, and then write. Bed at ten thirty.

15 September 1918

Up at three thirty. We leave at four thirty. We load up shells at Breuil and take them to the Dormant woods. It has been a very hard day without a break. I can feel the beginnings of enteritis, which is painful. I get back at ten in the evening, exhausted. I write and then go to bed at eleven thirty

16 September 1918

Up at four forty-five. Departure at five forty-five. We are taking provisions from the station at Épernay-Cumières to the farm at Presle, and then equipment to Faverolles. My enteritis is getting worse. I get back at six thirty. I try to eat, but I can't. Worn out, I go to bed at nine thirty.

17 September 1918

Up at eight thirty. My enteritis played up all night and I feel too under the weather to work on the car. At eleven, I learn that there is a departure tonight at six. I immediately go to my lieutenant and tell him

I'm feeling so lousy, I'm not sure I'll be well enough to go. I entrust my car to Lauzeral, and show him how to drive it, and he takes my place in the evening. I eat an egg and drink tea. I write and go to bed at nine.

18 September 1918

Up at eight. I have nothing to do and I am still very uncomfortable from the enteritis attack. Lauzeral gets back late afternoon. My lieutenant, in the meantime, has taken another car and does not get in until eleven at night. In the evening, I write and then go to bed at nine.

19 September 1918

Up at eight. Lauzeral and I immediately set to work on the car. There is a departure tonight for a service of five or six days. My lieutenant doesn't want me to go as he thinks I am not well enough for the service, which is to be operated from a small village, and will be rapid and extremely tiring. Lauzeral will go in my place. I watch them leave and I must admit, I feel a little regretful. In the evening, I feel a bit better, and I join in a game of roulette. I go to bed at eleven.

20 September 1918

Up at eight. Nothing to do. I am feeling a bit better. I spend my time rolling cigarettes. in the evening, I write and go to bed at ten.

21 September 1918

Up at eight thirty. I still have nothing to do. I roll cigarettes as I did yesterday. In the evening I write and go to bed at eleven.

22 September 1918

Up at eight. I pass the time by rolling even more cigarettes. In the evening, I write. I go to bed at ten thirty.

23 September 1918

Up at eight. In the afternoon at two o'clock, we are told that we will be leaving Port-à-Binson, for Mardeuil. We get there at eight even though it is so close. At nine thirty, we set up our barracks in a gymnasium and at ten, I go to bed.

24 September 1918

Up at seven thirty. I was cold in this great place. I spend the morning looking for more comfortable lodgings. Impossible to find anything. So we are obliged to find a corner in the gymnasium which takes us all afternoon. I write and go to bed at nine thirty.

25 September 1918

Up at eight. I was cold again all night. I have nothing to do and spend the time as I can. In the evening I write and go to bed at nine thirty.

26 September 1918

Up at eight. I was still cold, but I have just found a place where I'll be a little more comfortable, and tomorrow, I'll move in. I muck about all day and go to bed at ten.

27 September 1918

Up at eight. I set about moving in to my new digs. We have a place in a sort of laundry, which is spacious and clean. We learn that the 56th Light Infantry will be arriving at two in the morning; so no doubt, we will have quite a few men billeted on us. In the evening, I write and go to bed at ten.

28 September 1918

Up at eight. I have nothing to do. I spend the day reading. I write in the evening, and go to bed at ten.

29 September 1918

Up at eight. It is Sunday. In the afternoon, we walk as far as Cumières. At seven thirty in the evening, I am assigned to go out with a lorry. As I am now a touring-car driver, I refuse categorically. I am immediately summoned to the mess by Lieutenant Jobert, an extremely unpleasant paint salesman from St Cloud, who is in charge of the section in my lieutenant's absence. He is furious that I am doing nothing, and haven't even been given sick leave. He wants an explanation. I tell him that I am recuperating from an enteritis attack and I will not go out. He tells me that I'm not a very loyal Frenchman. My temper gets the better of me, and I answer back that I have seen nineteen months of active service and have the Croix de Guerre to show for it, which is more than most people can do and certainly worth more than some stripe. I repeat my refusal to take a lorry out. He then orders me to go to the doctor tomorrow and get an exemption order. I tell him that I will have no problem getting that first thing tomorrow morning. I go back to our billet furious, but I am not going out. I write a bit and go to bed at ten

30 September 1918

Up at seven. At nine, I go to the doctor on his rounds. It is Doctor Subert who knows me well and remembers me from when I served as a nurse for him at Igney. I tell him my story frankly, and at the same time have him examine me. He tells me the enteritis hasn't completely gone, and that I certainly need more time off. On strength of this, he exempts me from driving a lorry, and I am vindicated.

Lieutenant Jobert who is waiting to see the doctor's report, is put out, as he did not expect this. He takes his revenge by ordering me to work in the workshops. I tell him that I will go to the workshops if he wants me too, but I will not work, and I add that, if he insists, then I will ask to be sent to hospital and then he will see what happens when my lieutenant returns and finds he has been deprived of his driver. He is furious and tells me I am to go to the workshops anyway. I go over at midday and spend the time smoking – I also get frozen feet.

When I get back at five, the quartermaster comes to tell me that I am leaving at eight tomorrow morning for Jouy-sur-Martin, to rejoin my lieutenant and to take up my duties as driver again. I am delighted, and immediately pack my belongings. I write and then go to bed at ten.

1 October 1918

Up at six thirty. At seven fifteen, I go to the quartermaster's office to get my orders, and I am very upset to learn that my departure has been suspended as the lieutenant, will be shortly coming back here. I go back to the workshops in the afternoon, so that I don't have to look at Jobert's ugly mug. In the evening at eight a film is shown in a barn. We go and I get to bed at eleven.

2 October 1918

Up at eight. I am left in peace all morning. I go to the workshops in the afternoon; my only work is to get bored. In the evening I write. Bed at ten.

3 October 1918

Up at eight. At nine I go to the workshops. At eleven, my lieutenant returns, and I go over to see him at one o'clock. He shakes my hand effusively and wants to hear my news. He tells me he has missed me – well, that makes two of us. I immediately take up service with him and we leave at two for Try. On the way, I tell him about the Jobert incident. He tells me not to worry about it and that he will avenge me. We return at four. In the evening, I write. Bed at nine thirty.

4 October 1918

Up at seven thirty. At eight I leave for Courville and get back at one for lunch. In the afternoon, I work on the car. I go to bed at ten.

5 October 1918

Up at eight. We are waiting for orders to move to Argonne. We spend the day packing up. I go to bed at ten.

6 October 1918

Up at eight. We are still waiting to leave. I spend the day mucking about. In the evening, we go to the cinema. I go to bed at ten thirty.

7 October 1918

Up at five. Departure at six. We are moving to Gizancourt. I take the quartermasters with me so they can set up the barracks. We arrive at eight. I spend the day with the lieutenant and the quartermaster looking for suitable quarters. I have a place next to the lieutenant in a small stable. It is raining heavily. The men arrive at three thirty and settle in. Tonight, I shall write to the YMCA, which is a well-organized soldiers' hostel. We are warned that there are cases of Spanish flu in the village – cheerful news. I go to bed at ten.

8 October 1918

Up at eight. At eleven, I have to move from my spot, and I am obliged to sleep in barracks. I spend the day moving again. I go to bed at nine.

9 October 1918

Up at eight. At nine, the lieutenant tells me we are leaving at nine thirty. We are going to Suippes and Sommes-Suippes, but on the way, I notice a ball bearing is broken and we have to return to barracks so that I can fix it. An hour later, we set off again. We drive to Vitry-le-François, Vitry-la-Ville, Châlons, Suippes, and Sommes-Suippes. I have to drive back without lights and I am dead tired by the time we return at nine. I eat and then go to bed at ten.

10 October 1918

Up at eight. I work on my car. In the afternoon, I write. I've had a bit of an upset, because I was meant to be going on furlough tomorrow, and Lauzeral was to replace me. But his father has died, and he left this morning on compassionate leave, so I have to wait for his return before I can go myself – a delay of eight days.

At four, I drive to Sainte-Menehould and get back at five fifteen. In the evening, I take a look round the soldiers' hostel. I go to bed at nine thirty.

11 October 1918

Up at eight. I have nothing to do today, as I am not going out. In the afternoon, I write. Bed at ten.

12 October 1918

Up at six thirty. Departure at seven thirty. We are taking engineering equipment to Autry and to Ardeuil-et-Montfuxelles. It is a very bad road as it is so slippery. I get back at six fifteen. Bed at nine

13 October 1918

Up at eight. A day of rest for everyone. I work on the car all morning. I spend the afternoon writing. I go to bed at ten in the evening.

14 October 1918

Up at seven. Departure at seven thirty. We load up with provisions from the station at Somme-Suippes and take them to Semide on a very bad road. We get back at seven o'clock. I eat immediately and then go to bed at nine thirty.

15 October 1918

Up at eight. I am not going out today and I make use of the time by going to the workshops to have the carburettor and the clutch checked. This takes me until four thirty and we take it out for a test drive. It runs well. In the evening after supper, I go to the soldiers' hostel where they are showing a film. I stay until eight thirty. I go to bed at ten.

16 October 1918

Up at eight. I am not going out. I tidy my belongings. It has poured with rain all day. I write in the afternoon. In the evening, I go to bed at ten.

17 October 1918

Up at eight. I keep myself busy as best I can, as I am not going out today. I write and go to bed at ten.

18 October 1918

Up at eight. There is nothing to do. I spend the day tinkering and writing. Bed at ten.

19 October 1918

Up at four thirty. Departure at five thirty. We are taking provisions from the station at Somme-Suippes to Machault. We get back at seven o'clock. I eat and then go to bed at ten.

20 October 1918

Up at seven thirty. I'm summoned to the office by the lieutenant who tells me I am on furlough. Lauzeral has returned and I immediately hand the car over to him. A comrade and I take the one twenty-two train from Gizaucourt. It is raining without let-up. We go as far as Saint-Hilaire-au-Temple, and then change for Châlons where we arrive at five fifteen. There is no train until seven forty-one tomorrow morning – wonderful. We eat at a military canteen and then go to the cinema. Then we sit on a bench at a table and sleep with our heads on our arms.

21 October 1918

At two in the morning I wake up heavy eyed but I am no longer sleepy. We have a hot coffee at six, and at seven forty-one we board a packed train. I get to Paris at one twenty-five, and after all the formalities, I am out at two o'clock. I go to my wife's office, and then home, where I have a bit of a scrub up. In the evening, dinner with the family. Bed at nine thirty.

22 October 1918

Up at seven thirty. I think I have caught a bad cold. I don't want it to get any worse and I treat it immediately. My garden looks like a virgin forest, and I set about getting it tidied up. In the afternoon, I visit my sister Marie. I'm very tired in the evening and go to bed at ten thirty.

23 October 1918

Up at nine. I definitely have a cold. I work in the garden all day. In the evening, bed at ten.

24 October 1918

Up at ten. I potter around all morning. In the afternoon, my friend Mariot, Captain Gourragne's driver, drops in to see me. I go to bed at ten thirty.

25 October 1918

Up at nine. I still have a cold. In the afternoon, I go into Paris on an errand for a comrade. In the evening at six, I fetch my wife from the office and we return home together. Bed at ten.

26 October 1918

Up at eight. My cold is still with me. I stay at home to work. In the evening, bed at ten thirty.

27 October 1918

Up at nine. I visit my sister Marie, and find everybody there. Later, Jeanne and Georges pay us a visit and we spend the afternoon together, and they stay and have dinner with us. Bed at eleven.

28 October 1918

Up at nine. I potter about at home all day. Bed at ten thirty.

29 October 1918

Up at eight thirty. We have lunch at Puteaux and stay there all afternoon. In the evening my brother-in-law Edmond arrives at the house. He has a month's convalescent leave.

30 October 1918

Up at nine. Edmond comes with me to Place de Vincennes, to see if I can extend my leave, and we are sent to Invalides. We go in the afternoon, but there's nothing we can do to prolong it. We do a little shopping. At six, I have an aperitif with my friend Debout. At seven thirty we go home for dinner. I go to bed at eleven.

31 October 1918

Up at eight. I am not going out. I potter about all day. In the evening, I go to bed at ten thirty.

1 November 1918

Up at nine. Lunch with my sister Marie. We are twelve at the table and we stay until four in the afternoon. In the evening, we have dinner at home and set the table for tomorrow morning as we have invited the Felders for lunch. We also make a chestnut cake, which takes us quite a while. I go to bed at eleven thirty.

2 November 1918

Up at eight. We prepare lunch all morning – a real feast. We start at twelve, and don't leave the table until four thirty. The Felders are delightful people. In the evening we have very little to eat. I go to be at ten.

3 November 1918

Up at seven thirty. I have my leave papers endorsed at the Gare Saint-Mandé, and then go round to my two sisters and the Delapraz go say goodbye. We have lunch with the Felders and spend the afternoon with them. At six, we have an aperitif at the Grübers. We get back at eight and have dinner at home. I go to bed at eleven.

4 November 1918

Up at six thirty. I pack my bags, and I read in the paper that the armistice has been signed with Austria. Dear God, Germany surely cannot continue much longer on her own. Will the war soon be over? I dare not think it. However, the news has lifted my spirits a bit.

My wife comes with me to the station. I board the train at eight thirty. It leaves at nine fifteen and takes me to Faveresse, where at four forty-five I take another train to Valmy.

5 November 1918

I get to Gizaucourt at five fifteen and learn that the day before, everyone left for Sarry; Fortunately, there is a heavy goods train, which I can take. We leave at nine but with a change of direction as we are going into the Lorraine district. We will be billeted at Void-Vacon.

On the way, at Givry-en-Argonne I encounter my lieutenant whom I leave with Lauzeral for the rest of the day. We get to Void-Vacon at half past midnight. We have a bite to eat and then I find a corner in a barn where I stretch out on a hay bale.

6 November 1918

Up at six. Departure at seven thirty. My lieutenant tells me that while I was away Lauzeral has run the connecting rod on the car. I am astonished because he is a good driver. In any case the car is finished, and no doubt will have to be changed. I fetch it myself, climb in and am towed by a lorry to Damelevières where we arrive at eight in the evening. I have a bite to eat and then at nine thirty, go to sleep in a barn.

7 November 1918

Up at seven thirty. I settle in a little more comfortably and then look over the car. It doesn't seem quite as broken as I feared. At any rate, I think it can be repaired. I check with the workshops and they can work on it tomorrow. In the afternoon, I write. In the evening we go to the café. I turn in at nine thirty.

8 November 1918

Up at seven thirty. At eight I go over to the workshops. I go back at one and work there all afternoon. By four it is fixed. A dramatic turn of events. We learn that Germany has 72 hours to agree to the terms of the armistice. That is the most wonderful news, because she will have to accept. In the evening, we spend a little time at the café. Bed at nine thirty.

9 November 1918

Up at seven. I add the finishing touches to the car and in the afternoon, drive it to Lunéville. In the evening, I write. Bed at ten.

10 November 1918

We leave at one in convoy. We are to load up with artillery platforms and take them to Bauzemont. The trip takes all night driving in dense fog. We are greeted by the captain he asks us if we are mad, as according to him, the armistice will be signed tomorrow. Even so, we are in a region that has been bombarded incessantly since the start of the war. However, since this evening, there has not been one gunshot or cannon fired. We make another all night trip in dense fog and get back at four forty-five in the morning. I go to bed at five.

11 November 1918

Up at nine. A bit of a scrub up. At eleven o'clock, the town crier, beating his drum, confirms that the armistice has been signed. Everybody is half mad with joy. We don't know yet when we can return home, but just the fact that the cannons have stopped their firing, and that we can walk freely outside without fear of being hit by a shell or bullet, I can assure you, that in itself, is so wonderful that it is difficult to take it in.

In the afternoon, my lieutenant and I drive to Lunéville, where the euphoria of the population and military alike is impossible to describe. An extremely foolish aviator flies so low, that our kepis are blown off. People are hugging each other for nothing. It's crazy, but it is uplifting. I get back at five. At dinner, some mates and I drink a good bottle of wine. Worn out by all the emotion, I go to bed at nine thirty.

12 November 1918

Up at eight. I work a bit on the car. At ten, I go to Lunéville and return at midday. It's my feast day today, and we all go to the café where I buy a bottle of wine. I go to bed at ten thirty.

13 November 1918

Up at five. Departure at five thirty. We load up shells at Serres and Hoéville and bring them back to the depot at Tuvaux. It really is over. We are returning the merchandise. The weather is fine, but it is very cold. I get back at three. We spend some time at the café in the evening, and have a game of Manille. I go to bed at nine thirty.

14 November 1918

Up at eight. I tinker a bit. They have decided to change my car. At two I go to the Brigade Group at Mont-sur-Meurthe and I exchange my Delaunay-Belleville for a Théophile Schneider, which is just as big, but much lighter and therefore, easier to handle; it is also much faster and can reach ninety with ease. Its bodywork is in bad shape and needs a lot of work to restore it. I return at four thirty. We go to the café in the evening and have a game of Manille. bed at nine thirty.

5 November 1918

Up at seven. At seven thirty, I go over to the workshops and start cleaning up my new car, and I stay all day. In the evening we go to the café and have a game of écarté. I go to bed at ten.

16 November 1918

Up at seven. I go over to the workshops to go on with my work. At eleven o'clock, I leave with my lieutenant and two quartermasters to find a billet in the Vosges, as we are moving on tomorrow. We go to Vanémont which is twelve kilometres above Saint-Dié-des-Vosges. We return to Damelevières at eight in the evening. It is freezing hard. I have an excellent soup in the officers' mess, and a hot coffee, and I have a bed in a granary. I turn in at eleven.

17 November 1918

Up at six. We leave at eight for Vanémont. It is slow going. We make a stop at Raon-l'Étape and get to Vanémont at two. We set up in a barn. In the evening, we spend a little time at the café where I write. I go to bed at nine.

18 November 1918

Up at eight. I work on my car, which certainly runs extremely well. I go to La Chapelle and to Corcieux and return at four. In the evening we have a game of Manille at the café. Bed at ten.

19 November 1918

Up at three. Departure at four. We load up food and provisions at Raon-l'Étape to be distributed amongst the Alsatian population. We cross the border at Col de Hantz and go to Urmatt, where I spend the most incredible hour of my life.

The euphoria of the people in these liberated towns is indescribable. All the villages are decked with blue, white and red flags. Children clamber all over the car, and young girls kiss us. Men and old men particularly, welcome us with lifted hats. It is unbelievable.

In the evening, we load up French, Russian and Romanian prisoners. Their story is a painful one. The countryside is so beautiful that we have a wonderful trip. After a several eventful episodes, we get back at midnight. I go to bed at one thirty, worn out more from emotion than fatigue. It has been a tremendous day.

20 November 1918

Up at eight. We have to pack up as we leave at midday to billet at Fraize. We get there at two. I immediately find a place for five of us in an old butchery, where will be quite comfortable. I settle in and write. Bed at ten.

21 November 1918

Up at three thirty. Departure at four thirty. We load up with provisions at the Saint-Michel-sur-Meurthe station, to take to Saint-Peters – a marvellous drive. Once again, we receive a tumultuous welcome. Young girls take over my car and decorate the windscreen with tiny tricolour bouquets. The effect is lovely, and I return, decorated with flowers, at seven. I eat and then write a bit. I turn in at ten;

22 November 1918

Up at five thirty. Departure at six forty-five. We load up with food and provisions at Fraize station. We drive up through the Col du Bonhomme where there are two hairpin bends, and from there go to Guémar and Elsenheim.

On the way, we stop at Kaysersberg and my lieutenant invites me to lunch at an auberge where there is a very comely young maid called Kate, whom we tease unmercifully. She tells me she loves French humour which she finds is not in the least brutish.

From Elsenheim we go to Colmar, and are witness to the feast laid on by General de Castelnau for the populace. Here too, the town has a festive air and is bedecked with flags. We return to Elsenheim and get back at eight. I eat and go to bed at eleven.

23 November 1918

Up at seven thirty. At last, we are not going anywhere to day. I tinker a bit on the car and then in the afternoon, have a thorough and much needed wash. After that I write and in the evening we spend a little time in the café. Bed at eleven.

24 November 1918

Up at eight. Departure at nine. Once again, we go to Guémar and to Elsenheim and then push on to Schlestadt, making a stop at Kaysersberg, where my lieutenant again invites me for lunch. We see Kate again who has dressed up in Alsatian costume for our benefit, and very pretty she is too. Apparently our teasing is a little too noisy. So what? The war is over. We return to the auberge at four and have a kirsch, and then leave again at top speed because we are late. We get back at six. I eat, write, and then go to bed at ten.

25 November 1918

Up at seven thirty. I am not part of the convoy today. I work on my car, particularly on the brakes, which need attention, especially in this part of the world. At three in the afternoon, I drive a lieutenant who is on furlough to Saint-Dié. I get back at six. I eat, and then write a bit at the café. I go to bed at ten.

26 November 1918

Up at five thirty. Departure at six forty-five. We load up provisions at the station at Fraize for distribution at Guémar and Elsenheim. I have a good lunch of choucroute at Guémar.

From there I take a sub-lieutenant from the 8th Light Infantry to Schlestadt and then return to Guémar. After that I drive two captains from the 4th Artillery Regiment to Mackenheim, return to Marckolsheim, and from there go with my lieutenant to Sasbad to see the Rhine.

The river is 200 metres wide, but it is only about eighty metres wide, the rest being pebbles. It can be crossed by a pontoon bridge. We are one side and the Boches on the other – I go across in spite of the restrictions, and find my self in the land of the Hun. We go back and collect two sub-lieutenants from the artillery and take them to Fraize.

We stop at Kaysersberg on the way, to have a kirsch and to see Kate. We return at six. I eat, write a bit and go to bed at ten.

27 November 1918

I am not going out today. I work on the car. In the afternoon, I write. In the evening, a comrade from Marseille (Capuro) who is back from furlough, presents us with a cold rabbit, which we eat washed down with a good quarter litre of eau-de-vie, which is good, but is perhaps a little too fiery. Afterwards we go to the café to drink beer and play billiards. I have to go out for a call of nature, and return to the smoky and boozy atmosphere of the café. It is my turn to play, but I can't see the balls. My head is spinning and I am completely plastered. I'm overwhelmed and my comrades have to carry me back to our billet. They roll me onto my bed and go back to the café. Half an hour later, I vomit violently where I am and go to sleep in it. The comrades wake me up when they get back an hour later, and I see they are even drunker than I am. That Marseillais pig is overjoyed to have put a Parisian under the table – the shame of it is that Parisian is me.

28 November 1918

Up at seven. My head is so heavy it seems to roll about on my shoulders. I go over to the car, but it is raining and I don't do much work. In the afternoon, I write. In the evening after supper, I have a tedious fatigue duty. I have to meet up with two drivers at Saint-Dié and bring them back. I return in foul weather – pouring rain and a tempestuous wind. I go to bed at half past midnight.

29 November 1918

Up at seven thirty. I work on my car. At ten, I go to the Brigade Group at Saint-Dié and return at midday. I pack up my belongings in the afternoon as tomorrow, we leave for Mulhouse. In the evening, a little time at the café and bed at ten.

30 November 1918

Up at five. Departure at seven. It is a very difficult trip with a number of mishaps. We arrive at eight in the evening, at our billet in Brunstatt, two kilometres away from Mulhouse. Impossible to find anything at this time of night. I have a bite to eat in a café and then just for tonight, I find a place in a lorry, and turn in at eleven.

1 December 1918

Up at seven thirty. I fill the car up and at ten I drive my lieutenant and captain to Mulhouse to do some shopping. I get back at eleven. I have lunch at midday and then we take men on furlough and civilians to Montreux-Vieux. Various incidents on the road cause me to return in thick fog at ten in the evening. I have a quick bite to eat and then go to bed at ten thirty.

2 December 1918

Up at seven. I am not going out today and make use of the time by washing the car at the canal. In the afternoon, I have a bit of a scrub up. In the evening we go to the café. I go to bed at ten.

3 December 1918

Up at seven thirty. I am not going out today. I spend the day tinkering. At nine in the evening we are told that we leave tomorrow for Duppigheim. I pack and then go to bed at ten.

4 December 1918

Up at five, we pack up to leave. At seven everything is ready. We leave at eight. We do the journey quite rapidly. My lieutenant and I make a stop at Colmar. We arrive at Duppigheim at three, but, as usual, setting up the billet takes time and is not complete before four thirty.

All the villagers are so anxious to house us drivers, that in the end, there are only two of us to a house, and we are given proper beds. My motorcyclist and I have been taken in by some very pleasant people who unfortunately, don't speak a word of French. I have to make myself understood with the four words of German that I know. We have a warm, light, spacious room, which also has electric light. I write a bit, and then we join the family in the warmth. I go to bed at last, at nine.

5 December 1918

Up at seven thirty. I had a good night in a warm, comfortable bed and my comrade didn't disturb me too much, although I know he is infested with lice. I work on the car a bit. At one thirty in the afternoon, my lieutenant and I go to Strasbourg which is only about fifteen kilometres away. We make our way slowly through the main streets of the town, which look very much like those in Paris, particularly the embankments, which could be taken for those at the Hôtel de Ville. We go to the cathedral and take it in turn to visit it. We both make several purchases of postcards and other items. Then we drive back through dense fog and arrive at four. In the evening, I write and go to bed at ten.

6 December 1918

Up at seven thirty. I work on the car all morning. I read and write in the afternoon. In the evening, I learn a bit of German from my hosts. Bed at ten.

7 December 1918

Up at seven thirty. I spend the day tinkering. We are told in the afternoon, that our section has been designated to leave for Nancy on Monday. We get ready.

At seven in the evening, my lieutenant comes to see me and tells me that he is not leaving for Nancy but has to form a section with other drivers, which will probably be the 838, to take delivery of Boche lorries. He tells me he has to carry out his orders, and that although I am free to return to Nancy, he would miss me greatly and asks me if I will stay with him. If he only knew how much I would prefer to keep moving about in Alsace rather than being confined to barracks in Nancy. I tell him he can count on me and that I will follow him until the end of the clean-up operations. He thanks me very sincerely.

In the meantime, I am transferred to the 65 and I have to wait for whatever comes next. It certainly made me sad to take leave of my good friends, but I console myself with a few glasses of beer at the café. I go back to my digs to write and go to bed at nine thirty.

8 December 1918

Up at eight. At ten, I go to mass which is said in German. In the meantime, my lieutenant takes the car to do some shopping. It is the first time I have ever seen him drive. I have an uneventful afternoon. at four, I wander around Strasbourg, and on my return go to the Brigade Group at Duttlenheim. I get back at six thirty. I eat and then we go to a dance being held in the café. All the women want to dance with us. I return at ten and go to bed.

9 December 1918

Up at seven thirty. I work on my car. After a meal, I dress in full uniform as we are going to Innenheim to see where our new section is to be based. We go on from there to Strasbourg to take part in the celebrations. We get there in time to see the procession of the Poincaré-Clémenceau retinue. It is all magnificent. All the Alsatians from all the neighbouring villages are in costume and it is a lovely sight. They are amazed that the authorities are so approachable. When the Kaiser visited Strasbourg, hardly anyone bothered to go out, and the few spectators there were couldn't get close to him at all, as he was protected by troops four lines deep. The people here are genuine and sincere. We leave at five and give a lift to three Alsatian women. We take them to where they want to go and return at six. I eat, and then we go to the café until ten. I go to bed at eleven.

10 December 1918

Up at seven. So now, there are not many of us in this very peaceful little village. I dress. at nine thirty and I go to the Brigade Group at Duttlenheim and then to Innenheim to collect our quartermaster who is part of our new section. I return to the Brigade Group and then get back at three. After supper, we spend a little time at the café, and then I write and go to bed at nine thirty.

11 December 1918

Up at eight. I tinker all day on my car. In the afternoon, I write. We go to the café for a bit and at ten thirty, I go to bed.

12 December 1918

Up at eight. The morning goes by as usual. Three comrades and I go into Strasbourg, where I leave the car at the CRA (Centre de Réparations et d'Approvisionnements) and we visit the city on foot, and I can enjoy it at leisure. We get back at four and my lieutenant tells me that tomorrow, the quartermaster and I will spend the day in Mulhouse. It will be a treat. After dinner we go to the café. I go to bed at ten.

13 December 1918

Up at seven. At eight the quartermaster and I leave for Mulhouse. The weather is worse than disgusting. The wind and rain don't let up for an instant, and as we are driving straight into it, I have to stop every five kilometres to clean the windscreen. At eleven, we have lunch at Colmar. We arrive at Mulhouse at one thirty and leave again at three fifteen. We drive to Innenheim where we stop at six and have a bacon omelette and potatoes fried in oil, with some good people who my comrade knows. We return at eight thirty. I hand in my report to the lieutenant and then go for a glass of beer at the café. I go back to write and go to bed at ten.

14 December 1918

Up at seven thirty. I wash my car at the pond. In the afternoon, I have to go to the Brigade Group again, and I am livid because my car is dirtied again. In the evening, we go to the café. I go to bed at ten.

15 December 1918

Up at eight. at eight thirty my lieutenant tells me that we have to leave for the Brigade Group at ten. But there is a counter-order at the last minute. At ten thirty, I go to mass. At one thirty, the lieutenant, a couple of comrades and I drive to Strasbourg. We drop the two comrades off and the lieutenant and I push on to the Rhine which we view from the Kehl bridge. The bridge is a marvellous construction, but it has a military patrol on both sides. We go back to the city and explore its streets and districts more thoroughly. At four we pick up my comrades from the CRA and at four thirty, drive back through thick fog.

16 December 1918

Up at eight. At eight thirty, my car has to have a small repair done to it. I go to the Brigade Group in the afternoon and return at three. We go to the café in the evening, as the Rhine wines are excellent. When I get back, I write and go to bed at ten.

17 December 1918

Up at eight. I tinker a bit on my car. At one thirty, I go to the Brigade Group and return at three. in the evening I drive an officer back to the Brigade Group and return at nine. I go to the café for a bit and then to bed at ten.

18 December 1918

Up at eight. the 65th is leaving us to go to Metz, and those of us remaining, will join forces with the 407th. Another move, which is a bore because it means our mail will not get to us. I spend the morning doing nothing, or almost nothing. We go to the café in the evening. Then I write and go to bed at ten thirty.

19 December 1918

Up at eight. It appears that tomorrow, everyone is going to the 561st at Duttlenheim. The lieutenant and I go to the Brigade Group, and he gets permission for him and me to stay at Duppigheim, until further orders. To the café as usual in the evening, and then bed at ten thirty.

20 December 1918

Up at eight. At ten, we go to the Brigade Group, and learn that in spite of everything, we are all obliged to go to Duttlenheim tomorrow. I am really upset. We go back to the Brigade Group in the afternoon. In the evening we eat at the officers' mess and then join some young girls that we know for hot wine. We sit around chatting for some time. I go to bed at midnight

21 December 1918

Up at seven, I pack up my belongings. At nine, my lieutenant and I fetch his baggage which takes three trips. When we arrive, I find a small stable, which will take three of us. In the afternoon, I settle in. In the evening after supper, I go back to Duppigheim to see my ex-hosts and they are delighted to see me. When we get back, we go to the café for a bit. I go to bed at ten.

22 December 1918

Up at seven thirty. My lieutenant tells me that tomorrow we are leaving at eight for Schlestadt, where will wait for the arrival of the Boche lorries – an operation that could last for one to two months. I am delighted and repack my belongings. In the evening, we go to the café where they are having a dance. I go to bed at ten thirty.

23 December 1918

Up at seven. I get ready to leave. At one thirty, we go to Strasbourg and then Kehl to receive or orders from Captain Wickoff. The rain is lashing down and the wind is vile. We go on to Schlestadt where we arrive at five.

At eight, we go to the barracks to get a bite to eat. After that, we look for our own lodgings and we find a small building made up of two large rooms that belong to one Monsieur Spritz (an insurance broker from the Rhine and Moselle area) who will allow us to billet there. We immediately settle in with our beds. I turn in at nine thirty.

24 December 1918

Up at seven. We go to the auto park with the lieutenant, to help with the arrival of Boche lorries, and we are there all day without doing anything very much. What is interesting is that other than eating there, we are completely free to come and go as we please as we have no affiliation with the auto park at all. In the evening after supper, we go to a café. Bed at ten.

25 December 1918

Up at nine. It is Christmas Day. It is a day for rejoicing, but a sad one all the same, as we are not with our families. I wander about a bit in the morning. In the afternoon, we go for a walk and then return to the café for a game of cards, and we go back again in the evening as that is all there is to do. I write a bit and then go to bed at ten

26 December 1918

Up at seven thirty. I work on the car. At one thirty, the lieutenant and I go to the Brigade Group at Duttlenheim. We stay for a while and then return via Molsheim and Mutzig, which we admire as we drive through. I get back at five. In the evening, I write a bit and then go to bed at nine thirty.

27 December 1918

Up at eight. We go over to the auto park, but have nothing to do. In the afternoon, we have a little work as we have to make an inventory of five lorries. After supper, it snows so we stay in our room and make a good fire. I read and go to bed at ten.

28 December 1918

Up at eight. I work a bit on my car, as I have to check the carburettor. In the afternoon, we make a few more inventories of the lorries in the park. In the evening, it rains torrentially, so I stay indoors, read and write. I go to bed at eleven.

29 December 1918

Up at nine thirty. I do my Sunday scrub up. At one thirty, the lieutenant, two comrades and I fetch the post from Duttlenheim. We then go on to Duppigheim to look in on our old acquaintances. When I leave, Mathilde and Alois kiss me, and the lieutenant gives me an old-fashioned look. I return at five thirty. In the evening after supper, we spend a little time in the café. Then I return to read and write a little. I go to bed at ten thirty.

30 December 1918

Up at eight. I work on the car and fit it with a Boche headlamp, which certainly works better than the French ones. In the afternoon, I wander round the auto park. In the evening, I write for a bit and then go to bed at ten.

31 December 1918

Up at seven. At eight thirty, we leave for the CRA at Strasbourg and then from there to the Kehl Bridge. We return to Strasbourg for lunch. At two, we set off for Duppigheim and then to Duttlenheim to collect the post. I return at six fifteen. I have something to eat, and then read and to bed at ten.

1 January 1919

Up at nine. We all wish each other a happy and prosperous year, and it should be, as this time we will be returning home for good. At ten thirty, our lieutenant comes over to wish us the best. It's still sad that we can't be with our families. Happily, the release date has been announced.

We have champagne with our lunch. In the afternoon, we go for a long walk in the countryside and go as far as the neighbouring village. In the evening, we have a game of Manille in the café. I go to bed at ten.

2 January 1919

Up at eight. I tinker all morning. In the afternoon, I go over to the auto park for a bit. In the evening, I read and write and go to bed at ten.

3 January 1919

Up at eight. I work on my car. At one thirty, we collect the post from Duttlenheim and then go for a drive to Duppigheim. We return at six fifteen in torrential rain. I eat. I write and go to bed at ten.

4 January 1919

Up at nine. I am a little tired, as I have caught a heavy cold. I rest indoors in the morning. At two in the afternoon, my lieutenant comes to get me for a drive to see the Château Hohkönigsburg. It is a superb drive, and the view from the highest point is staggering. We drive down again and get back at four. After dinner, I write and go to bed at ten.

5 January 1919

Up at nine thirty. I have a bit of a wash. In the afternoon, I am writing by the fire, when the lieutenant calls me away at three, to go to Duttlenheim. As we go through Epfig, we spot the officers we were going to see. We retrace our steps and return. After supper, I write and go to bed at ten.

6 January 1919

Up at eight. At nine, the lieutenant and I go to Duttlenheim, as he is hoping to get leave. I have lunch there. After lunch, my lieutenant is down at the mouth, because he didn't get permission. We set off again at two. He didn't see the captain, and not being one to give in easily, he is going to come back tomorrow. I get back at three. In the evening, I write and go to bed a ten thirty.

7 January 1919

Up at seven thirty. At nine, we leave for Duttlenheim. At two, my lieutenant tells me he has permission to go on leave. We get back to Schlestadt at three, and then at five, we set off again and I take the lieutenant to Strasbourg where we arrive at six.

As I have to collect his replacement, Lieutenant Lautier, tomorrow, I stay the night at Duttlenheim with friends, where some comrades give me a place to sleep. We go to the café after dinner and I go to bed at eleven.

8 January 1919

Up at eight thirty. I fill up the car. At nine thirty, Lieutenant Lautier and I leave for Schlestadt and get there at ten. After lunch at two, we go to Strasbourg and get there at three. We leave the car at the CRA and walk round the town. We return to Schlestadt, and arrive back at six. I eat, write and then go to bed at ten thirty.

9 January 1919

Up at eight thirty. I am not going out and I have a thorough scrub up. In the afternoon, I tinker a bit on the car. In the evening, I write a lot of letters and go to bed at eleven.

10 January 1919

Up at eight. At nine, I go to Strasbourg and stay there for lunch. In the afternoon, we go through Duttlenheim, where I have to have an hour's repair done to the car. I get back at five. In the evening, I read a bit and go to bed at ten thirty.

11 January 1919

Up at eight. At nine Lieutenant Lautier, one of his comrades, and I visit Hohkönigsberg. We have a very nice outing and get back at eleven. At one thirty, the same crew and one of my comrades, set off again to the Sainte-Odile monastery.

It is a beautiful drive with a wonderful view. But I nearly have an accident. A horse attached to a wagon, takes fright and comes charging towards me. To avoid an accident, I have no choice but to immediately put the car and my passengers into a water-filled ditch. No one is hurt, but using jacks, it takes us three quarters of an hour to pull the car out again. Then we go on again as if nothing had happened.

I get back at five. In the evening after supper, I write a little and go to bed at eleven.

12 January 1919

Up at eight thirty. I have a thorough scrub up. In the afternoon, as the weather is not good, a comrade and I pay our twenty sous and go to the 'kinema'. We see a Boche film of which I did not understand one word, and a very good French film. We buy cakes when we leave to eat when we get back. In the evening after dinner, we have a game of Manille in a café where there is a concert given by a pianist and accordionist. It is excellent. I go to bed at eleven.

13 January 1919

Up at seven thirty. While I am washing, Mr Spritz our host comes over and invites us to go to his house in the evening. I accept. In the afternoon, I tinker a bit. At eight in the evening, we go to Mr Spritz's house where we are made very welcome by him and his wife. They give us ham sandwiches with butter, spicy biscuits and Alsatian wine. We don't leave until midnight. I go to bed at half past midnight.

14 January 1919

Up at eight. I have a bit of a wash. At half past twelve in the afternoon, three comrades and I take my car and make an illicit getaway to Hohkönigsburg. We have a very pleasant outing, but we had to make it short, in case we were discovered. We get back at two. I spend the afternoon tinkering a bit. In the evening after supper, I read and write and then go to bed at ten thirty.

15 January 1919

Up at eight. I tinker all morning. For something to do in the afternoon, we chop up a pile of wood for Mr Spritz. At two, his wife gives us each a glass of kirsch, and then at five, a big jar of preserves. After dinner, we go to the café for a game of manille. I go to bed at eleven.

16 January 1919

Up at eight. At one thirty, I leave with the lieutenant and two comrades to go on an outing to Colmar. I am delighted to bump into a friend, Charles Judlin, who has a wholesale grocery, and with whom I was at school at Saint-Michel and whom I haven't seen since 1906, when I was last in this area. It takes him a good two minutes to recognize me and then he throws his arms round me, but suddenly aware of his employees he stops.

He tells me a shocking story. When war was declared, he was taken by the Boches and forced to fight for them on the Russian front. In the meantime, his brother Albert, who was in Paris, joined the French army and is now a lieutenant. So they could easily have fought each other; what a terrible thought that two brothers could quite unwittingly have killed one another.

We go for a glass at the café and then he walks with me to the car. We leave at five and get back at five thirty. In the evening, we play manille at the café. I write and go to bed at ten.

17 January 1919

Up at eight. I go over to the auto park, because we are expecting a delivery of 15 Boche lorries. This takes up most of the day. We spend all afternoon helping those who have come to fetch them. We finish at four. In the evening I read and write and go to bed at eleven.

18 January 1919

Up at seven thirty. I work on my car, because in an hour and fifteen minutes, I have to leave for Strasbourg. There is a counter order at midday. Another lieutenant, whose name I have forgotten, has arrived to replace Lieutenant Lautier. He is a very pleasant man. After shaking my hand very politely, we talk most agreeably for a long time.

In the evening, we go to the café to celebrate the departure of two comrades who are going on leave. We see Mr Spritz there and he joins us for a drink. When the party is over, everyone is a little worse for wear, and Mr Spritz is more than happy that we are there to help him home. He is very amusing. When I get in, I write hastily and then go to bed at eleven.

19 January 1919

Up at eight and I have a very bad headache. I go to the station to send my trunk and all my personal belongings home. Things don't move any faster in France and I am there for an hour. Then I go to the office at the auto park to have my registration papers verified for my demobilization, because our release date is at last in the offing. I have such a bad headache that I lie on my bed all afternoon. In the evening, I feel a bit better and we spend a little time at the café. I go to bed at eleven.

20 January 1919

Up at eight. At ten, I go to the office to hand in my papers in anticipation of my demobilization. It seems there are some papers missing. I immediately enlist the lieutenant's help, who does the necessary to get them sent. He takes me to his room and while he is writing, he offers me a packet of Algerian cigarettes.

The weather has changed and there has been a hard freeze. As a precautionary measure, I empty the car's radiator. In the evening, we go to the café, and then I write and go to bed at eleven.

21 January 1919

Up at seven thirty. We go over to the auto park to make an inventory of the lorries that are leaving, and then in the afternoon, we lend a hand to the drivers who have to take them. In the evening, we go to the café. I go to bed at ten.

22 January 1919

Up at eight. We check over the lorries that have to leave tomorrow morning. As the lieutenant hasn't received anything back about my papers, he will go to Strasbourg tomorrow. At first, he was going to take the train, but in the afternoon, he tells me to get the car ready for tomorrow morning. In the evening, we go to the café. Then I go back to write and go to bed at ten thirty.

23 January 1919

Up at seven thirty. It is snowing, so before getting the car warmed up, I go and check with the lieutenant. In view of the weather, he prefers to take the train to Strasbourg. So I let him go. I spend the day busying myself with my own affairs. In the evening, we go to the café. As I am getting ready for bed, my lieutenant comes over to my room. He tells me that he has obtained the necessary papers for my demobilization. However, we have to leave for Strasbourg tomorrow morning at six thirty, to fetch the replacements. I tell him I will be ready and thank him for all that he has done for me. I go to bed at ten thirty.

24 January 1919

We can't leave at six thirty, as I don't wake up until six forty-five. The lieutenant doesn't make any comment and we leave at seven thirty. We get to Strasbourg at eight thirty and while the lieutenant is getting his business done, I fill up the car. We set off again at ten forty-five. I step on it a bit and we are back by eleven thirty. At one, I go out to look for the lorries that were following us, and find them at the village entrance. I lead them to where they need to go and then return. We spend a short time at the café and then I go to bed at ten thirty.

25 January 1919

Up at seven. At eight, I go to the office to be demobilized. I have to go to the clothing office, then to the registry office and lastly, to the accounts department. I am out of there at ten thirty. I am free for the afternoon, and use the time to scrub up from head to toe. In the evening, we go to the café for a farewell drink with the comrades who remain. I go to bed at eleven thirty.

26 January 1919

Up at seven. The big day has arrived. At last I am leaving the army and this time for good. I get a cold meal at the kitchen, and then go to the office to sign the last piece of paper and then it is goodbye to all my mates and – to my car.

It is ridiculous, but I am suddenly overcome with emotion; my only consolation is that I know I'm not the only one. At half past twelve, we assemble and we are given our papers. We shake hands for the last time and then we are off to the station.

What a wonderful, glorious, happy day. At one forty-five, we board the train. A last flurry of handshakes, a last look at Schlestadt, where we were not at all unhappy, and we are on our way to Haguenau the assembly point. We are travelling in cattle cars, of course. We get to Haguenau at five where, like a flock of sheep, we are herded into the barracks. More formalities, with two pieces of paper to hand over to the office. We are shown a room in D Building where we are to sleep. In the middle of the night, you have to grope your way through the maze of corridors. Eventually, we find pallets and find a corner to spend the night. We eat from our knees like beggars, which we really seem to be. It is nine o'clock when we finally doss down on our pallets

27 January 1919

Up at seven. My back is aching from sleeping on a hard surface. At ten, we are taken to the refectory for something to eat. There are over 2000 people and it is impossible to get served, so we end up by not eating.

At midday, we are assembled in the courtyard and there is an alphabetical roll call. We wait there for two hours with the snow falling down on us. Eventually, at two thirty, and led by a mounted cavalry officer, we leave the barracks for the station. On the platform, we wait a bit longer and then eventually board cattle cars, with thirty-two men to a car.

We are given rations for four days, which consist of two loaves of bread, two tins of corned beef and two litres of wine. How long is our journey for? No one can tell us. At four twenty, the train slowly starts to move, and does not pick up pace. We eat a bit and then cast around for a place to sleep . . .

At six in the morning, my back is breaking – and worse – we discover that during the night we have barely covered fifty kilometres. How long will it take us to get to Paris? We spend the whole day pondering this problem. Another night falls. All of us doze.

28 January 1919

At eight in the morning, we are at Marles, which means we are not far from Paris and we should get there not long after midday. I can hardly stand up straight I am so tired. Two days and two nights in cars heated only by straw bales – it really is a case of not giving a damn to the bitter end – wonderful army, how I hate you and your leaders. They say that we will disembark at Vaugirard and from there will be taken to the military college.

Suddenly, I see we are at the Gare d'Est-Ceinture, and are making a brief stop. I can't stand it a minute longer. I jump down from the train and run to the ceinture, where I take another train that takes me to Avenue Vincennes. I disembark – nobody asks where I have come from – and ten minutes later, I am home, at last! I am home and free. I have something to eat, and then oh happiness! I dress in civilian clothes, this time for good. I go over to my mother and my sisters and at five thirty, I fetch my wife from her office.

What joy it is to still be in one piece and to be together again for ever. I will finish with a few personal reflections, but I still have to be formally discharged and have my demobilization papers endorsed. Apparently, there are further formalities, which I would like to note down here – a little further on.

29 January 1919

I get up early and go to the Fontenoy military barracks, to be officially discharged and hand back army issue items. When I get there, there are about 1500 men all there for the same purpose as me. I make inquiries.

Apparently, it will take a few days for us all to be discharged, but we have to be present, in case our name is called. This is just too much. The war is over – well over and I do not see why this officious officer should walk all over me. I tell him that I'll come back when I'm feeling a little more amenable.

5 February 1919

Yesterday, my brother-in-law Edmond comes round and tells me that I should do something about completing my army discharge and offers to come with me. We go there and then to the Fontenoy barracks. The courtyard is empty. There are two soldiers standing near an orderly. I inquire and he tells me that I am several days late (as if I didn't know), and that we have to wait until there are six men before being admitted to the office. I question the two fellows and they tell me they have been there for nearly an hour. So that makes three of us and we have to wait for three more – not on your life. My temper takes hold. I take them along with me and knock on the first office door. Fortunately, it is the right one. Naturally, I am bawled out, but I refuse to engage. We have to go through seven offices in all.

The actual discharge process is hilarious. I hand over my military items and I am offered a civilian suit or fifty-two francs. You can only laugh. I ask to see the suit. They bring out blue dungarees, a pair of velvet trousers with the sort of baggy side pockets found on carpenters' trousers, and a straw hat. The squaddie then assures me that is all that is left. Well if that is so, I tell him, no doubt, at this time, someone from Nice or Cannes will be offered a loincloth. Naturally, I have no hesitation in taking the fifty-two francs.

When it comes to the subsistence allowance, although I have been officially demobbed since 29 January, the sergeant major pays me up to today, because it simplifies the books. So hey, a little army benefit after all. It takes two hours in all before I can finally rejoin Edmond outside. We have an aperitif on one of the boulevards... and here I am back at home and for ever this time.

Whatever the future holds for us, it can certainly never be as bad as what we have endured for these past 54 months. And now, without any doubt, the Boches will first have to pay damages, and then everything will have to be rebuilt, which will mean work for everyone. However tired I might be now, I aspire to just one thing – to work as hard as I can to make good the past.

May it be God's will to help me – Long live France.

René Besnard

Stretcher-Bearers (René top right)

Swimming in the Vezouze at Saint-Martin

Fishing at Saint Martin in the Vezouze

Making Aluminium Tags

Reillon

Trench rescue shelter (René on the right)

In a new trench (René on the left)

Digging a trench

Shelters in the woods. Rognelle, Saint Martin

Vého

Inside the church at Vého (René on the right)

Carrying a wounded man to a horse-drawn ambulance

Burial at Bélmery

Prisoners working

Making Coffins

A mobile kitchen

Made in the USA
Charleston, SC
13 December 2014